Elder Activities
for People Who Care

Volume One
January through June

by Pat Nekola

About the Cover

Ella Friess was born in Thorp, Wisconsin, on February 23, 1898. She passed away in September of 2000. Ella was the oldest of five children. Her entire elementary and high school education was at the school in Thorp.

Ella attended UW-Eau Claire for one year, where she studied business. Following school she was employed at the bank in Thorp where she met her first husband, Leland Nye. They had two daughters. At the age of 80 she remarried and resided in Cumberland with her husband, Everett Phillips, until his death five years later. Ella lived on her own, near her daughter, until she was 97 years of age, when she moved to the nursing home where Pat Nekola was the Activity Director.

Ella enjoyed life to the fullest; she was witty and smart. She loved fashions, sewing, and was very creative—taking up painting at the age of 65. She started taking art classes in Thorp at the age of 69, and continued her artwork until the age of 99. Ella did rosemauling (a Norwegian folk painting), knitting, and hooked and braided rugs. Pat would go to her room to push her to art class on the second floor every Wednesday. She would always say, "Be sure to get me to my art class on time." At the age of 99 she was still going on field trips and out to lunch. She loved animals and plants, and loved to show off pictures of her family. She could carry on a conversation on many topics and was very vital almost to the end of her life. Ella did the picture on the cover at the age of 99.

Pat provided the accordion music for Ella's 100th birthday party. Her great granddaughter sent her a lei from Hawaii for the party. She enjoyed every minute of that Hawaiian birthday party!

Ella lived in the nursing home for three years, and died at the age of 101.

Picnics

Catering on the Move:
A Cookbook and Guide
by Pat Nekola

Learn to cater your own picnic for family and friends, for church or service club gatherings, or open a catering business. This cookbook has a variety of recipes designed especially for picnics. View buffet layouts, decorations, and various styles of picnics from simple to elegant. Recipes serve groups of 12-100, some up to 1,500!

Snacks and beverages, salads, grilled meats, hot vegetables, and desserts recipes are all designed for the picnicker's appetite.

From the owner of Pat's Party Foods, Caterers.

Pat Nekola has a long history of fine catering with her own business, Pat's Party Foods, in Wisconsin. She cooked many delicious recipes in *Picnics, Catering on the Move*. Picnics were her favorite parties because she enjoyed watching families and friends relax and have fun.

Pat Nekola began writing *Picnics, Catering on the Move* when her mother was diagnosed with Alzheimer's disease. Alzheimer's is a progressive, degenerative disease of the brain causing confusion, personality, and behavioral changes. Eventually many people with Alzheimer's are not able to care for themselves. A family member loses them twice: first to Alzheimer's, then to death. Taking care of a person with Alzheimer's takes a lot of patience and love.

Pat is donating $3.00 of every book sold to the Alzheimer's Association. The funds are being used for research to find a cure for the disease and for educational programs that help caregivers.

242 pages, hard back with spiral binding.
ISBN: 0-9660610-0-4
February 2000, Catering by Design

- *Kitchen-tested recipes.*
- *Picnic ideas.*
- *Quantities shown for small to large groups.*
- *Decorations for theme parties.*
- *Diagrams to guide the reader.*
- *Buffet layout diagrams act as a learning tool.*
- *Heartwarming stories accompany recipes.*
- *Easy-to-follow instructions.*
- *Garnishes to make food attractive.*
- *Catering for crowds for fun and profit.*

Picnics

Catering on the Move:
A Cookbook and Guide
by Pat Nekola

Mail or fax to:	**Catering by Design** P.O. Box 181 Waukesha, WI 53187 Ph: (262) 547-2004 Fax: (262) 547-8594

Thank you for your order!

Customer Name _____
Library _____
Address _____
City State Zip _____
Phone _____ Fax _____

Qty:	Price @	Ext.
	$27.95	$
Shipping	$4.50	$
Total		$

MasterCard and Visa accepted.

WI residents please add 5.5% sales tax.

Signature _____

Date _____

Invoice Number _____

An *Alzheimer's* Guide

Activities and Issues for People Who Care

When Pat Nekola's mother and aunt were stricken with Alzheimer's disease, she found help and information from a number of public and private sources. She also found that there were many others—families, caregivers, residential facilities' staff—just like herself, that could make use of the same types of information. With this in mind, Pat set out to accumulate the education and information to write this handbook to help others going through the same trying personal experiences.

This handbook is easy to read and to understand. Pat's writing approach is like a one-on-one conversation with a friend that has "been there and done that". Everyone needs to read this book, we are all dealing with the disease whether on a personal level, or as members of our local communities. It is an informative and warm approach to helping the Alzheimer's patient live to their fullest and enjoy each day—no matter what their present situation.

242 pages, soft cover.
ISBN: 0-9660610-8-X
February 2002, Catering by Design

Information included in Part One of this Handbook:

- ■ *Easy to understand information on each stage of the disease.*

- ■ *How to deal with the different stages for families and caregivers.*

- ■ *Coping strategies when caring for the patient at home.*

- ■ *What to look for when selecting a care facility.*

- ■ *Resources including telephone numbers, websites, and questions to ask.*

Information and Activities Useful for the Care Facilities' Activity Directors included in Part Two of this Handbook:

- ■ *Directions for different craft activities.*

- ■ *Color graphics for use with the activities.*

- ■ *Recommended music for patient participation.*

- ■ *Recipes.*

- ■ *Patient assessment forms.*

An *Alzheimer's* Guide

Activities and Issues for People Who Care

Mail or fax to:	**Catering by Design** P.O. Box 181 Waukesha, WI 53187 Ph: (262) 547-2004 Fax: (262) 547-8594

Thank you for your order!

Customer Name _____

Library _____

Address _____

City State Zip _____

Phone _____ Fax _____

Qty:	Price @	Ext.
	$34.95	$
Shipping	$4.50	$
Total		$

MasterCard and Visa accepted.

WI residents please add 5.5% sales tax.

Signature _____

Date _____

Invoice Number _____

Acknowledgments

Thanks to Lynn Revoy Dean of Waukesha County Technical College for her sincere interest in my progress. She always has time to listen and encourage me. She had been my boss years earlier, and has helped to spur me onward in my career. She has always stayed "in touch" throughout the years.

I also want to thank my classmates for their sincere support and encouragement when I was the "new kid on the block". They approved of me changing careers and showed concern for me whenever I encountered new challenges. They also included me in their activities and helped me to try out and implement my ideas—and also gave me ideas—to use with the elderly. They have listened willingly as I've gone through the process of compiling my books. They celebrated when I completed my first book *Picnics, Catering on the Move*, and continued to inquire about the progress of the second book, *An Alzheimer's Guide, Activities and Issues for People Who Care*.

A special thanks to Marcia Lorenzen and Camin Potts of Graphic Liaisons LLC for their work and encouragement on both my second and third books.

My church family has been very supportive, and I would like to thank them for always being there for me.

A special thanks to my husband, Steve, for his encouragement and financial support while compiling my books. I wanted to be an author and he made it possible to fulfill my dream.

Dedication

I would like to dedicate this book to two very special teachers who taught the Activity Consultant, Trainee class, and Management class to prepare me for my third career.

Debra Wilkinson MSM, ATR, ACC Activity Consultant and Trainer
and
Sharon Krull, RMT, BC, ACC

These two ladies showed great patience, wisdom, and understanding. They embraced me, accepted me, and encouraged me to become an activity director. Their training helped me in compiling this material into a book.

Contents

Elder Activities *for People Who Care*

Volume One—January through June

Introduction

January Activities:

February Activities:

March Activities:

April Activities:

May Activities:

June Activities:

Color Section of Projects:

Preface

Activities are the hub of any care facility. The elderly look for something to brighten their day. The Activity Director not only needs to be creative, but also sensitive to the residents' needs. Administration, the entire staff, and families should be supportive of activities in the facility. Invite family members and staff to participate in the various activities. The leadership, team effort, enthusiasm, and follow through, of the Activity Director helps the programs succeed. The Activity Director needs to build a trust with the residents through actions and words. Give the residents time and space to develop this trust, and be supportive.

The Activity Director needs to consider the aging process. Think what it would be like to put Vaseline® over your eyes, ear plugs in your ears, lose control of your bladder, and set in a wheelchair day after day with nothing fun to do—there may be daily TV and a visitor once a week.

Take away the resident's independence and simple tasks become difficult to accomplish. Now the resident depends on someone to tend to their daily needs. Maybe the resident just doesn't like the worker that is helping he/she. The resident may be modest or doesn't want to accept help because of a sense of pride. The resident has stress because he/she doesn't know how far the money for their care will stretch. To make things even worse, a family member may take the loved one's money for their own gain. The resident simply has lost control. Yes, it is a big adjustment—attitude is everything!

An elderly person may be very crabby to a nurse or an aide, but very bubbly for the activity department person. That particular personal approach is entirely different because the activity person is not a threat. Most elderly want to be loved, understood, and needed like any other human being. Elderly folks desire self-worth. The activity department can build that self-worth and self-esteem through party activities and community based participation because the elderly are actively involved in the planning of the activities both in the care facility and in the community, and this activity fights the boredom the elderly may experience.

Activities in a care facility are a challenging, but rewarding, occupation. The knowledge gained from the elderly is a gift. As an activity person you will receive far more than you can give. You, as the Activity Director, can set the tone to make happy folks. The residents will relax and look forward to the activities. The more the residents become involved the easier it will be for the rest of the staff to care for the them.

As an Activity Director, I promoted the premise, "This is your home and we are a family. We need each other, and we should work together and love each other in our home. We are all in this together." This philosophy worked very well. People worked together to raise funds to give back to the community. The residents began fussing over each other. It was so neat to see residents bond and care about others.

The purpose of this book is to give information to activity staff personnel to help the elderly have fun while participating in the various activities. Each chapter describes activities for each month of the year. The parties help residents to exercise, reminisce, stimulate sensory skills, and maintain self-esteem. These activities give residents the opportunity to express their past and identify with the world of today. Activities with children, family, and animals play an integral part in remembering the past life. The activities and parties shared in this book also help support the residents' long-term memory.

Note: When I invited the residents to come for a history lecture or an educational activity I received very poor attendance. But when I called my "educational" activity a party my attendance soared. Every person old, or young, likes to eat and the smells made them curious enough to attend the party.

Methods, items needed, organization skills, recipes, and songs are included for the various activities. Many of them are unusual and promote not only goodwill, but also education, to keep the residents' minds alive and vibrant.

This ready-reference book is easy to follow. You can build in your own ideas making your activity as simple or elaborate as you desire. The information I have shared works. Observe the smiling faces in your facility while using the ideas in this book.

Good Luck!
—*Pat Nekola*

Disclosure

I do not proclaim to be an expert on dietary needs. However, my career began as a Home Economics teacher with strong emphasis in foods and diet. I have combined my studies with 18 years as a professional caterer, and Activity Director training specializing in Alzheimer's patients, and practical hands-on experience providing activities to the elderly population.

I share my experience and creative ability to meet the elder population's emotional and psychological needs. My mother had Alzheimer's for five years prior to her death.

I have authored *Picnics, Catering on the Move* and *An Alzheimer's Guide, Activities and Issues for People Who Care*. I implement information from both books during my work at care facilities. The *Picnics* book is a great tool to use when reminiscing with both Alzheimer's and higher functioning elderly residents.

I plan to continue to help families and activity personnel enrich the lives of the elder population, and I hope your facility will add this book to your library and apply some of my ideas in your activity planning.

—Pat Nekola

To touch an elderly
person's life
is God's precious
gift of love!

—Author unknown

Introduction

What an Activity Director Should Know
to Create and Sustain a Strong Activity Program

About the Recipes

One of the things I noticed was the amount of food being wasted day after day at care facilities. Soup is one item every elderly person will eat and enjoy. Granny's Soup Kitchen was a favorite activity because the elderly remembered soups made by their mothers, or the soups they made for their own families.

I have several heart healthy soup recipes and favorite old-fashioned soup recipes from residents' childhood. Soup is a healthy snack instead of always serving sweets. Although, I must admit sweets are a favorite of almost every elderly person.

About Mealtime

Many days, the three meals are all some residents live for. They look forward to eating a good meal. Unhappy residents often complain about the meals. It is the responsibility of each facility to serve good, wholesome, nutritional meals—and most do. But, color also plays an important part because the residents eat with their eyes.

As an activity director I remember holding a monthly resident's meeting. Usually the same people came month after month and food was always a well-discussed topic for half of the meeting.

Every two weeks the kitchen prepared a meal from a menu that the residents had selected, and for the most part the food was eaten on that day. The residents felt they were in control. Once a week I would dress up like a chef and make fried eggs for the residents. They grew up with farm-fresh fried eggs. Again, they ate the food and the smell of the eggs frying whet their appetites.

About Special Diets

As an activity person it is important to know about, and follow, each resident's diet.

On special occasions, such as a birthday, I feel they should be allowed to cheat a little on their diet unless someone is a brittle diabetic and it would cause them great harm.

Learn about the various diseases of the residents to make a decision about the foods to be served. I know—if I get to be 90, 95, or 100—I certainly will eat what I want for my birthday, if I have anything to say about it!

There are many arguments on this topic. I just feel that food can be a reward of happiness for that special birthday or party. Just use your good judgment. Check charts with the head nurse to see if the person can cheat for one special occasion.

Studying Residents' Past History

It is hard work to study the residents' background. The more you know about the person's past the better you can serve the individual.

Example:

If a person was a sport's fan make sure you become interested in their favorite sport. I brought in newspaper articles about their favorite teams, playing on the residents' interests is one of the best ways to keep them on your side—and this will help you get them to the various activities.

Above all, plan activities that interest the residents and don't forget to inform the families of their loved one's progress.

The Activity Calendar

Post activities monthly and send an activity calendar to each family's home every month. Invite family members to attend and participate in activities and field trips. I've included a sample of a monthly calendar (see page 7). The calendar must be inviting to gain family interest.

Get to Know Family Members

Talk to families at care meetings and also when you see them visiting their loved one. Show kindness and genuine support to each family member. You will be rewarded for this positive gesture.

I also had a "wish list" in my monthly calendar. Families often helped with supplies for the activity department.

Each year the activity department sponsored a family picnic. Families appreciate the invitation and some of them will volunteer to help at the picnic. I know I helped in activities for my mom at her care facility; I just appreciated any help for Mom.

About Volunteers

Use your community as a base for volunteers. You may have friends, neighbors, or the residents' family or friends that are willing to help.

I relied on area schools to come in and volunteer. Residents bond with young children easily. The two generations are great for each other.

Set up a schedule for the volunteer so he/she will come every week or month at the same time for the same activity.

I had a young lady help me every Monday. Her husband worked Monday nights so she brought her two young children and did one-on-one visits for a couple of months. (She did the one-on-one visits at the beginning to get to know the residents.) I also had some guidelines to help her get started on the activity. Then she set up a game night with her kids and told some stories. The residents enjoyed her children and looked forward to the volunteer's family visits.

Volunteer Appreciation Day

Select a month and plan a dinner or appetizer supper for the volunteers, either at the facility or going out to a restaurant. The residents helped me make an appetizer supper. They also picked a theme. (See April Activities page 151.)

The party was very meaningful for all involved. The head administrator spoke and praised the volunteers. I also spoke and expressed their value to our facility. Each volunteer was presented with a Certificate of Appreciation.

Bingo

Many facilities have bingo three times a week. Bingo is a big deal with the elderly. Most have grandchildren and they try to win a prize for them. Stuffed animals are one of the favorites.

When I first became an activity director, without thinking much about stuffed animals, I went to Goodwill Industries to buy bingo prizes. A lady at Goodwill informed me that she had a lot of 50-cent stuffed animals. I purchased a bunch and took them to the facility for Bingo Night.

Jeanine had twin granddaughters and her whole table knew that she wanted to send presents for their birthday. Residents helped her win two stuffed animals. She was so delighted! I found her two boxes and tape, and we wrapped the gifts. Her son delivered the gifts to the post office. A simple pleasure given to Jeanine became a "big deal" with several people involved to fulfill her wish.

Some other bingo prizes that are well received are:
> Jewelry.
> After Shave Lotion.
> Greeting Cards.
> Perfumes.
> Hand Cream and Lotions.
> Lap Shawls and Blankets.
> Bananas.
> Quarters.

Make your bingo prizes appropriate for each season and appropriate for both male and female residents.

About the Men Residents in a Care Facility

Elderly women outlive men throughout the U.S. In one of the facilities where I worked there were 85 women residents and only 10 men. It is the activity director's responsibility to have activities for men residents.

I formed a men's group. The men met for lunch on one Thursday a month. We had alcohol-free beer, a special lunch, and a speaker from the community. Some of the topics were:
> Fishing and Hunting.
> World War II.
> Guns.
> Fire Engine Collection.
> Coin Collecting.
> Clocks.
> Woodworking.
> Sports.

Being a Dad and Grandfather.

Trains.

You can choose any topics that will be of interest to your residents and that you can find a resource person familiar with the subject to be presented.

This gave the men a chance to participate and feel important.

Field Trips

Make sure families approve of their loved one going on a field trip. A permission slip needs to be signed by a responsible family member. You will need a bus or van with a chair lift.

Here are some suggested destinations:

- The county or city zoo.
- A picnic at the park with Head Start students from your community.
- Shopping at a local store or mall. You will need to make sure you have the following helpers along on this outing:
  - Someone to push wheelchairs (one for each chair-bound resident).
  - Two CNAs to assist with toileting needs.
  - Make arrangements ahead of time with the retailer as they sometimes have people to help push the wheelchairs and assist the residents in checkout. The residents will enjoy this outing greatly. Often family members set up a petty cash account for their loved one so they can make small purchases on the field trip.
- Going to a baseball game.
- Sightseeing at Christmas time to enjoy the Christmas lighting.
- A trip to a museum.
- Going fishing at the local river or lake.
- Going out for lunch at a local restaurant.
- Taking in a Dinner Theater or Concert.
- Taking a ride in the country to enjoy spring or to see the fall colors.

Network with Your Local Library

Call your local library and set up a system to checkout books for your residents' reading pleasure. Talking books are great for people with diminished eyesight. Arrange for the librarian to come to your facility and talk to the residents.

Arrange with people in the community to donate books and magazines to your facility.

Some residents may take the daily paper, which the facility staff will deliver to them.

A current events discussion group helps keep folks updated on local news and daily affairs.

Using Community Resources

Tap into business resources.

I wanted to do a greeting card, pasta, and Easter basket project using wallpaper. I called my local decorating center and asked if they had any old wallpaper books. Sure enough, he had many old books, which he gave me to use in the project. I saved old butter dishes to make Easter baskets and juice cans for making wishing wells.

Someone donated free heavy paper that I used to make little bags to stuff Kleenex® packets in for a Christmas present.

A grocery store donated brown paper bags to use for making Gingerbread men.

Just ask and someone will help you if it is for a good cause. Tell them what the project is about, and afterward take a sample or show a picture of the project. I also thank them in writing or personally.

Throughout this book you will find simple, inexpensive projects to keep residents happy. It takes so little to make them happy!

When a Resident Dies

Some families donate the clothing of a deceased person to the care facility. There are residents that are forgotten after being placed, and many times they can use these items. You can work with your social worker or caregiver to ascertain a resident's needs.

The activity department can get able residents to sew on buttons or mend clothing, if need be.

What to Remember as You Work with Residents

A care facility is a melting pot, with all kinds of personalities from every walk of life. Sometimes residents bicker, so you may need to be a mediator. Create an atmosphere that encourages everyone to get along.

At one facility, I encouraged Mavis to say, "Hi," to Wendy on her morning walk. Wendy was shy and declined most activities. Mavis became a friend to Wendy even though Wendy didn't attend the activities.

Also encourage residents to stay active in their community.

Finally, an activity director must be prepared to do a lot of charting and paperwork, and attend care conferences related to the nursing home setting. Divide some of the paperwork with the other activity staff. (Assisted Living paperwork is far less than that in a nursing home.) Get out with the residents and keep up with what is happening, so you can best serve them.

Don't try to do everything yourself. Get housekeepers, nurses, the doctor, administrator, and CNAs all involved in activities. It is everybody's business to make the residents happy and comfortable. Happy residents make for healthier residents. Diminish depression with heartfelt involvement in activities.

Client Satisfaction Survey

	Strongly Agree	Agree	Strongly Disagree	Disagree	N/A
Staff Attitude:					
The resident is treated with respect.					
The resident/family is included in decisions regarding care.					
Staff respects resident's personal belongings.					
Staff carefully answers all questions.					
Staff listens to concerns.					
Staff is friendly and courteous.					
Staff respects resident's privacy.					
Staff has a positive attitude.					
Staff responds to resident's needs promptly.					
Comments:					
Staff Skill:					
Family has confidence in the skill of:					
Nursing Staff					
Physicians					
Rehab Therapists					
Social Worker					
Others (please explain)					
Comments:					

Activity Calendar Sample

	BIRTHDAYS THIS MONTH:

SUNDAY	MONDAY	TUESDAY	WEDNESDAY	THURSDAY	FRIDAY	SATURDAY

THIS MONTH'S UPCOMING EVENTS:

(See example on page 16 in color section.)

January Activities

The Sunny Caribbean Party

Menu

Virgin Gorda Cucumber Sandwiches

∞

Caribbean Triscuit Snack

∞

St. Thomas Seafood Dip with Assorted Crackers

∞

Caribbean Beef Soup

∞

Island Meatballs

∞

Barbados Chicken Nuggets with Barbecue Sauce

∞

Grand Cayman Fruit Salad

∞

Recipes:

Virgin Gorda Cucumber Sandwiches
Yield: 96 sandwiches

    4   cucumbers, peeled and sliced
    2   jumbo loaves of white bread
    4   packages (8 ounces each) cream cheese
    1   teaspoon Worcestershire sauce
    1   teaspoon onion powder
         dill weed for garnish

Cream cream cheese, Worcestershire sauce, and onion powder together. Cut rounds of bread with the large end of a shot glass. Spread cream cheese mixture on bread round and place one cucumber slice on each round. Sprinkle dill weed on top of each cucumber. Place on serving tray, cover, and refrigerate until serving.

Note: Make sure each cucumber slice is dried with a paper towel. You will get 48 bread rounds from a loaf of bread.

Caribbean Triscuit® Snacks
Yield: 90-100 servings.

    3   cups shredded cheddar cheese
    2   cups chopped ripe olives
    2   cups chopped green onions
    2   cups mayonnaise
    2   teaspoons curry powder

Mix cheese, olives, onions, and curry powder and moisten with mayonnaise. Spread on Triscuits®. (There are 45 to 50 Triscuits® in a $9^1/_2$-inch box, expect some broken crackers in each box when deciding how many boxes you need to purchase.)

Place the crackers on a cookie sheet and broil for one minute or bake for 2-3 minutes until bubbly. You can microwave for 20 to 30 seconds rather than using the oven, if you wish.

St. Thomas Seafood Dip

Yield: 25-30 servings.

- 2 cans (6 ounces each) solid white tuna
- 4 packages (8 ounces each) cream cheese
- 2 teaspoons curry powder
- 2 tablespoons diced onion
- $1/4$ cup diced celery
- $1/4$ teaspoon onion powder
- $1/4$ teaspoon garlic pepper

Garnish:

red pepper

parsley

almond slices

green olives stuffed with pimento, sliced

Beat the cream cheese until smooth and creamy. Blend in tuna, curry powder, onions, celery, onion powder, and garlic pepper. Shape dip into a fish on your serving plate. Garnish with green olive slice for the eye and decorate the tail and fin with red pepper strips. Stand almond slices in a row across the body of the fish to simulate scales. Form the mouth with a piece of red pepper and garnish with fresh parsley. Serve with crackers. See page 1 in color section for color photo of St. Thomas Seafood Dip.

Caribbean Beef Soup

Yield: 24 servings.

- 10 cans (14 ounces each) fat free beef broth
- 2 pounds beef top round roast, sliced into strips
- 1 head Chinese cabbage leaves
- 2 cups red cooking wine
- 2 leaks sliced into onion rings
- 2 bunches green onions with tops, sliced thin
- 2 cups julienne carrots
- 3 large Portabella mushrooms, sliced and chopped
- 1 large red pepper, diced
- 1 can (8 ounces) water chestnuts, sliced
- 1 tablespoon Caribbean spice (see note)
- 2 cups long grain and wild rice, cooked separately

Place 6 cans of beef broth in a large crockpot. Add beef, wine, vegetables, and Caribbean spice and cook for 6 to 8 hours on low.

Cooking Directions for Rice:

6   cups water
1   tablespoon margarine
2   cups long grain and wild rice

Bring water and margarine to a boil, add rice and cover with lid. Stir occasionally until the rice is cooked and the water is absorbed. Add the rice to the soup after the 6 to 8 hours of cooking time. Transfer soup into a large kettle or divide it between two large bowls, as you will have quite a large amount of soup and it won't fit into one container. Add 4 cans of beef broth to the divided soup. The soup tastes best if served the following day, so refrigerate and reheat before serving.

Serve with cheese slices, assorted crackers, and salad.

Note: The Caribbean spice can be purchased at your local grocery store. If you cannot find it, ask the grocer to order it for you. Otherwise, call Penzey's Spices at 1-800-741-7787 and ask them to ship the spice to you directly. Penzey's Spices are excellent, and it makes this soup very tasty.

Remember to reserve 4 of the 10 cans of beef broth for the end of the cooking cycle. Grocery stores carry chicken stock in quart cans but not beef broth or stock.

Do not use the core of the cabbage—just the leaves. You can buy julienne style carrots at your local grocery store, or just dice the carrots finely.

Sweet and Sour Meatball Sauce #1

There are 95 to 100 meatballs per three-pound package.

1   jar (32 ounces) grape jelly
2   bottles (12 ounces each) chili sauce
$1/4$ cup concentrated lemon juice
3   pounds ready-made Swedish meatballs (mini size)

Place the grape jelly, chili sauce, and lemon juice in a large saucepan. Wire whip mixture over low heat until the jelly is melted and all the ingredients are blended together. Add pre-cooked meatballs. Continue to cook until meatballs are heated through.

Cranberry Sweet and Sour Meatballs

1   can (16 ounces) jellied cranberry sauce
1   bottle (12 ounces) chili sauce
1   cup honey
2   teaspoons lime juice
2   tablespoons white cooking wine
2   pounds ready-made Swedish meatballs

The same directions apply to this meatball recipe as to the previous recipe.

Barbados Barbecue Sauce

Yield: 4 cups.

2   teaspoons olive oil
$1/4$ cup water
$1/4$ cup finely diced onion
$1/3$ cup finely diced celery
2   cups tomato catsup
$1/4$ cup brown sugar
$1/3$ cup lemon juice
1   tablespoon Worcestershire sauce
$1/2$ teaspoon pepper
1   teaspoon prepared mustard
3   boxes (12 ounces each) breaded chicken nuggets

Place oil and water in a large saucepan and sauté the onion and celery until slightly tender. Add the catsup, brown sugar, lemon juice, Worcestershire sauce, pepper, and mustard and cook on low heat for 20 minutes stirring about every 5 minutes. Place sauce in portion control serving cups.

Heat the chicken nuggets according to the package directions just before the party. Serve with either hot or cold barbecue sauce.

Note: A 12-ounce box of chicken nuggets shaped like miniature patties has 18-20 nuggets. Figure 1 to 2 ounces of barbecue sauce per person.

Grand Cayman Fruit Salad

1   fresh pineapple
2   pints blueberries
2   mangos
1   pint strawberries
3   kiwi
2   star fruit for garnish
    parsley

*To prepare the pineapple cut off the leafy top. With the fruit upright, cut in half lengthwise, and cut each half in half again, lengthwise. Cut out the tough core. Lay the pineapple quarter skin side down on a cutting board and cut into bite-size pieces. Rinse the blueberries and dry on a paper towel. Peel the mango and cut into strips cutting around the stone in the middle of the fruit. Cut the strips into bite-size pieces. Mix cut fruit together and garnish with strawberries, kiwi, star fruit, and parsley.

*(Refer to author's cookbook *Picnics, Catering on the Move*, pages 64 and 65 for diagram.)

When we were in Jamaica we ate curried goat. It was delicious. The recipe calls for 2 large onions, 5 pounds of young goat meat, curry powder, red pepper, bay leaf, salt and pepper, chicken stock, and coconut milk. Squeeze lime juice on the hot dish just before serving. I have never tried to make the recipe, but instead, I've made curried chicken and reduced the recipe size. The Jamaican people eat pretty much what they find plentiful on the island. They raise goats and calves that roam freely along the roadside in the back country. Jamaica is a poor country. However, I admire many of these islanders living in shacks. They grow vegetable gardens and sew their own clothes. They help each other survive. It takes real skill to do so.

Curried Jamaican Chicken

Note: This recipe can be used for just a tasting party using portion control cups for each person. Coconut milk is hard to find, so I use the milk from a whole coconut for this dish.

Yield: 6 full size servings.

1   tablespoon canola oil
$1/2$ cup water
$1/4$ cup white wine
1   can (14 ounces) chicken broth
       (reserve half to use in the gravy)
$1/3$ to $1/2$ cup coconut milk
1   pound boneless chicken tenders

2	teaspoons canola oil (for sautéing vegetables)
2	teaspoons fresh garlic
1	red pepper, diced
1	cup fresh, sliced mushrooms
1	tablespoon curry powder
1	teaspoon allspice (Jamaica Ground)
2	teaspoons Jamaican Jerk Seasoning
	juice from a fresh lime
1	tablespoon cornstarch
1	pound cooked noodles or rice

In a 5-quart saucepan combine oil, water, wine, 7 ounces ($^1/_2$ of total) chicken broth, and coconut milk. Add chicken and steam until cooked through.

In separate pan add oil and sauté garlic, pepper, and mushrooms, and add to chicken mixture when cooked. Add the seasonings to the chicken/vegetable mixture. Squeeze the fresh lime into the mixture.

In a bowl wire whip the cornstarch into the remaining half of the chicken stock. Bring the hot dish to a boil and slowly add the cornstarch mixture. Cook and stir until the mixture thickens and serve over noodles or rice. (The Jamaicans serve many of their hot dishes over rice.)

The Jamaicans like Plantains. They can be either baked or fried. Jamaicans do not have very sweet desserts like Americans. Plantain Fritters are often served at a meal, they are like bananas, but firmer and not as sweet. The Plantains are cut in half the long way, and then in half cross-wise to make a larger-size fritter. Lime Juice is squeezed over the fritter. Americans like their fritters rolled in powdered sugar.

Plantain Fritters

Yield: 12 small fritters per plantain.

$^1/_4$	cup plus 1 teaspoon self-rising flour
$^1/_2$	cup plus 2 tablespoons regular flour
$^1/_2$	cup water
$^1/_4$	teaspoon cinnamon
$1^1/_2$	teaspoons sugar
2	plantains cut in half the long way and then cut into pieces

Mix both flours in a bowl. Pour in water and stir until a smooth paste is obtained. Add sugar and cinnamon and mix well. Heat oil in a deep pan until it is smoking hot. Coat each plantain section with the batter and slide into the hot oil. Fry until golden brown.

Coconut Bread is a Bajan favorite that is served for Sunday buffets in Barbados. This bread can be served plain, or with butter. It is like a heavy biscuit texture. Raisins or mixed fruits can be added to the batter if desired. I use $1/3$ each of craisins, raisins, and mixed fruit. I modified this recipe because many of the elderly do not care for big amounts of coconut. I also made it a little lighter and easier for the residents to eat. I buy baking raisins that are already soft—one box does equal a cup.

Coconut Bread
Yield: One 6 x 9-inch loaf.

1	cup brown sugar
1	cup shortening
2	large eggs
1	cup grated coconut
1	cup softened raisins
$1/2$	cup finely chopped almonds (optional)
1	teaspoon cinnamon
$1/2$	teaspoon nutmeg
$1/4$	teaspoon cloves
2	teaspoons almond extract
1	cup + 2 tablespoons milk
3	cups flour
3	teaspoons baking powder
$1/4$	teaspoon salt.

Cream together the sugar and shortening, beat the eggs and add. Add the coconut, spices, extract, raisins, almonds, and milk. Add the flour, salt, and baking powder and mix well.

Bake at 350 degrees for about an hour, or until a toothpick comes out clean.

Ideas for the Caribbean Party:

How to Decorate the Buffet Table

Place a plain blue (for the color of the sea) tablecloth on an 8-foot table and cover with a smaller tropical tablecloth. Next lay fishnet over the table and scatter fish and seashells at random over the net.

Display flags of the various islands.

Call your local travel agency and borrow a travelogue on the Caribbean. Show this to interested residents to begin to introduce the party theme.

Since my husband and I went to Jamaica, Bahamas, Puerto Rico, the U.S. and British Virgin Islands, and Aruba I can talk about my experiences. If you have not taken a cruise find someone in the community that would like to speak to the residents, or get some of the residents to talk about cruises they've taken.

I took pictures on our trips, and I put together an album and I use it as a one-on-one visit technique. It works very well because I have many scenery pictures. We visited the large fort in Puerto Rico and toured some of the shops and beaches. Much of the economy is helped through tourism.

Talk about Reggae and Calypso music in the islands, and play tapes of the various styles of island music.

While traveling in Jamaica, I found it very interesting that every Jamaican encountering a problem would immediately say, "No problem mon." As a tourist I decided to wear my "No problem" shirt. It started quite a conversation one day when my husband and I took a small fishing boat out into the bay. We ran out of gas, and I immediately yelled, "No problem mon!" We sat for two hours before someone came and brought gas.

One of the highlights is going to Dunn's River falls in Ocho Rios, Jamaica. We actually climbed the falls to the top. It was a rugged climb, but an accomplishment.

One Sunday we went to church in Jamaica. We sat in the front row. There are no doors on the churches—many buildings are very open. A lizard came crawling toward my feet, as he got closer and was almost ready to go across my feet I jumped up onto the church bench. The Irish priest, with vivid red hair, put his head down for he began to laugh. The entire church was filled with native people trying not to laugh. It is an encounter I will always remember.

We had the pleasure of going to an open-air restaurant; the stars and lights were ever so beautiful while dining. The atmosphere makes for a romantic evening.

The scenery is breathtaking and the culture is very interesting. Tourism helps keep the economy going. Many missionaries go to Jamaica to help build houses and teach the very poor people a trade.

Some of the islanders will follow you and beg for money, or try to sell you drugs. It is best not to travel alone in the back country, for your own safety.

We also went to Kingston for a day. The scenery is very pretty. Jamaica has lush greenery and waterfalls. It was a very interesting trip. We also visited the home of Bob Marley in Kingston. It is now a museum showing his music and life.

We enjoyed St. John's Virgin Island because we love to hike. The preserved land was a real treat, and we could also snorkel there.

We shopped in St. Thomas. The handmade embroidery tablecloths and napkins were beautiful. Needless to say I bought a couple of sets because the price was very inexpensive. I showed my tablecloths to the ladies that valued handiwork. They enjoyed seeing my find.

Aruba is a tiny island, but the beaches are so sandy and the weather was so sunny the entire time we were there. We enjoyed seeing the old church and the shopping.

Virgin Gourda was most memorable for us. We walked on the sandy beach to the baths—it is an encounter one must experience to get the full benefit.

I was so amazed at the beauty of the lush foliage, waterfalls, flowers, birds, and the deep blue color of the Caribbean Sea. Above all, the weather is so perfect.

Music in the Caribbean

Jamaica actually became familiar with reggae music back in the early 1970s. The Jamaicans invented a blend of rhythm and blues and mento music. The electric guitar and organ and steel drums produces the real sound of reggae music. Regge-regge means quarrel. Reggae is bass dominated and came from the slum of Kingston. The songs show the concern of the dissatisfied African-Jamaican youth. They did not respect the authorities. But also the reggae music of today emphasizes love, peace, and reconciliation.

Bob Marley was a supreme musician. Another Jamaican musician that has been successful is Jimmy Cliff. He is a singer and songwriter, and does a combination of soul music with traditional reggae. Some of his songs are: "Miss Jamaica," "Hurricane Hattie," "Wonderful World," and "Beautiful People." In the early 1970s he stared in a film called "The Harder They Come." He also appeared in the movies "Bongo Man," and "Club Paradise" in the 1980s. Other songs Jimmy Cliff made into reggae hits are "Sitting in Limbo," and "Rivers of Babylon."

Another native singer is Desmond Dekker. He had a hit called "Shanty Town."

Calypso music is considered slave music and was brought by the Africans to the islands in the 1600s. The plantation owners wanted the loud music and beating to stop, but the slaves continued their music as they worked the plantations.

Calypso started in Trinidad and influenced the Barbadian folk music in the early 20th century. At first Calypso artists were not very well received. However, today Calypso competitions play a major part in the carnival festivities and singers compete for the title of Calypso King.

Some Calypso music has a combination of folk and country music with Bajan Calypso, modern Calypso demonstrates political satire and biting social commentary.

The African folk music and drumming also had some influence from the English, French, and Spanish. Reggae and Calypso are very catchy tunes and are heard very often at restaurants and beach bars.

The Steel Drum is also called the steel pan. This instrument originated in Trinidad. The melodious sound of the steel drum accompanying the Reggae and Calypso music rings throughout the islands.

Tuk bands have a big log drum. These bands play at picnics and excursions and for private parties. Tuk bands usually travel from the various villages playing popular tunes. They get the villagers to join in and dance. There are also dancers on stilts called the "tiltmen". These tiltmen usually follow the tuk bands and ask the audience for contributions.

Invite a Music Appreciation Club to meet and listen to the music and pick out the songs for the party.

Suggested music and artists for the Caribbean party (music can be found on CDs).

"Be Happy"

"The Tide is High"

"Many Rivers to Cross" by Jimmy Cliff

"Caribbean Queen (No More Love on the Run)"

"Montego Bay"

"Pressure Drop"

"Limbo Bog"

"Gumbo Calypso"

"Jamaican Mambo"

"Grandma's Calypso"

"Everybody Limbo"

"Invader Mambo"

"Let's Calypso"

"Day-O"

Reggae Music from Bob Marley:

"Lively Up Yourself"   "Natural Mystic"

"Rebel's Hop"   "Rainbow Country"

"Fussing Fightin'"   "Trenchtown Rock"

"Soul Shakedown Party"   "Keep on Moving"

"Mellow Mood"   "Kaya"

Songs on the steel drum:

"Marianne"   "Caribbean Disco Show Medley"

"Reggae Night"   "Steel Drums Jam"

"La Bamba"   "Matilda"

"Tropical Bird"   "Down Presser Man"

"Bass Man"   "Sun of Jamaica"

"Wedding March"   "Barbados"

"Amazing Grace" (reggae style)   "Kingston Kingston"

"Red Wine"

The Sunny Caribbean Saying Sheet

Supplies needed:

White copy paper $8^1/_2$ x 11 inches.

The Sunny Caribbean saying.

Raised rainbow dye ink pad:

    calypso color.

    fresh greens.

Kit with fish stamps of various sizes and shapes, coral, leaves, and
    bubbles.

A separate stamp saying, "Let the "Fish"-tivities begin!"

(If you cannot find the above kit or stamp, ask the stamping shop if you
    can look in their catalog.)

1 pad to wipe off the ink.

Clear, plastic dropcloth for any paint spills.

Glue stick.

Be sure to wash off all the stamps after each use. When finished with the project rinse off each stamp with warm water. Dry with a soft towel. Wash off the pad and air dry. Store stamps in a box.

Directions:

Photocopy the sheet with the diagonal lines and The Sunny Caribbean saying. Glue the saying onto the sheet with the diagonal lines. Stamp the "Let the "Fish"-tivities begin!" above and below the saying. Using the various stamp pads and fish kit begin to stamp fish and place on the lined paper, at random.

Sample Two

Supplies needed:

White copy paper $8^1/_2$ x 11 inches.

Designer paper.

Map with saying "The Sunny Caribbean" on page 26.

Glue stick.

Photocopy the Sunny Caribbean saying and some of the islands using the sample. Cut out the saying and islands and glue them to the designer paper with the fish. Type on the date, time, and place of the party in the left-hand corner.

Refer to page 2 in color section for example.

How to Make a Shell Pin for the Caribbean Party

Involve children from the 4th to 6th grades to help with this project. The interesting part is the elderly and the children both believe they are needed to help. It becomes a win-win situation for both boost their self-esteem. It is beautiful to watch the interaction of the two generations.

Supplies needed:

Plain white shells about $2^1/_2$ inches in diameter.

1 fish frolic stamp.

1 raised rainbow dye ink pad with the calypso color (used for stamping).

1 paintbrush per person (medium fine).

1 pin for the back of the shell.

Hot glue.

Multipurpose glue.

2 teaspoons plaster of Paris mixed with 1 teaspoon of water, per pin.

$2^1/_2$-inch square of light tan felt.

Directions:

At the bottom of the shell, using the calypso pad, brush the purple pad with the paintbrush and paint the shell with a rainbow-effect line.

Next, paint the second strip using the orange-gold paint, then paint the blue-green strip, and finally the rose strip at the top of the shell. Using the fish frolics stamp, place individual fish on the blue-green paint. Place three fish on the gold strip, leaving some space between each fish.

Mix the plaster of Paris with water, making a heavy paste. Fill the shell with the plaster of Paris and level it off. Let plaster of Paris dry. Trace around the shell onto the felt with the backside down. Cut out the felt, and placing a small amount of multi-purpose glue in the middle and around the edges of the shell, place the felt, glue-side down, onto the plaster of Paris. Center the pin on the back and attach with hot glue. Refer to page 1 in color section for pin picture.

Caribbean Hat Band for Straw Hat for Party Leaders
Supplies needed:
Caribbean fabric.
Newspaper for pattern.
Pins.
Scissors.
Thread.
Wide-brimmed straw hat.

Make a newspaper pattern for the hatband and tie.

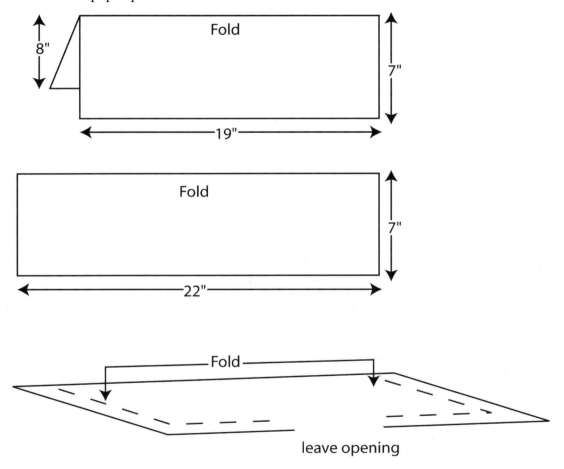

With right sides together, stitch pieces together, leaving a space on one long side so that you can turn it right side out. Turn the tie, and use a scissors to push out the points at the corner, but be careful to not make a hole in the cloth. Hand stitch the opening shut, or sew with the sewing machine and top stitch around the rest of the tie. Fold the band in half and wrap around the hat, tying in back with a square knot. Fan out the ends of the tie in the back of the hat.

Refer to page 1 in color section for finished hat project.

Decorations for the Dining Room

Purchase fish net and fish at the local party store. Hang the fish net around poles or from the ceiling. Open paper clips and use them to hang the fish from the net. Place the decorations around the dining room area to help get some conversation started.

Making Starfish for the Dining Room Ceiling
Supplies needed:

Light-weight construction paper in multi colors.

Multipurpose glue.

Glitter.

Newspaper.

Yarn.

Large paper clips.

Paper punch.

Lay newspaper on the worktable. Trace starfish onto cardboard and cut out. Swirl glue around the starfish and sprinkle with glitter. Repeat the glue and glitter technique on the backside of the starfish. Punch a hole in the tip of the starfish, cut yarn at various lengths and string through the hole in the starfish. Tie the yarn to a paper clip and hang from the ceiling.

Place the excess glitter into a throwaway dish and, using a funnel, pour the excess glitter back into the glitter bottle. Refer to page 3 in color section for starfish.

Making Caribbean Flags for the Party

Supplies needed:

Fabric with Caribbean print.

24-inch dowel.

Thread to match the fabric.

Newspaper for a pattern.

Make a 14 x 16-inch rectangle from the newspaper. Place the pattern on the material and cut it out. Fold edges over twice on all four sides and stitch $1/4$ inch from the edge. Roll the fabric over the edge of the dowel. Using a zipper foot on the sewing machine, stitch the flag fabric close to the dowel to secure the flag and dowel in place. Refer to page 3 in color section for examples.

Caribbean Napkins

Supplies needed:

Newspaper pattern.

Fabric with a Caribbean print.

Thread to match the fabric.

Make a 14 x 16-inch rectangle from the newspaper. Place the pattern on the material and cut out. Fold the edges over twice on all four sides. Press and stitch around the entire napkin to form a hem. Fold the napkin in half on the 14-inch side to meet the edges. On the 16-inch side, fold the napkin into thirds. (You can use this same pattern to make place mats.)

The napkins can be used as accents on the buffet table, or on the guests' table. Just lay the napkin flat in the center of each table. Place vases of flowers or tropical birds in the middle of the napkin.

You can also buy paper napkins and plates to match your theme at your local party store. The advantage of making your own supplies is that the entire facility gets involved in the project, and you can use them again next year. Refer to page 3 in color section for examples.

The Sunny Caribbean Island Word Search

```
D O M I N I C A G H E T Y O R K B A R B A D O S T O O A R U B A J
R E E D O Y B N O O N S T C R O I X M O O M J O H N G R E N A D A
T J A M T Y R H N M N M V I N E V I S T N H O H V I S O P H I S W
R M A T N V B Q A E R I U H N E S I T N V I O W Q M T T O H B E S
I M M M N V I T A I E E P B A R B U D A Q W C O L A J H O N K V T
N A L Q A N G U N V T E W O O C U R A C O A I S I C O O O Y U P K
I U A R E I E I O T Q I C E W Q B T G P N B C U B A H H T Y P K I
D A I P A C C I T O C M M A I N Y V N M I E T Y F I N N N V E R T
A M C P P Y A A A N S A T O B A G O W M I I Q W E R Y O P K R E T
D E R V I S O P K J C A R R I A C O U G R A N D C A Y M A N E O S
O P A K D O M I N I C A N R E P U B L I C H I J K O Y P A A H T A
S T M O M A R T I N I Q U E O I U P Q I V I H I S T M A A R T E N
S T Q H I T O R T O L A B A U B O D A U A N T I G U A P O W R A I
T S S I T H I O W A M A T C A M U I C A K E E T D B A D W X U C U
V V T I I O Y T E Q C S W U U F A B A N G U I L L A V K D H R A H
I Q I T H I A E I H H A U W E B D T Y U I H W W S W H R T H G E W
N O K L H H V E I A A D E W E G A E D E D A D E C E T O R T O L A
C I P O Q O U H D O M I N I C A E Q D R T G U K U U D D E Y F G W
E D U K L J M G F D S A Z X Y T E U I T G R S W S W B T U I L F R
N U N V I U M A U I O P G R E N A D I N E S E R E R B A G U E L I
T R B V E W Q A S E S W T Y D G Y E Y H I E E P U E R T O R I C O
T A B A U O P Q S S T L U C I A A V E R T K D F D F W W E D E E L
T P H L I P M O N T S E R R A T D T I K G U A D E L O U P E A T T
```

Names of Islands in the Caribbean to Search for:

Nevis	Montserrat	St. Thomas	St. Lucia
St. Kitts	Grenada	St. Maarten	St. John
Trinidad	Grenadines	Tortola	St. Croix
Curacoa	Carriacou	Anguilla	Dominica
Aruba	Barbados	Jamaica	Grand Cayman
Tobago	Antigua	Cuba	Guadeloupe
Puerto Rico	Martinique	Haiti	
St. Vincent	Dominican Republic	Barbuda	

The Sunny Caribbean Island Word Search Answer Key

```
D O M I N I C A G H E T Y O R K B A R B A D O S T O O A R U B A J
R E E D O Y B N O O N S T C R O I X M O O M J O H N G R E N A D A
T J A M T Y R H N M N M V I N E V I S T N H O H V I S O P H I S W
R M A T N V B Q A E R I U H N E S I T N V I O W Q M T T O H B E S
I M M M N V I T A I E E P B A R B U D A Q W C O L A J H O N K V T
N A L Q A N G U N V T E W O O C U R A C O A I S I C O O O Y U P K
I U A R E I E I O T Q I C E W Q B T G P N B C U B A H H T Y P K I
D A I P A C C I T O C M M A I N Y V N M I E T Y F I N N N V E R T
A M C P P Y A A A N S A T O B A G O W M I I Q W E R Y O P K R E T
D E R V I S O P K J C A R R I A C O U G R A N D C A Y M A N E O S
O P A K D O M I N I C A N R E P U B L I C H I J K O Y P A A H T A
S T M O M A R T I N I Q U E O I U P Q I V I H I S T M A A R T E N
S T Q H I T O R T O L A B A U B O D A U A N T I G U A P O W R A I
T S S I T H I O W A M A T C A M U I C A K E E T D B A D W X U C U
V V T I I O Y T E Q C S W U U F A B A N G U I L L A V K D H R A H
I Q I T H I A E I H H A U W E B D T Y U I H W W S W H R T H G E W
N O K L H H V E I A A D E W E G A E D E D A D E C E T O R T O L A
C I P O Q O U H D O M I N I C A E Q D R T G U K U U D D E Y F G W
E D U K L J M G F D S A Z X Y T E U I T G R S W S W B T U I L F R
N U N V I U M A U I O P G R E N A D I N E S E R E R B A G U E L I
T R B V E W Q A S E S W T Y D G Y E Y H I E E P U E R T O R I C O
T A B A U O P Q S S T L U C I A A V E R T K D F D F W W E D E E L
T P H L I P M O N T S E R R A T D T I K G U A D E L O U P E A T T
```

Names of Islands in the Caribbean to Search for:

Nevis	Montserrat	St. Thomas	St. Lucia
St. Kitts	Grenada	St. Maarten	St. John
Trinidad	Grenadines	Tortola	St. Croix
Curacoa	Carriacou	Anguilla	Dominica
Aruba	Barbados	Jamaica	Grand Cayman
Tobago	Antigua	Cuba	Guadeloupe
Puerto Rico	Martinique	Haiti	
St. Vincent	Dominican Republic	Barbuda	

The Sunny Caribbean

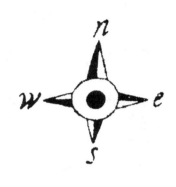

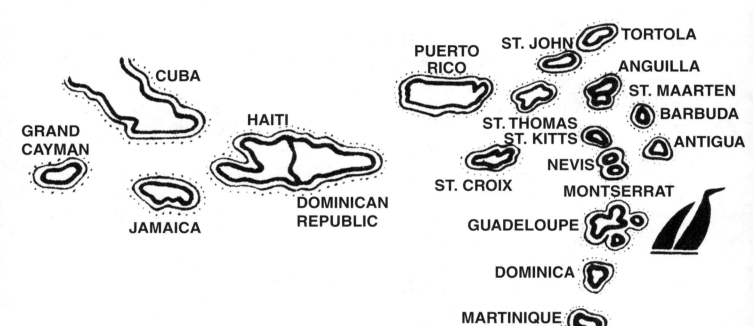

CUBA

GRAND
CAYMAN

JAMAICA

HAITI

DOMINICAN
REPUBLIC

PUERTO
RICO

ST. JOHN

TORTOLA

ANGUILLA

ST. MAARTEN

BARBUDA

ST. THOMAS

ANTIGUA

ST. KITTS

NEVIS

ST. CROIX

MONTSERRAT

GUADELOUPE

DOMINICA

MARTINIQUE

ST. LUCIA

ST. VINCENT

BARBADOS

ARUBA

GRENADINES

CURACAO

CARRIACOU

GRENADA

TOBAGO

TRINIDAD

The Sunny Caribbean Island Game
Tell how many islands start with each letter.

1. Which of the following islands start with "A"?
2. Which of the following islands start with "B"?
3. Which of the following islands start with "C"?
4. Which of the following islands start with "O"?
5. Which of the following islands start with "S"?
6. Which of the following islands start with "T"?
7. Which of the following islands start with "Z"?
8. Which of the following islands start with "J"?
9. Which of the following islands start with "H"?
10. Which of the following islands start with " M"?

Answers:
1. A (1) Aruba
2. (2) Barbados, Barbuda
3. (1) Curacao
4. (0) none
5. (5) St. John, St. Maarten, St. Lucia, St. Thomas, St. Croix
6. (2) Trinidad, Tortola
7. (0) none
8. (1) Jamaica
9. (0) none
10. (2) Montserrat, Martinique

Following the map of the Caribbean Islands, which of the following islands are located in the North, South, East, or West?

1. Puerto Rico =
2. St. John =
3. Trinidad =
4. Dominica =
5. Aruba =
6. Jamaica =
7. Grand Cayman =
8. Barbados =
9. St. Maarten =
10. Guadeloupe =
11. St. Lucia =
12. Tortola =
13. St. Thomas =
14. Montserrat =
15. Curacao =
16. Martinique =
17. St. Croix =
18. Barbuda =
19. Puerto Rico =
20. Grenadines =

1. Puerto Rico=N
2. St. John=N
3. Trinidad=S
4. Dominica=E
5. Aruba=W
6. Jamaica=W
7. Grand Cayman=W
8. Barbados=E
9. St. Maarten=N
10. Guadeloupe=N
11. St.Lucia=E
12. Tortola=N
13. St. Thomas=N
14. Montserrat=E
15. Curacao=S
16. Martinique=E
17. St. Croix=N
18. Barbuda=N
19. Puerto Rico=N
20. Grenadines=S

Caribbean Island Trivia Questions

The following trivia questions are from only a few of the Caribbean Islands.

Little tidbit notes to talk about to the residents:

The Jazz Festival is in January.

Holetwon Festival in February.

Oistins Fish Festival is Easter weekend and celebrates the island's fishing folk.

Decongaline Carnival is in April and is a competition of steel bands and a parade.

Crop Over Festival is in mid-June and celebrates the harvest.

National Independence Festival of Creative Arts is in November and recognizes talents in writing, art, music, singing, dancing, and acting.

In addition there are sports festivals such as:

The Mountain Bike Festival in February.

The Banks Hockey Festival in August.

Dominica:

1. The national tree of Dominica is:
    a. maple b. scotch pine c. baobab tree d. palm tree.
2. This flower is grown in Dominica and Hawaii:
    a. hibiscus b. snapdragon c. cattail d. dried forget-me-not.
3. The poinsettias bloom in Dominica in
    a. November b. December c. January.
4. Dominica has products of:
    a. Guava jelly b. coffee c. bay rum and hot sauce d. "a, b , & c".
5. Which Caribbean island would Christopher Columbus recognize today, if he would return?
    a. St. Thomas b. Dominica c. Virgin Gorda d. Barbados.
6. The island that is located between the French Islands of Guadeloupe to the north and Martinque to the south is:
    a. Dominica b. St. Maarten c. Trinidad d. Puerto Rico.
7. In Dominica the word "main" means:
    a. no trespassing b. stop on the main street c. two ordinary vehicles can pass each other d. two cars can not pass.

Martinique:

1. Martinique is owned by:
    a. Britain b. America c. France d. Cuba.
2. Martinque is known as the island:
    a. Little Paris b. Big London c. Big Blue d. Great America.
3. Martinque is found on which of the following seas?

a. Black b. Red c. Caribbean d. Baltic.

4. Martinque is under the rule of the:

   a. French b. British c. Dutch d. Germans.

Barbados:

1. The tree with the largest trunk is found in:

   a. Barbados b. Africa c. Dominica d. "a, b, & c".

2. Barbados grows many spices used by the entire world in baking, such as:

   a. cinnamon b. ginger c. nutmeg d. "a, b, & c".

3. The official language in Barbados is:

   a. Polish b. German c. English d. French.

4. Bajan is a Caribbean dialect and is known as what kind of language?

   a. Pinocchio b. Cinderella c. Donald Duck d. Mickey Mouse.

5. An example of Bajan An' yah still wan' rice … means:

   a. and you still want rice b. an yo still wan rice c. and you still want rice d. and you want rice.

6. Bajans like to tell what kind of stories?

   a. mystery b. ghost c. legends and myths d. "b & c"

7. The lyrics from the Barbados National Anthem were from:

   a. Irving Berlin b. Irving Burgie c. Irving Bugie d. Irging Berling.

8. The two types of music most often heard in Barbados restaurants and beach bars is:

   a. rock and roll b. soul c. reggae and calypso d. Lawrence Welk.

9. Soca music is:

   a. blend of soul with calypso b. dance music with bold rhythms c. played at carnivals
   d. "a, b, & c.".

10. Steel drums are very popular in Barbados but originated in:

    a. Trinidad b. Jamaica c. St. Thomas d. St. Maarten.

11. The Barbados people are big on festival celebrations. Besides Christmas and Easter they host how many other festivals?

    a. 10 b. 5 c. 3 d. 6.

12. Cou-cou is a Bajan national dish made of cornmeal and okra and found in:

    a. Trinidad b. Barbados c. St. Maartin d. Martinique.

13. The favorite meat served in Barbados is:

    a. beef b. fish c. pork d. lamb.

14. Barbados' tropical climate has fruits such as:

    a. bananas and guavas b. avacados and coconuts c. mangoes and papayas   d. "a, b, & c".

15. One of the favorite Bajan breads found in Barbados is:

    a. coconut b. raisin c. nut d. banana.

16. The social drink of Barbados is:

    a. vodka b. rum c. whiskey d. brandy.

Jamaica:

1. Popular drinks made in Jamaica use:
   a. coconut b. water c. goat's milk d. "a, b, & c".

2. The beverage most served in Jamaica is:
   a. coffee b. tea c. milk d. juice.

3. To save fuel for cooking many Jamaicans use:
   a. gas stoves b. wood fires c. barbecue d. paraffin stoves.

4. The saying most Jamaicans use is:
   a. no problem b. Jamaican juivan c. keep the beat d. "b & c".

5. Foods grown locally are:
   a. breadfruit and bananas b. coconuts c. pineapples d. "a, b, & c".

6. Jamaica makes a living mostly through:
   a. high-tech industry b. computers c. tourism d. acting.

7. The famous artist in Jamaica known for reggae music is:
   a. Bob Marley b. Jimmy Cliff c. Jimmy Carter d. Bill Marley.

8. A product that is known as marijuana in the U.S. is called what in Jamaica?
   a. ganja b. hanya c. ganyia d. ganjia.

9. Most of Jamaicans live in poverty and the largest ancestry population is made up of:
   a. Africans and Europeans b. East Indians c. Caucasians d. Chinese.

U.S. Virgin Islands:

1. The names of the three U.S. Virgin Islands are:
   a. St. Lucia, St. Vincent, St. Maarten b. St. Thomas, St. John, St. Croix
   c. St. Martin, St. Vincent, St. Maarten d. none of the names.

2. Which of the U.S. Virgin Islands has national forest preserves:
   a. St. John b. St. Thomas c. St. Croix.

3. Which of the U.S. Virgin Islands has a lot of shopping:
   a. St. John b. St. Thomas c. St. Croix.

4. Which of the three U.S. Virgin Islands is the largest:
   a. St. John b. St. Thomas c. St. Croix.

5. St. Croix has approximately how many square miles:
   a. 50 b. 82.2 c. 95.3 d. 100.1.

6. Which of the three islands has the least tourism:
   a. St. John b. St. Thomas c. St. Croix.

7. How much of St. John Island is owned by the National Parks Service (12,900 acres):
   a. 1/4 b. 1/3 c. 2/3 d. 3/4 .

8. St. John is beautiful with:
   a. great beaches b. 22 walking trails c. snorkeling and underwater trails d. "a, b, & c".

9. St. Thomas became the great place for French perfumes and designer fashions as far back as:
   a. 1400 b. 1550 c. 1691 d. 1700.

Nevis:

1. Nevis island was known as the:
   a. queen b. king c. high style d. "a, b, & c".
2. In Nevis a tourist can pick up some of the finest:
   a. pottery b. jewelry c. shells d. "b & c".
3. Many of the plantations have been turned into:
   a. private homes b. hotels c. government estates d. tourist sites.
4. St. John's Fig Tree Church was founded in:
   a. 1665 b. 1668 c. 1679 d. 1680.
5. The story of St. John Fig Tree Church goes…there is something displayed of Horatio Nelson and Fanny Nisbet:
   a. jeweled crown b. wedding certificate c. a picture of their wedding day
   d. death certificate.
6. Alexander Hamilton was born in the 18th Century in the capital of Charlestown on Nevis island. He is the statesman with his portrait on which of the following American money:
   a. $5.00 b. $10.00 c. $20.00 d. $100.00.

Antigua:

1. The largest of the leeward islands is:
   a. Nevis b. Antigua c. Dominica d. Haiti.
2. Antigua is known for their fine:
   a. ports b. harbors c. sword fishing d. "a & c".
3. They say that Antigua has how many fine beaches:
   a. 300 b. 325 c. 350 d. 365.

Trinidad and Tobago:

1. Trinidad and Tobago are two small islands in the Caribbean Sea and located:
   a. southernmost b. north c. east d. west   ... of the end of the West Indian Island chain.
2. Christopher Columbus discovered Trinidad in:
   a. 1398 b. 1450 c. 1458 d. 1498.
3. Political influences on Trinidad and Tobago are largely:
   a. British b. U.S. c. French d. Dutch.
4. There are over a million people with mixed cultures in Trinidad and Tobago. These cultures have enhanced unique:
   a. traditions b. harmony c. respect d. dignity   ... instead of racial violence.

5. The main source of revenue comes from the following products:
   a. sugar b. cocoa c. oil fields and natural gas d. "a, b, & c".

6. Trinidad and Tobago are independent and industrialized nations. The government is working with its people to continue to have:
   a. education and opportunity b. jobs c. modern transportation d. "a, b, & c".

Anguilla:

1. The word angulla could have come from the Spanish word anguila or French angulle meaning:
   a. heel b. hill c. eel d. foot.

2. In the 1600s farming was a main source of earning a living by raising:
   a. tobacco b. cotton c. sugar cane d. "a, b, & c".

3. Anguilla is mostly of what country influence:
   a. British b. French c. Dutch d. Spanish.

British Virgin Islands:

1. The name of the British Island that has the baths is:
   a. Anegada b. Tortola c. Virgin Gorda d. Jost Van Dyke.

2. The two British Virgin Islands known for their sandy beaches are:
   a. Tortola and Virgin Gorda b. St. Thomas and St. John c. Martinique and St. Maarten
   d. Trinidad and Tobago.

3. The British Virgin Islands are scattered 1,000 square miles to the east of:
   a. Puerto Rico b. Trinidad c. Aruba d. Grenada.

4. The largest British Virgin Island, which is 11 miles x 3 miles is:
   a. Virgin Gorda b. Tortola c. Jost Van Dyke d. Anegada.

5. Virgin Gorda received what nickname from Christopher Columbus:
   a. Slender Virgin b. Fat Virgin C. Naughty Virgin d. Funny Virgin.

General Questions about the Caribbean Islands:

1. South of the Virgin Islands are the following islands consisting of Anguilla, St. Maarten, Saba, St. Eustatius, St. Bathelemy, St. Kitts, and Nevis, Antigua and Barbuda, Monsterrat, Guadeloupe known as the:
   a. leeward islands b. westwood islands c. windward islands d. adjacent islands.

2. Dominica, Martinique, St. Lucia, St.Vincent, The Grenadines, and Grenada, are known as the:
   a. leeward islands b. westwood islands c. windward islands d. adjacent islands.

3. The lesser Antilles islands Barbados, Trinidad, and Tobago and the Venezuelan Islands plus Aruba, Curacao, and Bonaire are often called the:
   a. westwood islands b. ABC islands c. windward islands d. sea islands.

4. Which of the following islands is known as the great Antilles Island:
   a. Cuba b. St. Vincent c. St. Maarten d. "b & c".

5. Aruba has beautiful sandy beaches and began under the influence of the:
    a. British b. Dutch c. Spanish d. French.
6. Aruba's size compared to other Caribbean islands is:
    a. smallest b. largest c. second smallest d. second largest.
7. In the middle of town, Aruba has a beautiful church of what faith:
    a. Catholic b. Methodist c. Lutheran d. Episcopal.

Grenada:
1. The capital of Grenada is:
    a. St. Mark b. St. Mary c. St. George d. St. Ann.
2. What conditions make it hard to travel in Granada:
    a. mountainous terrain b. no railroads c. gravel and narrow roads d. "a, b & c".
3. Less than half of the population own automobiles, but people that do own a jeep-like vehicle called:
    a. mini-moke b. mini-poke c. mini-jeep d. none of the choices.
4. Gas in Grenada costs how much a gallon:
    a. $1.00 b. $1.50 c. $2.00 d. $2.50.
5. Most of the Grenada population is:
    a. Catholic b. Christian Scientist c. Lutheran d. Presbyterian.
6. Approximately 95 percent of the Grenadians are descended from African slaves brought to work on what kind of plantations:
    a. corn b. sugar c. cotton d. tobacco.
7. A very important tradition in Grenada that comes from African roots is:
    a. folk singing b. story telling c. dancing with family d. playing tag with the children.

Caribbean Island Trivia Questions
Answer Key:

Dominica
1. c.
2. a.
3. c.
4. d.
5. b.
6. a.
7. c.

Martinique
1. c.
2. a.
3. c.
4. a.

Barbados
1. d.
2. d.
3. c.
4. b.
5. a.
6. d.
7. b.
8. c.
9. d.
10. a.
11. d.
12. b.
13. c.
14. d.
15. a.
16. b.

Jamaica
1. d.
2. a.
3. c.
4. a.
5. d.
6. c.
7. a.
8. a.
9. a.

U.S. Virgin Islands
1. b.
2. a.
3. b.
4. c.
5. b.
6. c.
7. c.
8. d.
9. c.

Nevis
1. a.
2. a.
3. b.
4. d.
5. b.
6. b.

Antigua
1. b.
2. b.
3. d.

Trinidad and Tobago
1. a.
2 c.
3. a.
4. a.
5. d.
6. d.

Anguilla
1. c.
2. d.
3. a.

British Virgin Islands
1. c.
2. a.
3. a.
4. b.
5. b.

General Questions
1. a.
2. c.
3. b.
4. a.
5. b.
6. a.
7. a.

Grenada
1. c.
2. d.
3. a.
4. d.
5. a.
6. b.
7. b.

Facts About the Baobab Tree

The baobab is also called the upside-down tree. The oldest known living specimen is 45 ft. in diameter and 3,000 years old. The tree originated in Africa.

The baobab tree has the widest trunk in the world. It takes 15 people to reach around the entire trunk of the tree. It is considered the national tree in Dominica and is also found in Barbados. It is not a tall tree, usually grows no higher than 9 feet, but it is very wide at the trunk. The tree has leaves of deep yellow and green and has white flowers. Each year, new foliage appears in late spring or early summer.

The baobab tree has many uses. Its fruit, which is egg shaped, is known to fight fever and the bark is a source of quinine. It is also used to fight malaria. The seeds found in the fruit of the baobab are high in protein and oil. The leaves can be used in salad. The inner part of the trunk has strong fibers, which are used for making sacks, baskets, ropes, and nets. They also make waterproof hats from this remarkable tree. The tree can survive even when large amounts of the bark is removed—it just grows back, and it makes the trunk of the tree look like an old elephant skin.

Would you believe, the tree's large trunk contains 30,000 gallons of water? Let's make a big circle stretching out our arms to get an idea of the size of the baobab tree.

The story goes, that in Dominica, Hurricane Hugo took one of the baobab trees and laid it right down on a school bus. Now tourists come from all over to witness this tree.

Story

In Barbados there was a baobab tree named Bab with wrinkled elephant skin. The tree had only one eye, but when the tourists walked by and gave the tree a big squeeze, the tree winked and jiggled his trunk a tad.

You see, this tree was very vain and always looked in the mirror. He was so proud because he said God made him very different from any other trees in the entire world. He had fun letting tourists give him many hugs. He enjoyed the comments of the tourists. Some would say, "Boy, are you ever big!" One time he winked at me. I sure hope he does not fall on me. His skin is so funny and his leaves are so small in comparison to his trunk.

Eventually the tree got tired of the comments from the tourists and began to complain to God. Then one day the tree was uprooted and became upside down. The big old tree never looked in the mirror again.

Tourists continued to come and see the tree, feeling sorry for Bab.

At this point, the tree made up his mind to make the best of his upside-down situation. Today, he continues to greet the tourists from all over the world. He realizes it is wonderful to stand out and not to be just different, but outstanding!

Granny's Soup Kitchen

Select volunteer residents to participate in making the meal. This meal is sized for a 20-patient residence such as Assisted Living. It is a great time for residents to come together to socialize. Use a theme to set the table and decorate, it could be a farm theme or any subject that seems appropriate. You can do this activity six months out of the year. The residents enjoy the good meal and the creativity.

Menu

Chicken Chili

Raspberry Spinach Salad

Cheese, sliced and chunks

French Bread and Butter

Coffee and Milk

Recipes:
Note: Use small portions.

Chicken Chili
Yield: 20 one-cup servings.
- 1 pound chicken tenders, cooked and diced
- 1 jar (48 ounces) great northern beans (fully cooked)
- 1 can (3 pounds $1^1/_2$ ounces) chicken broth (99% fat free)
- 1 can (15 ounces) corn 'n peppers (southwestern style)
- 1 can ($14^1/_2$ ounces) diced tomatoes
- 1 cup diced celery
- 1 small onion, diced
- 3 cloves fresh garlic, minced
- 2 teaspoons chili powder
- 2 teaspoons cumin
- 1 teaspoon onion powder
- $^1/_2$ teaspoon pepper

Boil the chicken in water for about five minutes. In a large stock pot or crockpot add the chicken broth, chicken, beans, corn, celery, onion, tomatoes, and garlic. Add the spices. Cook over low heat in the crockpot for five to six hours. Serve with bread and crackers and cheese.

Raspberry Spinach Salad

Yield: 20-25 servings.

2 pounds fresh spinach
3 hard-cooked eggs, diced
1 pound bacon, diced
$^1/_2$ red onion, sliced
$^1/_2$ pound seasoned croutons
2 pints grape tomatoes
1 red pepper, diced
1 cup diced celery
1 pound mushrooms, sliced
1 bottle (8 ounces) Fat Free Raspberry Vinaigrette salad dressing

Clean spinach and drain thoroughly. Fry bacon and drain on a paper towel. Add the celery, mushrooms, and dressing. Toss. Place in your serving bowl and garnish with bacon, eggs, red pepper, and croutons.

Fantastic Brain Tickler Word Game

The following words have the letters "e" and "a" in each word. See how many words you can figure out by reading the description.

1. E_ _ Something most people like to do at a picnic.
2. H _ _ _ If you are cold you turn up the.
3. S_ _ _ _ Commit robbery.
4. S_ _ _ _ _ Date one person exclusively.
5. S_ _ _ _ _ _ A way of taking action designed to escape notice.
6. S_ _ _ _ Boiling water or a hot iron produces.
7. S_ _ _ _ _ _ A white crystalline fatty acid used to make candles or soup.
8. S_ _ _ _ A thick slice of beef.
9. B_ _ _ Winning a game or keeping time with the music.
10. S_ _ _ _ _ _ _ Solid part of fat found in many vegetables.
11. G_ _ _ _ A grandparent whose grandchild has a baby becomes a _____grandparent.
12. G_ _ _ _ _ The squeaky wheel gets fixed with this.
13. C_ _ _ _ _ _ _ _ _ A popular music using steel drums and played in the islands.
14. B_ _ _ _ A favorite picnic food known as musical fruit.
15. B_ _ _ _ String these objects into a group to make a design on a wedding gown or into a necklace.
16. B_ _ _ _ Made from yeast and known as the staff of life.
17. K_ _ _ _ Working the bread dough.
18. R_ _ _ _ _ _ Something existing in fact.
19. R_ _ _ _ Kingdom, Province, or Domaine.
20. R_ _ _ Estate
21. R_ _ _ _ _ _ _ _ _ _ Politics that deal solely in terms to do with national interests.
22. R_ _ _ _ _ _ One of the three "Rs".
23. R_ _ _ _ _ _ _ _ Clothes sewn to a stock size.
24. R_ _ _ _ _ _ _ A surprised response.
25. R_ _ _ _ _ _ _ _ _ To be active again.
26. R_ _ _ _ Complete a goal.
27. P_ _ _ A point at the top.
28. R_ _ _ _ _ _ _ _ _ _ To encourage a person.
29. R_ _ _ _ _ A person may not act for a good _____.
30. R_ _ _ In the Bible it says, "You will ____ what you sow. Also pertains to ripe grain.
31. R_ _ _ _ _ _ A temperature scale on which the freezing point of water at one atmosphere is zero and its boiling point is 80 degrees at the same pressure.
32. P_ _ _ _ A popular fruit grown in Georgia.

33. P_ _ _ _ _ _ An English novelist and poet who wrote "Nightmare Abbey" in 1818. Also a name of a bird.
34. P_ _ A name of a green vegetable that is small and round.
35. W_ _ _ _ _ An automobile usually has a set of four (two in front and two in back).
36. E_ _ _ When traveling you can go south, north, west or ____.
37. Y_ _ _ _ Helps bread to rise.
38. P_ _ _ A greenish-yellow fruit, wide at the bottom and narrow at the top.
39. P_ _ _ _ At the end of war there is a treaty made.
40. P_ _ _ _ _ _ _ A minister is also known as a ____.
41. P_ _ _ _ Another name for Margaret.
42. P_ _ _ _ _ _ _ Pleasing or agreeable.
43. P_ _ _ _ _ Interweave stems or branches.
44. P_ _ _ _ To beg with emotion.
45. P_ _ _ _ _ Asking for something in a polite manner and a thank you if the person obliges.
46. Q_ _ _ _ _ Sick stomach.
47. E_ _ _ The opposite of a hard task.
48. T_ _ A popular hot beverage served in England.
49. C_ _ _ _ Served in coffee.
50. C_ _ _ _ Squeaking noise.
51. I_ _ C_ _ _ _ Made with cream, sugar, and vanilla and comes in a frozen state in several flavors.
52. C_ _ _ _ _ _ _ A living animal or human being.
53. C_ _ _ _ _ _ _ Imaginative.
54. B_ _ _ _ _ Breaking of a legal contract or a moral obligation.
55. B_ _ _ _ _ _ _ _ _ A tropical fruit that is edible, round, and sticky.
56. B_ _ _ _ Drop and shatter a glass.
57. B_ _ _ _ _ _ The linear dimension measured side-to-side.
58. B_ _ _ _ _ _ _ _ _ _ Earns the living for the family.
59. B_ _ _ Part of a bird's body.
60. B_ _ _ _ _ A light in a tower.
61. C_ _ _ _ _ _ _ A business that washes and presses clothes.
62. H_ _ _ _ _ Well being of a person.
63. B_ _ B_ _ _ _ _ A part of the human's body that has an odor after eating garlic or onions.
64. H_ _ _ _ A symbol associated with Valentine's Day.
65. S_ _ _ A technique used for browning a roast.
66. M_ _ _ Food you eat three times a day.
67. B_ _ _ _ _ _ _ _ Food eaten early in the day.
68. C_ _ _ _ _ _ A kitchen tool to cut a big piece of meat.
69. D_ _ _ Got an item for a good price, or something a person does when handing out playing cards.
70. R_ _ _ _ _ _ _ To study on a topic such as cancer.

71. S_ _ _ _ _ _ A person who addresses a group about a topic.
72. F_ _ _ _ _ _ A special movie or an article in a newspaper.
73. F_ _ _ _ _ _ _ Found on a bird's body such as a chicken or turkey.
74. E_ _ _ _ _ _ Clip on, or pierced style of jewelry.
75. C_ _ _ _ _ _ A product like window wash solution.
76. T_ _ _ _ _ _ _ _ How a person acts toward another person, or an application by a doctor.
77. T_ _ _ _ _ _ Works with students in school.
78. L_ _ _ Grows on a tree—and not money!
79. B_ _ _ _ Facial hair on a man.
80. Y_ _ _ 365 days make up one.
81. H_ _ _ If you don't use your_____, you will use your feet.
82. D_ _ _ _ _ _ _ _ _ A deed is made void.
83. D_ _ _ _ _ Conquer in a sport or a war.
84. C_ _ _ _ Bring to an end.
85. C_ _ _ _ _ _ _ _ A last name of a Rumanian statesman. Secretary General of the Communist Party.
86. B_ _ _ A long, heavy, piece of wood.
87. B_ _ _ _ _ A drinking vessel.
88. B_ _ _ A large furry brown or white animal.
89. B_ _ _ _ There is a children's movie called "Beauty and the ____".
90. B_ _ _ _ _ _ _ _ Majestic mountains are said to be _____.
91. D_ _ _ Introduction word when writing a letter.
92. S_ _ _ _ Trim wool from a sheep.
93. H_ _ _ _ An object too hard to pick up due to its weight.
94. H_ _ _ _ _ Comes after life on this earth and thought as eternal life.
95. H_ _ _ _ _ _ A person who does not worship the God of Christians, Jews, or Moslems.
96. H_ _ _ _ _ _ _ A pain in the head.
97. H_ _ _ C_ _ _ _ _ _ A census taker.
98. H_ _ _ C_ _ _ _ _ A meat from a pig's or calf's head that is boiled and pressed in a mold in a natural aspic.
99. H_ _ _ B_ _ _ Worn around the head, sometimes while exercising.
100. H_ _ _ L_ _ _ A hold in which the opponent's head is held between the arm and body.
101. H_ _ _ Q_ _ _ _ _ _ _ A command post.
102. H_ _ _ R_ _ _ A support for the head, often in a reclining chair.
103. H_ _ _ S_ _ _ _ _ Obstinate.
104. H_ _ _ S_ _ _ _ Is erected at the head of a grave.
105. H_ _ _ S_ _ _ _ A program developed by the government for low-income families.
106. H_ _ _ _ _ _ Used for listing to the radio that only you can hear.
107. H_ _ _ A material piled high.

108. H_ _ _ To get better after surgery.
109. D_ _ _ A name of a sea near Israel.
110. B_ _ _ _ _ A part of a women's body used for feeding milk to her newborn baby.
111. H_ _ _ _ _ Vigorous.
112. H_ _ _ _ _ _ _ Not concerned for anyone's feelings.
113. H_ _ _ r_ _ _ _ _ _ A feeling of pity.
114. H_ _ _ _ _ The floor of the fireplace.
115. H_ _ _ _ _ _ Not based on facts.
116. H_ _ _ _ _ A vehicle that carries a corpse.
117. H_ _ _ _ _ _ _ A burning sensation that causes indigestion.
118. H_ _ _ _ _ _ A deep and sincere feeling.
119. H_ _ _ _ _ _ _ Depressed.
120. H_ _ _ _ S_ _ _ _ _ _ To appeal to someone's feelings of affection or pity in order to gain something they desire.
121. H_ _ _ _ _ _ _ _ The innermost non-living portion of xylem of vascular plants that serves primarily as mechanical support.
122. H_ _ _ _ A plant usually found growing in open, barren, poorly drained soil.
123. H_ _ _ _ _ _ A female name.
124. H_ _ _ E_ _ _ _ _ _ _ _ _ Too much sun causes fainting and dizziness.
125. H_ _ _ S_ _ _ _ _ An acute condition marked by inactivity of sweat glands and very high body temperature.
126. H_ _ _ P_ _ _ _ _ _ _ _ Heated industrial waste that causes environmental changes.
127. H_ _ _ _ W_ _ _ _ _ A professional boxer.
128. B_ _ _ _ _ T_ _ _ _ _ Thrilling.
129. B_ _ _ _- T _ _ _ _ _ _ Successful achievement.
130. B_ _ _ _ _ _ A huge wave with a white crest.
131. B_ _ _ _ _ B_ _ _ The sternum.
132. W_ _ _ _ _ Uses a loom to make fabric.
133. W_ _ _ _ _ Rich with lots of worldly possessions.
134. W_ _ _ Take a baby off the bottle.
135. W_ _ _ _ _ _ Temperature of the day, sunny or cloudy.
136. W_ _ _ _ _ _ B_ _ _ _ _ Sun burned.
137. W_ _ _ _ _ A small mammal found in the northern hemisphere. He does well in cold weather.
138. W_ _ _ _ _ _ _ _ Mental, of physical fatigue.
139. Z_ _ _ _ _ _ Showing zeal.
140. Z_ _ _ _ _ Someone that acts for a cause.
141. Z_ _ _ Devotion to a cause.
142. Z_ _ _ _ _ _ Largest island located in Denmark.
143. Z_ _ _ _ _ A substance with self-dividing properties that enables plants to grow.

144. Y_ _ Indeed, agreeing, often used in oral voting.
145. Y_ _ _ _ _ _ Statistics, activities, events, published by high schools.
146. Y_ _ _ Irish poet with the first name of William.
147. J_ _ _ _ _ A predatory bird that lives in the northern seas.
148. J_ _ _ _ _ Envious of others.
149. J_ _ _ _ _ _ A female name. Stephen Foster wrote a song about her hair.
150. J_ _ _ _ A type of pants worn by men, women, and children.
151. G_ _ _ _ A faint light, or faint trace of hope.
152. G_ _ _ _ To gather grain leftover little-by-little.

Answer Key to Fantastic Brain Ticklers

1. Eat
2. Heat
3. Steal
4. Steady
5. Stealth
6. Steam
7. Stearic
8. Steak
9. Beat
10. Sterarin
11. Great
12. Grease
13. Caribbean
14. Beans
15. Beads
16. Bread
17. Knead
18. Reality
19. Realm
20. Real
21. Realpolitik
22. Reading
23. Readymade
24. Reaction
25. Reactivate
26. Reach
27. Peak
28. Reassurance
29. Reason
30. Reap
31. Reaumur
32. Peach
33. Peacock
34. Pea
35. Wheels
36. East
37. Yeast
38. Pear
39. Peace
40. Preacher
41. Pearl
42. Pleasant
43. Pleach
44. Plead

45. Please
46. Queasy
47. Easy
48. Tea
49. Cream
50. Creak
51. Ice Cream
52. Creature
53. Creative
54. Breach
55. Breadfruit
56. Break
57. Breadth
58. Breadwinner
59. Beak
60. Beacon
61. Cleaners
62. Health
63. Bad Breath
64. Heart
65. Sear
66. Meal
67. Breakfast
68. Cleaver
69. Deal
70. Research
71. Speaker
72. Feature
73. Feathers
74. Earring
75. Cleaner
76. Treatment
77. Teacher
78. Leaf
79. Beard
80. Year
81. Head
82. Defeasance
83. Defeat
84. Cease
85. Ceausescu
86. Beam
87. Beaker
88. Bear
89. Beast

90. Beautiful
91. Dear
92. Shear
93. Heavy
94. Heaven
95. Heathen
96. Headache
97. Head Counter
98. Head Cheese
99. Head Band
100. Head Lock
101. Headquarters
102. Head Rest
103. Headstrong
104. Headstone
105. Head Start
106. Headset
107. Heap
108. Heal
109. Dead
110. Breast
111. Hearty
112. Heartless
113. Heartrending
114. Hearth
115. Hearsay
116. Hearse
117. Heartburn
118. Hearten
119. Heartsick
120. Heart Strings
121. Heartwood
122. Heath
123. Heather
124. Heat Exhaustion
125. Heat Stroke
126. Heat Pollution
127. Heavy Weight
128. Breathtaking
129. Break-Through
130. Breaker
131. Breast Bone
132. Weaver
133. Wealth
134. Wean

135. Weather
136. Weatherbeaten
137. Weasel
138. Wearisome
139. Zealous
140. Zealot
141. Zeal
142. Zealand
143. Zeatin
144. Yea
145. Yearbook
146. Yeats
147. Jeager
148. Jealous
149. Jeannie
150. Jeans
151. Gleam
152. Glean

Log Cabin Fever Party

The purpose of this event is to raise funds for a favorite charity in the community.

Contact your local council of Scouts and invite them in to help set up and serve for a community based pancake breakfast. Saturday is a very good day. Ask merchants for prizes to give out to participants at the breakfast.

Sell tickets in advance and hire a company to come in with their pancake equipment to do the work.

You can give out, or sell, hot pads or T-shirts with the facility's name on them.

Invite crafters and quilters to rent a booth at the breakfast and have a craft show. Get a band to come in and play music.

People will enjoy the day with their loved ones.

Suggested Menu: Pancakes, Sausages, Applesauce, Syrup, Milk, Coffee

Music Bingo

Name that tune: Listen to the song and cover the board space that lists that title.

B	I	N	G	O
You Are My Sunshine	Tea For Two	Bye, Bye, Blackbird	Baby Face	I Love You Truly
Sidewalks of New York	I'm Looking Over A Four-Leaf Clover	I Found a Million-Dollar Baby	Let Me Call You Sweetheart	Goodnight, Irene
Harbor Lights	The Sound of Music	**FREE**	Blue Hawaii	Battle Hymn of The Republic
When Irish Eyes Are Smiling	Oh! Suzanna	Tick Tock Polka	Red River Valley	My Wild Irish Rose
On Top of Old Smoky	Home on the Range	Bicycle Built For Two	Take Me Out To The Ballgame	God Bless America

Wishing Well Activity

The idea is to make a Wishing Well showing something the participants are wishing for.

I wish I could grow flowers.

I wish I could golf.

I wish I could have a dog.

I wish I could play Bingo three times a day.

The residents can display their wishing well in their room, or at coffee hour—or even trade when they are wishing for something they like to do or something they can no longer do, such as gardening or golfing. It is a memory to hold dear. While making the wishing well they can do a lot of wishing.

Supplies needed: Refer to page 4 in color section for finished project in color.

- 1   orange juice can, cleaned and dry.
- 11   clothes pins taken apart for around the bottom of the wishing well. (*Save the clips.)
      Glue.
- 2   clothespins for holding the roof (1 on each side).
- 6   clothespins for the roof (6 half pins on each side).
      Various decorative items to trim the wishing wells to match the resident's wishes.

*You can use the leftover clothespin's clips to string together to make a plant hanger.

1. The juice can is $11^1/_2$ inches high and clothespins are $3^1/_2$ inches high, so cut the can down to 3 inches so the clothespins stick up above the top edge of the can.

2. Hot glue the clothespins to the side of the can with the flat side against the can, and leaving $1/_2$ inch of the pin sticking up over the top of the can.

3. To form the roof, place two single pieces of the clothespins together at the thicker end of the pin piece, and hot glue. Repeat until you have glued six pins together side by side, forming a peaked roof.

4. Using two single pieces of pin, glue the flat sides together, leaving a single pin sticking out at both ends. You use this single space to hot glue the pin post to the inside of the roof and the other end of the post is glued to the inside of the can.

5. Decorate roof and wishing well in any theme you choose.

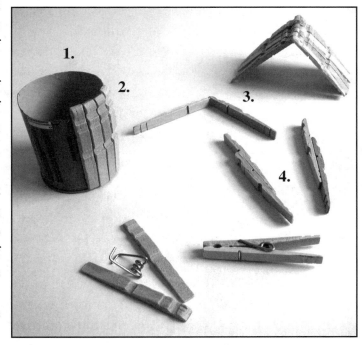

February Activities

Groundhog's Day Shadow Party

A groundhog is also called a woodchuck. It is a round-like furry animal that lives in the ground. The groundhog is found throughout North America and hibernates during the winter.

Groundhog's Day is celebrated on February 2nd. It is a tradition that started with a Christian festival associated with farmers planting their spring crops. It was believed that if the groundhog saw his shadow he would go back into his den for six more weeks of winter.

If it was a cloudy day, spring would come early. In the old days, crowds gathered to see the groundhog and make a big celebration out of this event. If winter was extended six more weeks, the crowd would show great disappointment with loud noises. But if the groundhog didn't see his shadow—spring would come early and the band would play and the people would cheer.

In America, Groundhog's Day began in 1887 in Pennsylvania. People from Punxsutawney would gather to see the appearance of the groundhog. But, some folks say the custom really started in Scotland. Legend has it that the person who saw the groundhog first would follow him as a reminder to the animal that spring was coming early. At any rate, Groundhog's Day is famous for predicting how much longer winter will last.

Now, let's talk shadows. What really is a shadow? How can we actually see our shadow? You can see your shadow in the sunlight or with candlelight. A shadow is an outline of an object. You can make a shadow and chase it. If you are out in the sun with your feet on the ground your feet will touch the shadow. A shadow copies what you do in the sun. If you put a light on your hand in a dark room you will see the shadow of your hand on the wall or floor. If you use a projector, you can create a shadow.

Get the residents to wave and help them exercise their hands and arms as they seek their shadow and other residents' shadows.

Ask for volunteers from the group to see their shadow. Turn a movie projector light on a screen and get the volunteers to put their hand up toward the screen to see their hand shadow.

Get a local weather report about whether the groundhog saw his shadow. If he didn't, and spring is predicted to come early, lead the residents in a cheer—if he did see his shadow and winter is going to continue for six more weeks, act out being disappointed.

At the end of the program sing or play some spring music to celebrate the end of winter.

The Groundhog Dance

This is an actual North American Native American dance from the Cherokee tribe.

Get a person in the audience to volunteer to be the groundhog. Select seven more "volunteers" to act like wolves. (If you have invited elementary school children to the party include them in the "volunteers". Prepare the children by practicing with them in school beforehand. You can also have one student beat a drum to add suspense to the story.)

Have the groundhog stand in the middle of the circle of wolves. Have some of the residents use rhythmic instruments to create the mood. The bongo drum can be used when the wolves get too close to the groundhog.

The story goes ...

Seven wolves caught a fat groundhog. The wolves said they were going to eat the groundhog. The groundhog said, "Tsk, Tsk, Tsk," as he scolded the wolves, and stalled for time by saying, "When you find good food you should dance first, before you eat it."

The wolves agreed to dance like human beings do. But the groundhog informed the wolves they were not dancing properly, and he let them know that they looked funny dancing in such a manner. The groundhog said, " I will be your teacher—here is how it really goes. I will sing and you will dance far away from me. Whenever you run toward me, I will sing until you get far away from me." Here is the groundhog's song.

The Groundhog Song
a folk song by Laura Booseinger

(19th Century Sing-Alongs, $9.95. Native Ground Music, 109 Gell Road, Asheville, NC 28805 [1-800-752-2656]
ISBN: 1-883206-21-9) website: www.nativeground.com.

Ha wi ye-a hi

Ya ha wi ye a hi

Ha wi ye-a hi

Ya ha wi ye-a hi

(Cherokee Indian version.)

Type these lyrics up and hand out the sheets to the residents and then do a little rehearsal. You will get the residents laughing as they try to say this very quickly.

Back to the story ...

Finally the groundhog persuaded the wolves to get farther and farther away from him, and he made a beeline to his burrow. The groundhog shouts a loud "Yu," to the audience.

The storyteller should tell the groundhog, "I can't hear you!" Get the school children to say it louder, and the storyteller should repeat, "A little louder!" "Yu! Yu! Yu! Yu!" The groundhog was saved and survived.

The End!

Groundhog's Day Dance and Chant

Accordion Music by Pat Nekola

Ha Ha Wi   Ye a Hi   Shout Yu

Ya Ya Ya Ya   Ha Ha   Wi Ye a Hi   Shout Yu

Ha   Wi   Ye   a   Hi   Shout Yu

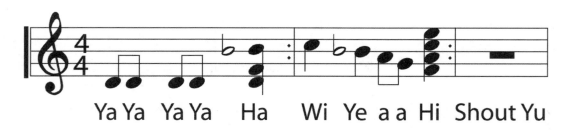

Ya Ya Ya Ya   Ha   Wi Ye a a Hi Shout Yu

Bellow shakes repeatedly for the last chord of the song. This is an alert the groundhog is getting away from the wolves. The air button on the accordion makes for a sigh of relief for the groundhog's get away. The groundhog shouts Yu! because he is getting the wolves away from him.

Serve coffee, milk, and shadow cake to the residents and children.

Recipe:

Chocolate Shadow Cake

2	dark chocolate cake mixes
$1/2$	cup almonds, finely chopped
$1/2$	teaspoon cinnamon
$1/4$	teaspoon cloves
6	eggs
$2^1/2$	cups water
$2/3$	cup cooking oil

Topping:

4	cups (2 pints) whipping cream
2	cups powdered sugar
1	cup cocoa
1	teaspoon almond extract
$1/2$	cup slivered almonds

Follow directions on cake mix. Preheat oven to 350 degrees. Grease 11 x 17-inch cake pan.

In a large bowl, combine all the cake ingredients at low speed until moistened. Beat for 3 minutes at the highest speed. Pour batter into cake pan and bake for 30-40 minutes or until toothpick comes out clean. Cool cake on a large rack.

When cake is cool combine all the topping ingredients except the almonds in a large chilled bowl. Beat at the highest speed until topping forms stiff peaks. Spread over cake and sprinkle almonds at random on top, to form a shadow.

Without A Shadow Of A Doubt, It'll Be A Happy Groundhog Day!

Granny's Soup Kitchen

For a great Soup and Sandwich event serve Split Pea Soup and Grilled Cheese Sandwiches.

Split Pea Soup

12   cups water (4 quarts)

1   pound ham, diced or a ham bone with meat

2   pounds dry split peas

$^2/_3$ cup onions, diced

3   tablespoons ham flavor seasoning (optional)

3   tablespoons finely diced celery

$^1/_2$ cup julienne carrots

2   teaspoons garlic pepper

2   bay leaves or 1 teaspoon bay leaf seasoning

In a 6-quart crockpot mix all the ingredients. Cook on low heat for 6 to 8 hours, or until soup is thickened. If the soup is refrigerated overnight it will thicken, add a little water when reheating.

The Eggplant-Ravioli Soup is nice to serve for Valentine's Day, as it is red. People don't think they like eggplant, but it is diced small and cooked and no one knows what it is.

I grow my own tomatoes, onions, peppers, and zucchini for soups. Zucchini bread is great with this soup—you can make mini cream cheese sandwiches with it. The ladies like this better than the men, men prefer bread and crackers. This soup is best cooked for at least 8 hours on low heat—the liquid will cook up. I, personally, like to stir the cooked ravioli into the soup—be sure to cool the ravioli before adding to the soup, so it doesn't fall apart. If you need to stretch the soup, add more ravioli and V-8 juice or chicken stock, and more seasonings, to taste.

Go through the method with the residents in the Granny's Soup Kitchen activity. Get their opinion about which method they prefer to use for soup. I did some soup with two different methods so the group could decide which method tasted better to them. Giving choices to the residents always makes them feel special, because, for once, they are in control.

Eggplant-Ravioli Soup

Yield: 24 servings.

1   can (49-ounces) fat-free chicken broth

4   cans (11.5-ounces each) V-8 juice

1   eggplant, peeled and diced

1   cup vermouth cooking wine

2   cans (14.5-ounces each) diced tomatoes

2   leeks, sliced into onion rings

$^1/_2$ white onion, diced

2 bunches (1-ounce each) fresh Italian basil, chopped—or you can substitute 2 teaspoons dried basil

1 package (16-ounce) frozen pepper stir-fry vegetables

3 cups frozen whole kernel corn

3 teaspoons minced dehydrated garlic

2 teaspoons onion powder

4 bay leaves

3 teaspoons white pepper

1 teaspoon salt

2 teaspoons Italian seasoning

3 teaspoons thyme

3 teaspoons fennel seed, or $2^1/_2$ teaspoons ground fennel

2 tablespoons olive oil (reserve 1 tablespoon for cooking the ravioli)

$^1/_3$ cup water

2 pounds ground veal

2 packages (9-ounces each) sun-dried tomato ravioli

Combine the broth, juice, and wine in a large stockpot. Add the vegetables and seasonings and stir thoroughly. Divide the soup into a large and small crockpot and cook for 8 hours over low heat. When the soup is thoroughly cooked combine the two crockpots into one large pot.

Method One: *Personally, I prefer to stir the cooked ravioli into the cooked soup.*

For cooking the ravioli:

Add 3 quarts of water to a large saucepan, and bring to a boil. Add 1 tablespoon olive oil and the 2 packages of ravioli to the boiling water. Cook for 6-8 minutes. Do not overcook the ravioli. Drain, rinse, and set aside. Add to thoroughly cooked soup.

Method Two:

One hour before serving time, cook the ravioli as directed in Method One. Heat the soup and place in a shallow full-size hotel pan. Place the ravioli on top of the soup and sprinkle with Parmesan cheese. Bake for 8-10 minutes at 350 degrees, or until the cheese melts.

Serve with assorted crackers, French bread, and cream cheese zucchini bread mini sandwiches.

As a Side Dish: Cheesy French Bread

butter or margarine

2 packages (12-ounces each) grated Parmesan or Mozzarella cheese

Slice the French bread into thin slices. Butter each slice and sprinkle with cheese. Place on a cookie sheet and bake at 400 degrees for 4-5 minutes, or until the cheese melts and the bottom of the bread is toasted. Serve with the soup.

♥

Zucchini Bread

Note: It is best to use smaller zucchini. The very large ones have large seeds. If your zucchini has large seeds, cut them out. It takes about $6^1/_2$ to 7 small zucchini to make two loaves of bread. You can grate the zucchini by hand, or use a Kitchen Aid slicer and shredder attachment. The zucchini should be very finely grated. Try adding a small can of crushed pineapple-per loaf, drained well, to the batter—it is delicious. You can also substitute black walnut flavoring for vanilla and walnuts for pecans. If the bread browns too quickly, halfway through the baking time reduce the heat to 325 degrees.

Yield: one loaf.

3	eggs
1	cup oil
$1^3/_4$	cups sugar
2	cups peeled and grated zucchini
3	teaspoons vanilla
3	cups flour
1	teaspoon salt
1	teaspoon baking soda
2	teaspoons cinnamon
$^1/_4$	teaspoon baking powder
$^3/_4$	cup chopped pecans (optional)

Yield: two loaves.

6	eggs
$1^3/_4$	cups oil
3	cups sugar
4	cups peeled and grated zucchini
4	teaspoons vanilla
6	cups flour
1	teaspoon salt
2	teaspoons baking soda
1	tablespoon cinnamon
$^1/_2$	teaspoon baking powder

Grease and flour $9^1/_2$ x $5^1/_2$-inch bread pans for either one or two loaves. Beat eggs until light in color. Add oil, zucchini, vanilla, flour, salt, cinnamon, baking soda, and baking powder. Stir until the batter is smooth. If making two loaves, divide the batter evenly between the two loaf pans. Bake at 350 degrees for 1 to $1^1/_2$ hours, or until toothpick inserted in the center of loaf comes out clean. Cool in pan for 5-8 minutes before turning bread out onto counter or serving plate. Serve warm or cold with butter. Refer to page 4 in the color section for a color picture.

Sweetheart Dinner-Dance

Get the residents to sign up in advance. They can invite their families to attend the party. Hire a band to play for the evening. Contact community businesses and citizens for donations for a silent auction. (One independent living facility made a quilt and sold raffle tickets.) Select a favorite charity to give the proceeds to, such as the Alzheimer's Association, Heart Association, or the Diabetes Foundation.

Menu

This menu is designed for Independent and Assisted Living Facility residents.

Fresh Fruit Cup

❤

Chicken Cordon Bleu

❤

Wild Rice Pilaf

❤

California Blend Vegetables

❤

Tossed Salad with French and Italian Dressing

❤

Rolls and Butter

❤

Red Velvet Cake

❤

Coffee and Milk

Recipes:

Red Velvet Cake

1   Red Velvet Moist Deluxe Cake Mix 18.25 ounces
1   12-ounce frozen whipped topping
2   cans (21-ounces each) cherry pie filling

Follow directions on the cake mix. When the baked cake is cool, frost with the whipped topping and top with the cherry pie filling.

❤

Heart-Shaped Cookie Bake Sale

The purpose of the bake sale is to raise money for the Heart Association. Select a date and time. It has been my experience that cookies sell best at lunch and supper time. Set up a table with a "Valentine" tablecloth and display the cookies in heart-shaped baskets. Residents and staff will purchase cookies, and even donate cash to the cause.

Have a meeting with the residents to set a price for the cookies. Organize the group on times to make and bake cookies. You can get some staff members to donate sugar or flour to help make more for the Heart Association.

Compose a letter to the Heart Association explaining your donation. Have the residents read and sign the letter. When you get a "Thank You" note back, be sure residents get to see it. Residents will feel good about their accomplishment. They are very much a part of the community for this kind of work. Refer to the color section page 4 in the back of book.

Sugar Cookie Recipe

Yield: $3^1/_2$ dozen.

1	cup butter
1	cup sugar
1	egg
1	teaspoon vanilla
$2^1/_2$	cups flour
1	teaspoon baking soda

Cream butter and sugar together. Add egg and flavorings. Add the baking soda to the flour and add flour mixture to butter mixture.

Flour your board and rolling pin. Roll dough out to $^1/_4$-inch thick. Using a $2^1/_2$ x 3 inch heart-shaped cookie cutter cut out cookies. Sprinkle with red sugar topping and place on ungreased baking sheet $1^1/_2$-inches apart. Bake at 350 degrees for 8 to 10 minutes, or until golden brown on the bottom. The top of the cookie should stay light even though it is baked through. Do not over bake. Do not over flour the board or rolling pin or your cookies will become very hard.

Hand and Heart Cookies
For the Heart Bake Sale

Follow the sugar cookie recipe on page 54. If you do not have a hand cookie cutter trace the pattern onto cardboard and cut out. Use this pattern to trace and cut out cookies with a paring knife. With a mini cookie cutter, cut a heart out of the center of the hand cookie. Bake the hand cookies at 350 degrees for 8 to 10 minutes. Bake the heart cookies for 5 to 6 minutes. Use the frosting glaze recipe on page 78. Add red food color to $1/4$ of the glaze to use for the hearts. The remainder of the frosting will be white for the hand. Use red hot candies for the fingernails on the hand cookies.

Place one hand and one heart cookie in a Ziplock® bag and attached a colored tag with the following message.

"With my heart in my hand, I offer to you,
All of my love in all that I do.
The bond that we share, forever will stand.
I give you this gift, my heart in my hand."
Punch a hole in the corner of the tag and attach to the bag with ribbon.

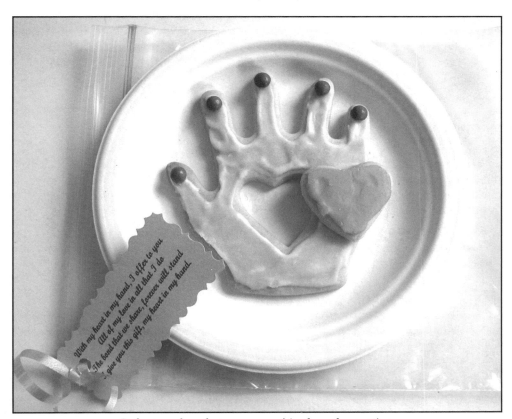

Refer to color photo on page 4 in the color section.

A Valentine Word Game
Using the words "Happy Valentine's Day Sweetheart" create other words.

Rules:
No female or male names.
Do not use the words more than once.
Do not exceed the letters in the phrase.

Example:
Pepper has three letter "p" and there are only two letter "p" in the phrase, therefore pepper does not count.
Remember there is only one "l" and one "i"—do not use these letters more than once in each word.
Count the number of each letter before forming a word.
Do groups of three, four, five, etc. letters for each word.

Answer key of three-letter words:
Ace, aid, and, ant, any, ape, art, car, den, die, dry, ear, eat, end, eye, fir, for, gas, had, has, hat, hay, hen, hip, hot, ink, key, kit, lad, lap, lay, lie, lip, low, may, nap, nip, pal, pan, pat, pay, pea, pen, per, pet, pie, pin, pit, ran, red, sad, sap, sat, see, set, she, shy, sip, sky, sly, tan, tea, ten, war, was, way, wee.

Answer key for four-letter words:
Ants, band, bear, cape, care, clan, darn, dart, date, dead, dear, deer, dent, dine, draw, drew, earn, ease, east, easy, fern, fire, glad, hair, hand, hard, head, heal, hear, heat, heel, heir, help, here, hips, host, laid, last, late, lawn, lead, lend, lent, line, loop, loud, made, maid, nail, neat, nest, note, paid, papa, pare, pain, peak, peep, pine, pipe, plan, play, rage, rate, read, reed, rent, rude, said, sand, seal, sear, seat, seed, send, ship, side, silt, slit, spit, star, step, stew, stir, swan, tale, teal, teen, tent, then, tire, tool, wade, wait, want, weed, weep, were, west, whip, wide, wind, wine, wing, wish, with, wits, wrap.

Answer key for five-letter words:
Apply, atlas, devil, drawn, dread, eaten, entry, erase, ether, ideal, later, leach, lease, least, nasty, noise, paint, paper, pearl, pipes, plaid, plain, plane, press, reeds, river, ruled, saint, sales, sandy, Santa, sense, slate, speed, stain, stand, stale, start, steal, steer, stool, super, sweat, sweep, tarts, taste, tease, tenth, their, there, three, tiger, tired, train, tread, treat, valet, water, wheel, which, white, wings.

Answer key for six-letter words:
Active, answer, easily, handle, happen, heated, health, hearth, hearts, intent, lessen, lesson, lenten, letter, nestle, pledge, steady, stripes, sweets, sweeten, thread, treaty, waiter, wanted.

Answer key for seven-letter words:
Hearten, instead, lantern, lateral, leather, pretend, shipped, starved, weather.

Answer key for eight-letter words:
Elephant, entrance, interest, Internet, pleasure, separate, treasure, waitress.

Answer key for nine-letter words:
Apprehend, essential, president.

Love Word Game

Fill in the blank with words that pertain to love, or can be found in love songs.

1. _ _ _ e
2. C u _ _
3. A _ _ h a
4. _ r i e _ _ s _ _ p
5. L _ i
6. D i a _ _ _ _
7. R o _ _ _ _ _
8. H _ _
9. _ a s _ i _ n
10. H o _ _ _
11. V _ n _ s
12. H _ _ _ t
13. F l o _ _ _ _
14. S w e _ _ h _ _ _ _
15. A n n i v _ _ _ _ _ _
16. X _ X
17. M _ s _ c
18. V a l _ _ _ _ _ _
19. _ _ i r t
20. A m o r _ _ _
21. F i _ _ _ e

22. S _ _ _ _ s
23. J _ _
24. G _ _ _
25. _ _ s s
26. S h a r _ _ _
27. L o y _ _
28. W _ _ _ _ _
29. _ _ _ s h i n e
30. M _ _ _ l i g _ _
31. M _ _ _ _ a g _
32. H a p _ _
33. L o v _ _
34. A _ _ e c t _ _ _
35. K i n _
36. S w e e t _ _
37. W o n d _ _ f _ _
38. T _ _ e
39. C _ _ i n g
40. T e n d _ _ l y
41. F _ _ _ _ f u l
42. S _ _ t o r

Key to love word game:

1. Love
2. Cupid
3. Aloha
4. Friendship
5. Lei
6. Diamond
7. Romance
8. Hug
9. Passion
10. Honey
11. Venus
12. Heart
13. Flowers
14. Sweetheart
15. Anniversary
16. XOX
17. Music

18. Valentine
19. Flirt
20. Amorous
21. Fiance
22. Smiles
23. Joy
24. Gaze
25. Kiss
26. Sharing
27. Loyal
28. Warmth
29. Sunshine
30. Moonlight
31. Marriage
32. Happy
33. Lover
34. Affection

35. Kind
36. Sweetie
37. Wonderful
38. True
39. Caring
40. Tenderly
41. Faithful
42. Suitor

Sweetheart Songs Music Bingo

B	I	N	G	O
Let Me Call You Sweetheart	How Deep Is Your Love?	Bridal Chorus	Wedding March	True Love
Let's Fall In Love	Anniversary Song	If I Loved You	My Romance	Why Do I Love You?
Love Can Make You Happy	You Needed Me	**FREE**	All The Things You Are	I'm Looking Over a Four-Leaf Clover
That's Amorè	Funiculi Funicula (A Happy Heart)	Volarè	Three Coins in the Fountain	O Sole Mio
You are My Sunshine	My Chinatown	I'll Take You Home Again Kathleen	My Wild Irish Rose	The Rose of Tralee

Help the Girl Scouts Earn a Badge

Every month Troop 1234 meets after school to plan an activity. I visited their school in January to train them on how to entertain and better serve the elderly. We talked about the physical problems some elderly people have such as not hearing or seeing very well. We discussed not walking up behind them as they might be frightened if they didn't see or hear you coming. We also discussed presenting a program for the elderly. The girls made up cards from construction paper and wallpaper, and we rehearsed songs we would sing at the program.

We met at the care facility in February, but you can do this activity at any time of year. I planned to get to the facility a little early so I could hand out hats and rhythmic instruments to the residents, and we sang a few songs to set the mood for the program. When the Girl Scouts arrived their leader introduced them to the residents. We recited the "Pledge of Allegiance" and "Scout's Honor."

We involved the residents by asking how many of them had been scouts or scout leaders. After this discussion, everyone joined in singing songs. When we played the "Battle Hymn of the Republic" the scouts marched around and interacted with the residents. For the "Grandfather's Clock" song the scouts did a swing of arms and hands and ticktock sounds.

When the singing was finished the scouts distributed their cards and visited with the residents.

You might want to continue with background music while the scouts and residents are visiting. You can use live accordion or piano music, or taped music.

Suggested Music:
"Jimmy Cracked Corn"
"B I N G O"
"Amazing Grace"
"The More We Get Together"
"You Are My Sunshine"
"Let Me Call You Sweetheart"
"Grandfather's Clock"
"She'll Be Coming 'Round the Mountain"
"For He's a Jolly Good Fellow"
"On Top of Old Smoky"
"America"
"God Bless America"
"Yankee Doodle"
"You're a Grand Old Flag"
"Michael Rowed the Boat Ashore"
"Kumbaya"
"Oh Suzanna!"
"Oh My Darling, Clementine"
"Dixie"
"Home on the Range"
"Marine's Hymn"
"Anchors Away"

Presidents' Day Tea

U. S. Presidents' Trivia Game

Refer to the following list of U.S. Presidents to formulate your own trivia questions for a Presidents' Day Trivia Tea. Serve juice and coffee. Reserve 15 to 30 minutes for this activity. Or use the questions for a Mens' Lunch discussion. Men enjoy talking about how they served their country in the military, and the hard times of the Depression.

Examples:

The 16th President of the U.S. was known as "Honest Abe".

The President known as "Old Hickory".

The President known as the "Bachelor President".

1. **George Washington**—1788-1797. He served his country eight years without pay. He said: "The love of my country shall be the ruling influence of my conduct."
   "To please everybody is impossible."
   "It is better to be alone than in bad company."
2. **John Adams**—1797-1801. He was the first president to live in the White House. He was known as the "Son of Liberty".
3. **Thomas Jefferson**—1801-1809. He was the author of the Declaration of Independence and one of the greatest scholars of his time.
4. **James Madison**—1809-1817. He was the "Father of the constitution". He was Secretary of State under Jefferson. Madison declared the war of 1812. As the defender, he became the greatest American constitutional statesman.
5. **James Monroe**—1817-1825. Served as Governor of Virginia. He purchased Florida from Spain. He served during the era of good feeling and is known for the Monroe Doctrine.
6. **John Quincy Adams**—1825-1829. He was the son of the second president. He served as minister to various foreign countries and as Secretary of State.
7. **Andrew Jackson**—1829-1837. Also known as "Old Hickory". He was known as the people's president. He became a soldier at the age of 14, and was the hero of the battle of New Orleans in the War of 1812.
8. **Martin VanBuren**—1837-1841. This president was known as "King Martin the First". He was a U.S. Senator, Governor of New York, and Vice President. He was known as "The Red Fox" in politics and revolutionized banking and business in the U.S.
9. **William Henry Harrison**—1841. "Old Tippecanoe" defeated the Indians at Tippecanoe in 1841. He died one month after being inaugurated.
10. **John Tyler**—1841-1845. He became president due to the death of Harrison and was known as the "Accidental President". He supported the south and annexed Texas.
11. **James K. Polk**—1845-1849. "Young Hickory" was also the Governor of Tennessee. He was

known as the first "dark horse" to be president. He annexed California and New Mexico.

12. **Zachary Taylor**—1849-1850. "Old Zach" was known to be rough and ready. He fought in the War of 1812 and served 40 years in military service.

13. **Millard Fillmore**—1850-1853. Fillmore became president upon the death of Zachary Taylor. He was known as a tariff advocate in Congress and he passed the fugitive slave bill.

14. **Franklin Pierce**—1853-1857. Known as "Poor Pierce" he was a Brigadier General in the Mexican War. His abilities were better served as a soldier rather than a president. He favored slavery until the beginning of the Civil War.

15. **James Buchanan**—1857-1861. President Buchanan was the only president that never married, and was known as the "Bachelor President". "Old Buck" served as a Private in the War of 1812, and also as a minister to England. He believed in states' rights.

16. **Abraham Lincoln**—1862-1865. "Honest Abe" is noted for the Gettysburg Address. He was known as the great emancipator. He was president during the Civil War and was assassinated by John Wilkes Booth while attending the theater.

17. **Andrew Johnson**—1865-1869. President Johnson was known as "Sir Veto". He became president upon the death of Lincoln. His wife taught him to read and write.

18. **Ulysses S. Grant**—1869-1877. Known as the "American Caesar". He accepted the surrender of Robert E. Lee at the end of the Civil War.

19. **Rutherford B. Hayes**—1877-1881. Hayes defeated Tilden for the presidency by one vote. "He serves his party best who serves his country."

20. **James A. Garfield**—1881. He was mortally wounded six months after his inauguration by a disappointed office seeker.

21. **Chester A. Arthur**—1881-1885. Arthur became president upon Garfield's death. He was known as the "First Gentleman of the Land". He favored civil service merit promotions.

22. **Grover Cleveland**—1885-1889 and 1893-1897. He served two non-consecutive terms. He was also the Mayor of Buffalo, New York. Known as "The Man of Destiny", he favored tariff reduction and expanded civil service. He was excellent in dealing with foreign policy.

23. **Benjamin Harrison**—1889-1893. Known as "Backbone Ben", he was the grandson of William Henry Harrison. Six territories became states during his term.

24. **Grover Cleveland second term.**

25. **William McKinley**—1897-1901. "Little Mack" and "Our Martyred President" were titles used for this president. He was assassinated while president. He was a Private and Major in the Civil War.

26. **Theodore Roosevelt**—1901-1909. Roosevelt was a Colonel in the Spanish American War, Governor of New York, and Vice President. He became president upon the death of McKinley. He was a trustbuster and great conservationist. He also built the Panama Canal. He said, " Speak softly and carry a big stick."

27. **William H. Taft**—1909-1913. He was known as "Big Bill Taft". He was a legal genius and a great jurist. He served as the Governor of the Philippines and Secretary of War. As president he

sponsored high tariffs and caused a party breach.

28. **Woodrow Wilson**—1913-1921. Wilson was the Governor of New Jersey. He served as president during World War I. He attended the Versailles Peace Conference, which helped end World War I.

29. **Warren G. Harding**—1921-1923. Harding was greatly admired, but imposed upon by trusted friends. He made a noble stand for reduction of armaments. He served as an editor and U.S. Senator. He died in office.

30. **Calvin Coolidge**—1923-1929. Coolidge went up the political ladder step-by-step. Serving as Governor of Massachusetts and Vice President. He became president upon Harding's death. He stood for economy in government and was known as the "Prosperity President".

31. **Herbert C. Hoover**—1929-1933. Hoover was known as "The Great Human Engineer". He was a mining engineer and head of the Belgium Relief Commission. He was also Food Administrator and Secretary of Commerce. His presidency had problems due to the Depression. He was known as "The Great Humanitarian", and said, "The thing I enjoyed most were visits from children."

32. **Franklin D. Roosevelt**—1933-1945. His New Deal helped get the country out of the Depression. He had served as Secretary of the Navy and Governor of New York. He died in his third term of office. He said, "We have nothing to fear, but fear itself." He was president during World War II.

33. **Harry S. Truman**—1945-1953. Truman became president upon the death of Franklin Roosevelt. He had served as a Senator from Missouri and Vice President. Truman had a rocky road when he became president, but he had unshakable faith in his country and his countrymen. He gave the order to drop the atomic bomb on Japan and brought an end to World War II.

34. **Dwight D. Eisenhower**—1953-1961. Eisenhower was commanding General in Europe during World War II. He sought armistice in Korea, and helped ease the cold war between the U.S. and the communists. He said, "The future of this republic is in the hands of the American voter."

35. **John F. Kennedy**—1961-1963. Kennedy was the first president born in the 20th century. His famous saying was, "Ask not what your country can do for you, but what you can do for your country." Kennedy and Nixon were the first presidential candidates to debate political issues on TV. Kennedy was assassinated in November 1963 in Dallas, Texas.

36. **Lyndon B. Johnson**—1963-1969. Johnson was sworn into office while flying back to Washington, DC, after the death of President Kennedy. Johnson was a Senator from Texas. He worked for peace in Viet Nam. He was a backer of the NASA space program. He said of NASA, "You've taken all of us, all over the world, into a new era."

37. **Richard M. Nixon**—1969-1974. Nixon served as Vice President under Eisenhower, but had to resign his presidency in disgrace due to the Watergate scandal.

38. **Gerald R. Ford**—1974-1977. Ford was appointed president upon the resignation of Nixon. He said, "Our long national nightmare is over. Our constitution works. Our great republic is a government of laws and not of men. Here, the people rule." Ford worked with Leonid Brezhnev to slow down the nuclear arms race. He served as a ranger, sailor, and congressman.

39. **James Carter Jr.**—1977-1981. Carter worked to make government competent and compassionate. He was highly criticized in public office as being too "imperial". He wrote a book entitled *Why Not the Best?* His administration had problems with world-wide inflation, unemployment, and an energy crisis at home. His most famous quote was: "A world in which human beings can live in peace and freedom, with their basic needs adequately met."

40. **Ronald Reagan**—1981-1989. Reagan was a movie star early in his career. He also served as the Governor of California before becoming president. Reagan was the oldest man ever elected to the presidency. He said, "It is not my intention to do away with government, it is rather to make it work—work with us, not over us. Stand by our side, not ride on our backs." He played Knute Rockne in the movies and gained the nickname "The Gipper" from that performance.

41. **George Bush**—1989-1993. President Bush came from a wealthy, close-knit family who were no strangers to politics. He attended private schools and was very athletic. He joined the Navy during World War II. He served in the U.S. House of Representatives and as Vice President. During his presidency the country was involved in Desert Storm. He said, " We cannot hope only to give our children a bigger car, a bigger bank account. We must hope to give them a sense of what it means to be a loyal friend, a loving parent, a citizen who leaves his home, his neighborhood, and town better than he found it."

42. **Bill Clinton**—1993-2001. Clinton served as Governor of Arkansas. When he became president the U.S. was facing problems with unemployment and the economy. He laid out a plan to make major changes in the health care system. It wasn't successful, but it brought attention to the health care problems. He said, " There is no more fundamental value than the American family. There is no more important job than raising a child."

43. **George W. Bush**—2001-   . George W. is the son of the 41st president. Before becoming president he was Governor of Texas. He won the presidency by a slim five-vote margin in the electoral college. The terrorism at the World Trade Center in New York (9-11-01) happened during his presidency. He is a devoted supporter of literacy programs.

President's Triple Cherry Cheesecake Bars

Note: I use fresh cherries, but you can use canned cherries instead. Filo dough comes in a one-pound box in the freezer department. You can omit the whipped topping, black cherry and mint leaf and substitute 1 cup mini chocolate chips. Once the sour cream has set, sprinkle the chocolate chips over the sour cream. Leave in the oven with the oven turned off to melt the chocolate chips. Spread melted chocolate chips to form the topping. The filo dough will come up on the sides of the pan somewhat. Sour cream should be room temperature. You can also omit the sour cream and use one pound of ready-made vanilla or chocolate pudding over the cheesecake.

Yield: 30 servings.
Bake in a $9^1/_2$ x $12^1/_2$-inch lasagna pan.

Crust:

12	sheets filo dough
6	tablespoons butter, melted

Melt the butter and place half of it (3 tablespoons) in the bottom of the baking pan, brushing evenly over the bottom of the pan. Place six sheets of filo dough over the butter; add six more sheets over the first layer of filo sheets. Brush the remaining 3 tablespoons of butter over the top of the filo sheet layer.

Cherries:

$1^1/_4$	cup white Queen Ann cherries
$1^1/_2$	cup black cherries
$1^1/_4$	cup tart cherries
3	tablespoons instant tapioca
1	cup sugar

Combine all three types of pitted cherries. Add the tapioca and sugar and set aside for five minutes.

Filling:

2	packages (8-ounces each) cream cheese
3	eggs
$1/_2$	cup sugar
1	teaspoon almond extract

Beat softened cream cheese, eggs, sugar, and almond extract until smooth. Fold the cherry mixture into the cream mixture by hand. Pour cream mixture into the baking pan on top of the filo sheets. Bake at 300 degrees for 45-50 minutes, or until a toothpick comes out clean.

Topping:
>2   cups sour cream
>2   teaspoons vanilla
>2   tablespoons sugar
>2   cups whipped topping

Mix sour cream, sugar, and vanilla together and spread over the top of the cheesecake. Return to turned off oven, to set sour cream topping. Leave in oven for about one hour. Cool thoroughly.

For Garnish:
>   genuine chocolate flavored topping
>30   black cherries
>30   mint leaves
>30   cupcake liners (optional)

Spread whipped topping over the sour cream topping. Swirl genuine chocolate flavor topping over the whipped topping, making a creative design. Cut into bars. Top each bar with a cherry and mint leaf. Place into individual decorative cupcake liners, or serve on a pretty plate.

Patriotic Art Projects:

Presidents' Patriotic Windsock
Supplies needed:
A cylinder-shaped oatmeal container.
Blue and white fabric, felt, or pre-pasted wallpaper.
Red, white, and blue $1^1/_2$-inch wide ribbon.
White yarn.
Scissors.
Hole punch.
Fabric glue, if using felt.

Instructions:
- Cut and remove the top of the oatmeal container (it will become the bottom of the windsock).
- Glue the blue fabric, felt, or wallpaper around the container.
- Cut a number of stars from the white material, felt, or paper depending on the size selected. Glue the white stars to the blue fabric, felt, or wallpaper in a random design. (I use 12 to 14 stars.)
- Cut 8 lengths of red, white, and blue ribbon, making them 18 inches long.
- Glue the ribbon to the inside of the bottom of the container.
- Punch four holes in the flange of container's top, making sure the holes are spaced evenly across from each other, so that the windsock will hang evenly.

- Cut two 12-inch pieces of yarn.
- Cut another piece of yarn that is longer to use for hanging the windsock.
- Using the two shorter pieces of yarn, tie opposite ends of the yarn to holes on opposite sides of the windsock.
- Use the longer piece of yarn to tie the smaller pieces together, using the other end of the yarn and a paperclip as the hanger.
- Residents can hang windsocks in their room or window. See finished windsock in colored section on page 5.

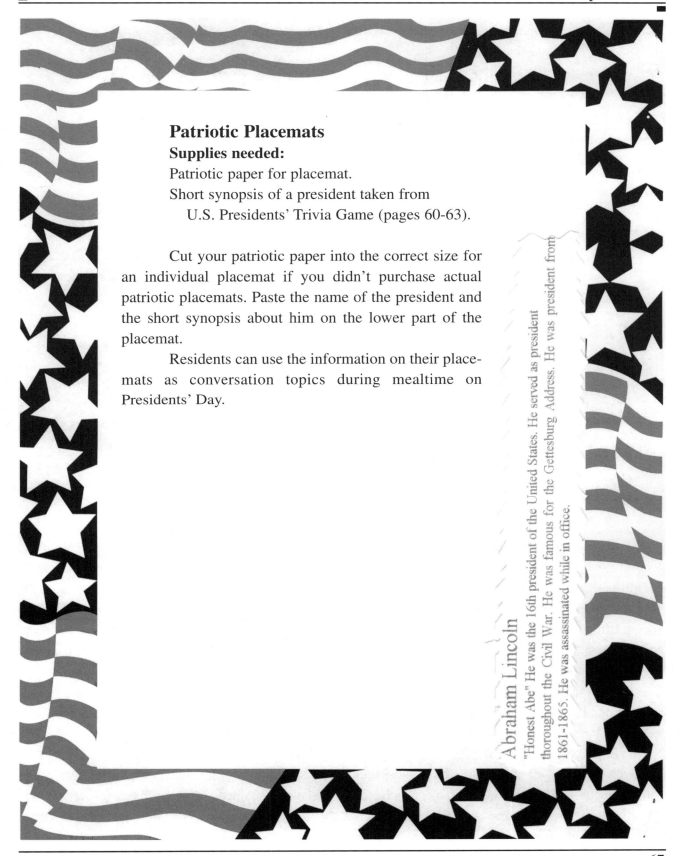

Patriotic Placemats

Supplies needed:

Patriotic paper for placemat.

Short synopsis of a president taken from
U.S. Presidents' Trivia Game (pages 60-63).

Cut your patriotic paper into the correct size for an individual placemat if you didn't purchase actual patriotic placemats. Paste the name of the president and the short synopsis about him on the lower part of the placemat.

Residents can use the information on their placemats as conversation topics during mealtime on Presidents' Day.

Abraham Lincoln
"Honest Abe" He was the 16th president of the United States. He served as president throughout the Civil War. He was famous for the Gettesburg Address. He was president from 1861-1865. He was assassinated while in office.

March Activities

Who Was Saint Patrick?

Several people have asked me about the background of Saint Patrick. Saint Patrick is the patron saint of Ireland, and the following is his story. *Note: The story of Saint Patrick can be part of the Irish Poetry Reflections Party.*

The Story of Saint Patrick

Saint Patrick lived in Britain near the Irish Sea with his noble family. He was captured by some fierce Irishmen and they brought him back to Ireland where he was sold to a man named Miliucc. Patrick became a slave to his owner. Patrick was used to fine clothes and good food, but these things weren't available to him as a slave. His job as a slave was to attend to Miliucc's sheep, which was a lonely job. He was alone every day, but he became aware that God loved him and was with him.

One night during his sleep he heard a voice tell him that he should go back to his country. The voice told him he would board a ship that was located more than two hundred miles away from him. Patrick believed the voice and the next day he set out to find his way to the ship. Finally Patrick came to a ship that was headed for France. It had many hunting hounds aboard and they were barking and very noisy. However, when Patrick approached the ship the dogs became very quiet.

Patrick asked the captain if he could board his ship, and offered to pay for his passage. The captain refused the money, and told Patrick to get off his ship as he feared that Patrick was a runaway slave. Of course, Patrick was disappointed but he got off the ship. Patrick didn't give up hope and he prayed for guidance on his journey.

After Patrick left the ship the dogs began barking again and were making a big fuss. Soon the captain came hurrying up to Patrick and asked him to board his ship because he quieted the dogs. Patrick's prayers were answered.

The ship traveled for three days before landing. The country was deserted as there was a war going on there. Patrick, the captain and crew, and the dogs traveled through this deserted land for twenty-eight days on very few provisions and they were getting hungry. The captain challenged

Patrick to pray for the group by saying, "Why can't your God find food for us?" Patrick answered that nothing was impossible for his God.

Soon there were a number of pigs ahead of them on the road. They killed and roasted the pigs over an open fire to feed themselves and the dogs. The pigs provided enough food for two days.

Later Patrick left the group and traveled for two years to get back to Britain. His faith carried him through this time. His family was so happy to have him home, and they begged him never to leave them again.

Once again Patrick had a dream. Victoricus appeared to him, he had traveled from Ireland with letters for Patrick. These letters were "The Voice of the Irish". Patrick heard the voices of the Irish saying "Come and walk among us again." A second time Patrick had a dream with more voices calling to him and he knew that God wanted him to return to Ireland and spread the word of God.

He left his family and homeland and hired a boat to take him to Ireland to study to be a missionary. Not long after Patrick arrived in Ireland he met a kind, good man named Dichu. Patrick spoke to Dichu about his love of God, and Dichu asked Patrick to baptize him in the new faith. In return Dichu gave Patrick his barn, which became the first church in Ireland.

Odran usually drove the chariot for Patrick. But Odran planned to kill Patrick and one day he asked Patrick to drive the chariot because he was too tired to drive. While Patrick was driving the chariot the king threw a spear and killed Odran. Patrick was very sad because he thought Odran gave his life for him.

Patrick was actually threatened with the loss of his life twelve times during his travels through Ireland baptizing thousands of people.

Patrick died on March 17, 461. His great love of God was recognized all over the country and many churches were built across the land because of Patrick's work. Many people followed in his footsteps by becoming priests and nuns and Patrick was made a saint.

One legend concerns Saint Patrick and snakes. They say that Saint Patrick drove the snakes to the sea by beating a drum hard and fast.

Another story is about Patrick and the lost horses.

It was very dark and Saint Patrick had lost his horses and chariot. As he raised his hand and stuck out his fingers they lighted up and he was able to find his horses and chariot.

The legend of Saint Patrick and the shamrock came about when he was preaching about the Holy Trinity of the Father, Son, and Holy Ghost. The people did not understand the trinity concept so Patrick reached down to the ground and picked a shamrock with one stem. He held it up and said there is only one stem, but three leaves. Instantly the people understood the teaching of the Holy Trinity.

In some pictures Saint Patrick is pictured holding a staff in one hand, a shamrock in the other, and green snakes at his feet.

Saint Patrick's Day is celebrated on March 17. A true Irishman will say with zest "Erin go bragh!", which means "Ireland forever!"

A Wee Bit of Irish Party

- Place pictures of Ireland around your party area to announce the celebration. Don't forget to note the date and time on the pictures. Plan the decorations for the dining area and hang them two days in advance to help get the residents in the mood for a festive occasion.
- Show a slide presentation on Ireland, or you can get videos from your library to use.
- Read an Irish greeting card to the residents and share good Irish cheer.
- Ask the residents what they used to do on Saint Patrick's Day.
- Have the attendees do the Word Search game.
- Discuss various Irish foods eaten on Saint Patrick's Day.
- Sing Irish songs and do the Irish Jig.
- I obtained Irish dice that said, "carefully, get lucky, eat cabbage, loudly, playfully, foolishly, quietly, sing, dance a jig, kiss me". The residents roll the dice and have to do whatever the dice turn up.
- Have an Irish sing-along. Refer to the songs on pages 84 and 86.
- Invite the dietician to participate in the resident council meeting to help plan an Irish menu for the main meal on Saint Patrick's Day.

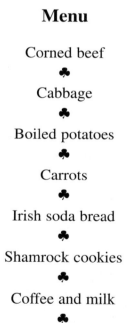

Menu

Corned beef

♣

Cabbage

♣

Boiled potatoes

♣

Carrots

♣

Irish soda bread

♣

Shamrock cookies

♣

Coffee and milk

♣

For a snack at the Saint Patrick's Day party, serve cake with green frosting and coffee. You can also serve pretzels or popcorn and green non-alcoholic beer, green punch, or Irish cream coffee. *Have plain decaf coffee on hand—not every resident likes flavored coffee.*

Recipes:

Green Punch

1   can (1 quart) pineapple juice
1   quart 7up
     green food color
     lime sherbet to float in the punch

Green Cake

White cake mix
Green food coloring
Pistachio Frosting

Follow the directions on the cake mix and add a few drops of green food coloring to the mix. Bake in a 9 x 13-inch cake pan. Bake according to the box directions and frost with Pistachio Frosting.

Pistachio Frosting

1   box ($^3/_4$ ounce) instant pistachio pudding mix
1   pound frozen non-dairy whipped topping, thawed

In a large bowl, mix the pudding and whipped topping together, beating until smooth. Spread over the cake. Frosting will keep in the refrigerator up to 3 days. Do not freeze.

The Irish Blessing

May the road rise to meet you.
May the wind blow at your back.
May the sun shine warmly on your face.
May the rain fall softly on your fields.
And until we meet again,
May God hold you
In the palm of His hand.
Amen.

Irish Poetry Reflections Party

As the residents are entering you can play Irish ballads. One of my favorite CDs is called "Home to Ireland". It has 28 Irish favorite ballads with the Clancy Brothers and Tommy Makem. You can purchase it at your local department store or through the Madacy Music Group, Inc., P.O. Box 1445, St. Laurent, Quebec, Canada Hal 421.

Menu

Blarney Stones

Reuben Cocktail Sandwiches

Saint Patrick Florentine Artichoke Appetizers

You can pick other Irish foods for the party—the residents will enjoy the Irish foods that are only served on Saint Patrick's Day.

Recipes:

Blarney Stone Bars
Yield: 30 bars.

4	eggs
1	cup brown sugar
1	cup granulated sugar
1/4	teaspoon salt
1	teaspoon vanilla
2	tablespoons butter, melted
1	cup hot milk
2	teaspoons baking powder
2	cups cake flour

Preheat oven to 350 degrees.

Beat the eggs by hand until light and then beat in both the sugars. Add the salt, vanilla, butter, and milk and mix thoroughly. Add the baking powder to the flour and add to the liquid mixture and blend. Pour into a greased 9 x 13-inch pan. Pound the pan on a hard surface several times to remove the air bubbles. Bake 30 to 35 minutes.

When the cake is cool cut 5 lines on the 9-inch side. On the 13-inch side cut 6 lines.

Frosting
Yield: 30 bars. The frosting is like a thick glaze.

6	cups powdered sugar
6	tablespoons water
3	teaspoons almond flavoring
$^1/_2$	teaspoon salt
$2^1/_2$	cups unsalted peanuts, finely chopped
15	green maraschino cherries, halved, drained, and dried with a paper towel

Add water, flavoring, and salt to the powdered sugar and beat by hand until smooth. Frost each bar on all sides and roll in the peanuts. Top each with a green cherry.

My Blarney Stone Story

My husband came home from work and sampled a blarney stone bar. (I must tell you that he is a chocolate lover.) He immediately asked me if I could make these with chocolate. I replied, "I'm sure I can, Steve. For now I'll just sprinkle on some mini chocolate chips." Once the chocolate chips were on the Blarney stones he said, "Wait—where are the cherries for my blarney stones?" At that point I began to laugh. My husband is just a big kid with a "big" chocolate sweet tooth.

Reuben Cocktail Sandwiches
Yield: 45 servings.
Note: You can substitute mozzarella cheese for the Swiss cheese to save calories. 30 slices of party rye bread will fit on a baking sheet 13 x $16^1/_2$ inches. There are 45 slices of party bread in a loaf.

1	pound loaf cocktail pumpernickel bread
2	cans (14-ounces each) sauerkraut, drain and squeeze dry
$^1/_2$	pound deli corned beef, sliced thin
$^1/_2$	pound Swiss cheese
	soft butter for spreading on bread

Sauerkraut Mixture:

1	tablespoon brown mustard (tangy and creamy with horseradish)
2	teaspoons Bavarian seasoning
6	tablespoons Thousand Island Dressing

Mix all ingredients together. Place 1 heaping teaspoon of mixture on each piece of buttered party bread. Cut the corned beef and cheese to fit the bread slice and place one slice of meat and then one slice of cheese on the sauerkraut mixture. Bake at 400 degrees for 5 minutes, or until the cheese melts. You can microwave for 30 seconds, or until the cheese melts. *Be sure to use a micro-wavable pan for the microwave.*

Bavarian Seasoning

Note: Your local grocery store may not have the Bavarian spice. So here is the recipe to make your own! It's also excellent as a rub on pork roast.

4	bay leaves, crushed
1	tablespoon thyme
2	teaspoons sage
1	teaspoon minced dehydrated garlic
2	teaspoons basil
2	teaspoons rosemary
$^1/_2$	teaspoon granulated white onion powder

Mix all ingredients together.

Saint Patrick Florentine Artichoke Appetizers

Note: There are eight large tortillas per package of Garden Spinach and Herb Style.

1	package (10 ounces) frozen, chopped spinach, thawed
2	jars ($6^1/_2$-ounces each) marinated artichoke hearts, drained and chopped
1	package (8 ounces) cream cheese, softened
2	cups Parmesan cheese, freshly shredded (reserve 1 cup)
1	cup light mayonnaise
4	large cloves garlic, pressed
1	can (4.25 ounces) tiny shrimp, drained
1	package (8 ounces) sliced fresh mushrooms
1	cup chopped pecans
1	cup sliced black olives
1	bunch green onions, diced

Drain the spinach and press between layers of paper towels to remove excess moisture. Combine the spinach, artichoke hearts, cream cheese, 1 cup of the Parmesan cheese, mayonnaise, garlic, shrimp, mushrooms, pecans, black olives, and green onions. Blend together well. Place in greased 11 x 17-inch baking dish. Top with the remaining Parmesan cheese. Cover with foil and bake at 350 degrees for 25 minutes. Cool and refrigerate overnight.

The next day, lay out the tortillas and spread $^1/_4$ cup of mixture over each tortilla. Sprinkle 3 tablespoons of mozzarella cheese over each shell. Bake in oven, open-faced, uncovered. Cut the baked tortillas into pie-shaped pieces and roll each pie shape to make individual appetizers. Or you can fold the baked tortilla in half and eat like a sandwich.

You can make the appetizers using refrigerated crescent rolls from the dairy department. Bake the rolls following the package directions. When cool slice the crescent in half, leaving it hinged in the back. Lightly butter and fill each roll with the Florentine Artichoke Mixture. Sprinkle cheese over the mixture, place on baking sheet and heat for 1 to 2 minutes at 350 degrees. Top each sandwich with a green olive on a frilled toothpick. *Be sure to dry the green olives with a paper towel before using.*

Poetry to Read:

I've listed some with the poems I've used on these occasions. There are several other good books of Irish poetry.
New Oxford Book of Irish Verse edited by Thomas Kinsella. I particularly liked "Saint Patrick's Breast Plate" on pgs. 12-14.
The Collected Poems of W. B. Yeates. It was originally published in 1903 and has had seventeen reprints. The poems I particularly liked are: "An Irish Airman Foresees His Death" on page 133 and "To An Isle in the Water" on page 20.
A Child's Treasury of Irish Rhymes, compiled by Alice Taylor and illustrated by Nicola Emoe. Some of my favorites from this book are "The Irish Student and His Cat" page 20, "The Little Elf Man" page 27, "The Wood of Flowers" page 34, "Good People" page 35, and "A Prayer" page 47. Use the rhymes in this book for reminiscing with the residents.
Note: People who kiss the blarney stone are said to have the gift of gab. Ask the residents if they might know anyone who has the gift of gab.

I Am a Tall Leprechaun
by Pat Nekola

Some people say I am short—or small,
Believe it—that does not bother me at all!
I wish you could see,
I am tall as a tree.

A bee is a creature smaller than me.
As a leprechaun, I enter my plea.
It is a pity
To think of me as "itsy-bitsy".

I am an Irishman
Feeling ever so grand.
I am witty, smart, charming,
And I say with glee—
I am a leprechaun as tall as a tree!

An Irish Dream
by Pat Nekola

To have a dream
In the Suncatcher face,
To travel in an Irish place.

To have a dream
With Irish fortune and fate,
To meet an Irishman at the gate.

To have a dream
To fall in love with an Irishman.
To fulfill this dream,
Makes life so grand.

To dream to find a book
With a pot of gold,
To note so many
Beautiful stories untold.

For the stories are shared with a mate
With sweet memories and love so great.

The following poems are from the Poolbeg Book of Irish Ballads *by Sean McMahon. The author has approved the printing. Thank you, Sean McMahon.*

The Cod Liver Oil

Anonymous

A cure-all, most efficacious in every case, that ante-dated Lily the Pink's by sixty years.

I'm a young married man
And I'm tired of my life,
For lately I married,
An ailing young wife,
She does nothing all day,
Only sit down and sigh,
Saying I wish to the Lord,
That I only could die.

Till a friend of my own,
Came to see me one day,
And told me my wife
Was just pining away,
But he afterwards told me
That she would get strong
If I'd buy her a bottle
From Doctor de Jongh.

So I bought her a bottle
'Twas just for a try,
And the way that she scoffed it,
You'd swear she was dry;
I bought her another,
It went just the same,
Till I own she's got
Cod Liver Oil on the brain.

My house it resembles
A big doctor's shop
With bottles and bottles
From bottom to top
And when in the morning
The kettle's a-boil
Ye'd swear it was singing out
"Cod Liver Oil!"

O Doctor, dear Doctor,
O Doctor de Jongh,
Your Cod Liver Oil
Is so pure and so strong,
I declare to my life,
I'll go down in the soil,
If my wife don't stop drinking
Your Cod Liver Oil.

The Flower of Sweet Strabane
Anonymous

*Another nostalgic nineteenth-century song of lost love and forcible emigration,
with a tribute to the beauty of the women of a very friendly town.*

Were I the King of Ireland with all things at my will,
I would roam for recreation, new comforts to find still,
But the comfort I would like best you all may understand,
Is to win the heart of Martha, the flower of sweet Strabane.

Her cheeks are like the roses red, her hair a lovely brown,
And o'er her milk-white shoulders it carelessly hangs down.
She's one of the finest creatures of the whole Milesian clan,
Oh, my heart is fairly captured by the flower of sweet Strabane.

I wish I had my darling far down in Inishowen,
Or in some lonely valley in the wild woods of Tyrone.
I would do my best endeavor, I would work the newest plan,
To gain the heart of Martha, the flower of sweet Strabane.

I've often been in Phoenix Park, and in Killarney fair,
In blithe and bonnie Scotland, on the winding banks of Ayr;
But yet in all my travels I never met with one
That could compare with Martha, the flower of sweet Strabane.

But since I cannot win your love, no joy there is for me.
So I will seek forgetfulness in lands across the sea;
Unless you chance to follow me, I swear by my right han',
Macdonald's face you'll never see, fair flower of sweet Strabane.

Adieu, then, to the Liffey's banks, and Mourne's water's sided.
I'm sailing for America, whatever may betide;
Our ship is bound for Liverpool, straight by the Isle of Man,
Adieu, my dearest Martha, the flower of sweet Strabane.

The Old Bog Road

Teresa Brayton

This grand old standard of parties of fifty years ago was written at the end of the nineteenth century by an exile from County Kildare.

My feet are here on Broadway this blessed harvest morn,
But O the ache that's in them for the spot where I was born.
My weary hands are blistered from work in cold and heat,
And O to swing a scythe today, thro' fields of Irish wheat.
Had I the chance to wander back, or won a king's abode,
'Tis soon I'd see the hawthorn tree by the Old Bog Road.

When I was young and restless, my mind was ill at ease,
Through dreaming of America, and gold beyond the seas,
O sorrow take their money, 'this hard to get that same,
And what's the world to any man, where no one speaks his name.
I've had my day and here I am, with building bricks for load,
A long three thousand miles away, from the Old Bog Road.

My mother died last spring tide, when Ireland's fields were green,
The neighbors said her waking was the finest ever seen.
There were snowdrops and primroses piled up beside her bed,
And Ferns Church was crowded, when her funeral Mass was said.
But there was I on Broadway, with building bricks for load,
When the carried out her coffin, from the Old Bog Road.

There was a decent girl at home, who used to walk with me,
Her eyes were soft and sorrowful, like sunbeams on the sea,
Her name was Mary Dwyer; but that was long ago,
And the ways of God are wiser, than the things a man may know.
She died the year I left her, with building bricks for load,
I'd best forget the times we met, on the Old Bog Road.

Ah! Life's a weary puzzle, past finding out by man,
I take the day for what it's worth and do the best I can.
Since no one cares a rush for me; what needs to make a moan,
I go my way, and draw my pay and smoke my pipe alone,
Each human heart must know its grief, tho' little be its load,
So God be with you Ireland, and the Old Bog Road.

Irish Word Search

```
S A C X H K O I T A B L A R N E Y S I S E
I G E T L U C K Y B N L O O I U Y T R T A
N F U T R D T L E P R E C H A U N O I P T
G V J F G R R F O B A G P I P E S N S A C
I B H G R E E N B E E R P I D F G E H T A
R C O R N E D B E E F N O R O P L I A R B
I H F G R E E N C T G B T I T R E R T I B
S I D P B V F V L S F N O S H G F I T C A
H R S I C J V F O H C M F H Y L T S I K G
S I S P E K G O V A R V G B U U G H R ' E
O S E E R L N D E M D C O R H C B W E S K
N H C O F F E E R R V X L O R K N H F D J
G B N R B A G K S O I U D G E O M I D A H
S K V G C S D J V C O Y J U F F K S C Y G
U M C F R D Y L B K P T M E I T I K V A F
E L X D A N C E A J I G T T J H L E B Q B
R I R V D H I M M A H R R G H E U Y N R N
G G O L D C O I N S G E G F G I R I S H M
I R I S H B E E R B T W V I F E R F D C I
```

Irish Sayings, Names and Words to Search for:

Shamrock	Irish whiskey	Get lucky
Luck of the Irish	Green beer	Dance a jig
Blarney stone	Corned beef	St. Patrick's Day
Irish beer	Eat Cabbage	Leprechaun
Irish coffee	Gold coins	Green clover
Bagpipes	Irish brogue	Pipe
Pot of gold	Irish attire	Sing Irish songs

Irish Word Search Answer Key

```
S A C X H K O I T A B L A R N E Y S I S E
I G E T L U C K Y B N L O O I U Y T R T A
N F U T R D T L E P R E C H A U N O I P T
G V J F G R R F O B A G P I P E S N S A C
I B H G R E E N B E E R P I D F G E H T A
R C O R N E D B E E F N O R O P L I A R B
I H F G R E E N C T G B T I T R E R T I B
S I D P B V F V L S F N O S H G F I T C A
H R S I C J V F O H C M F H Y L T S I K G
S I S P E K G O V A R V G B U U G H R ' E
O S E E R L N D E M D C O R H C B W E S K
N H C O F F E E R R V X L O R K N H F D J
G B N R B A G K S O I U D G E O M I D A H
S K V G C S D J V C O Y J U F F K S C Y G
U M C F R D Y L B K P T M E I T I K V A F
E L X D A N C E A J I G T T J H L E B Q B
R I R V D H I M M A H R R G H E U Y N R N
G G O L D C O I N S G E G F G I R I S H M
I R I S H B E E R B T W V I F E R F D C I
```

Irish Sayings, Names and Words to Search for:

Shamrock	Irish whiskey	Get lucky
Luck of the Irish	Green beer	Dance a jig
Blarney stone	Corned beef	St. Patrick's Day
Irish beer	Eat Cabbage	Leprechaun
Irish coffee	Gold coins	Green clover
Bagpipes	Irish brogue	Pipe
Pot of gold	Irish attire	Sing Irish songs

Granny's Soup Kitchen
This is an ideal soup for Saint Patrick's Day.

Potato Leek Soup
Yield: 24 one-cup servings.

- 5 pounds potatoes, cooked in jackets, peeled and diced
- 2 cups thinly sliced leek, including the green
- 2 cans (48-ounces each) chicken stock
- 1 pound bacon, diced, fried, and drained
- 2 cups heavy cream (optional—may substitute milk)
- 1 bunch scallions (green onions) reserve tops for garnish
- 2 teaspoons black pepper
- 1 teaspoon granulated garlic

Ingredients for Thickening Soup:
- 2 cups milk at almost room temperature
- 6 tablespoons cornstarch

Fry bacon to almost crisp. Add the leeks and scallions and sauté. Drain grease off and dab up excess grease with a paper towel.

Boil the potatoes in jackets until tender, then drain, peel, and dice.

Place ingredients in soup kettle and add chicken stock and cream.

In a separate bowl mix the cornstarch and milk and wire whip until smooth. Add this mixture slowly to the soup while stirring constantly to prevent lumps. Remove from heat and store in several small containers to cool. Refrigerate overnight. This soup is best when it's reheated the next day. Serve with Irish Soda Bread and Dilly French Bread and crackers.

Irish Soda Bread
Yield: 2 loaves.

4	cups flour
$1\frac{1}{2}$	teaspoons baking soda
$\frac{3}{4}$	teaspoon salt
$\frac{3}{4}$	cup shortening
1	tablespoon sugar (optional)
$1\frac{1}{3}$	cups buttermilk

Place flour, soda, and salt into a bowl, cut in shortening. Add buttermilk and mix well. Divide the dough and shape into $1\frac{1}{4}$-pound loaves (recipe will make two loaves) in a football or round shape. Place in greased 9 x 5-inch baking pan or on a greased cookie sheet.

Bake at 375 degrees for 40 to 50 minutes or until toothpick comes out clean. Cool on racks. Serve with butter, it is also tasty with jelly.

Note: You can substitute one cup of rolled oats for one cup of the flour. You can also add 1 cup of raisins or currants to the dough. You can also brush with melted butter when the bread is warm and sprinkle the top with cinnamon and sugar. If someone is diabetic this bread is ideal because you can omit the sugar.

Dilly French Bread
Yield: 3 loaves.

3	loaves (one pound each) French bread—loaves should be 20 inches long and sliced part way through lengthwise.

Dill Butter Spread:

1	pound butter, softened
4	teaspoons dill weed
$\frac{1}{2}$	teaspoon granulated onion powder
$\frac{1}{4}$	teaspoon Worcestershire sauce

Beat all ingredients until well blended and whipped. Butter both sides of bread slices lightly. Also spread some of the butter mixture across the top of the loaves. Wrap each loaf separately in foil and place in 350-degree oven until butter is melted and bread is warmed.

Irish Songs Word Game

Fill in the blanks with the names of Irish songs.

Danny Boy _____ _____ (Londonderry Air)

H_____(Harrigan)

I'll Take You _____ Again, Kathleen (Home)

Irish _____ (Washerwoman)

McNamara's _____ (Band)

My _____ _____ Rose (Wild Irish)

Sweet _____ O'Grady (Rosie)

The Wearing of the _____ (Green)

Little Bit of _____ Sure They Call it Ireland (Heaven)

The _____ I Left Behind Me (Girl)

_____of Coleraine (Kitty)

The _____ Dance (Kerry)

The Minstrel _____ (Boy)

Where the _____ Shannon Flows (River)

The Rose of _____ (Tralee)

Too-ra- _____-ra- _____-ra That's an Irish Lullaby (loo, loo)

Mother _____ (Machree)

The Galway _____ (Piper)

Rory _____ (O'Moore)

Has Anybody Seen _____ (Kelly)

Shamrock Pin Art Project

Supplies needed:

Green fun foam (9 x 12-inch sheets).

Hot glue gun, or glue sticks.

Pin backs (they are packaged 8 to a package).

Trace shamrocks on the fun foam and cut out (you should get 12 shamrocks from one sheet of fun foam). Glue the pin back onto the shamrock. Let dry for 24 hours. Every resident should have a shamrock pin for the party. Also, get as many residents as possible to wear something green to the party.

Shamrock Pin Pattern

Irish Songs Music Bingo

B	I	N	G	O
When Irish Eyes are Smiling	My Wild Irish Rose	Danny Boy	The Rose of Tralee	A Little Bit of Heaven (Sure They Call it Ireland)
I'll Take You Home Again, Kathleen	Kitty of Coleraine	Irish Washer Woman	Harrigan	Sweet Rosie O'Grady
Molly Malone (Cockles and Mussels)	Too-ra-loo-ra-loo-ra (That's an Irish Lullaby)	**FREE**	Wearing of the Green	Mother MacCree
Kilarney	Believe Me If All Those Endearing Young Charms	Tourelay	Where the River Shannon Flows	The Kerry Dance
McNamara's Band	The Harp That Once Thru Tara's Halls	Has Anybody Seen Kelly	The Galaway Piper	The Girl I Left Behind Me

Word Game Social

I served chocolate chip cookies and decaf coffee. The recipe for the cookies can be found in my Picnics Catering on the Move *book on pages 142-143. You can also purchase the cookies from your local bakery, or buy the dough pre-made, or ask the kitchen to make them for you if time permits. It depends on your type of facility.*

Pass out the refreshments and get the residents to relax before you start the word game. Explain the word game to the residents:

> Each person must use their first name.

> They must use the initial of their name to come up with a city name, kind of transportation, food, and an event.

Examples: My name is Delores. I am going to Denver. I will drive my Dodge to get there. On the way I will stop and pick up donuts. My grandchild lives in Denver. My son has a dog. I will attend a dance in Denver.

Delores loved to dance in her younger days!

Name: Jeanne
City: Jacksonville, Florida
Transportation: Wasn't sure how she was going to get there.
Food: Junk food.
Event: Meeting a "Jack of all trades" and they were going to jump in the river and swim.
Jeanne was a good swimmer when she was young. She never drove in her entire life, and she loves snacks!

Name: Beatrice
City, Baraboo, Wisconsin
Transportation: Bus
Food: Beer
Event: Barbecue.
She loved family gatherings.

Name: Mary
City: Milwaukee
Transportation: Mustang
Food: She said she will take money so she can stop on the way and buy milk.
Event: She was going to pick up a friend and go to a musical.
Mary drove a mustang in her younger years.

Name: Steve
City: St. Louis
Transportation: Space shuttle.
Food: Sandwiches
Event: Space demonstrations.
Steve was very fascinated with space.

Now you can add to the list at your own facility.

Pig Day Party

Make sure you have enough time for party preparation and cleanup. The residents enjoyed this event very much and gave their completed pictures to their grandchildren.

The purpose of the party is for all the residents to have a good time and to honor farmers, past and present.

Residents still like to color pictures once in a while. One week prior to the party run off copies of the pig pictures. Hand them out to the residents and assist them whenever needed. When they're finished, put their names on their pictures, collect them, and hang them in the dining room for all to enjoy.

On the day of the party judge the coloring contest. Announce the winners at the party. Prizes should be awarded for the prettiest pig, the most original pig, the most colorful pig, and so on. Get the staff involved and have them color pigs, too. Let the residents judge the best picture colored by the staff.

Have a hog-calling contest. You will be surprised how the shy residents get into this event.

Have a "Pin-the-tail on the Pig" game. Make an enlarged pig using an overhead projector, make the tail separate so the residents can take turns pinning the tail on the pig. Blindfold the residents and assist them in placing their tail on the pig. *Get the staff to help the residents with this game.*

Make, or buy, prize ribbons like they'd win at the County Fair to give out as prizes to the best coloring winners and the game winners.

Menu

Pigs-in-a-blanket

Raspberry Punch

Recipes:

Raspberry Punch

Yield: Serves 20 people.

2   quarts Cranapple juice

2   quarts 7UP

1   quart raspberry sherbet

Mix juice and 7UP together and scoop sherbet into the punch before serving.

Pigs-in-a-Blanket

Yield: 20 servings.

20   all beef hot dogs

20   slices bacon

20   slices American cheese

Slit the hot dog making a hinge. Cut the cheese into thin strips to fit into the hot dog slit. Wrap a piece of bacon around the hot dog to cover the entire surface to seal in the cheese. Broil until the bacon and hot dog are done. Drain. *You can use precooked bacon to cut down on the grease and cooking time. You can also use turkey bacon and turkey hot dogs for less fat.* Wrap each hot dog into a bun or piece of bread and serve with mustard and ketchup.

April Activities

Easter Gathering

Cover a card table with an Easter tablecloth. Arrange Easter eggs, Easter lily, and stuffed bunny animals on the table.

I have a Mrs. Easter Bunny with an apron. Her ears are poking through her hat and she has a basket of carrots and flowers. She makes a nice display—you probably have a similar Easter animal you can use in your arrangement.

I grow daffodils. I use a soda can wrapped with ribbon to hold the flowers, and use the flowers as a door prize. Pick a card from a deck of cards and whoever guesses the card gets the prize—or mark a plate or chair and the person sitting in the spot gets the prize. Residents have fun guessing the correct number and enjoy the flowers in their room later. See picture in An Alzheimer's Guide— Activities and Issues for People Who Care *page 200.*

Many residents get flowers for Easter. If they wish, the flowers can be displayed in the dining room for the party. Residents can tell the group, "I got this plant from my daughter." This time of sharing can ignite the conversation.

Talk about the signs of spring, flower names, and about your table arrangement. In my case, we talked about Mrs. Bunny and how she had her apron on because she was making Easter dinner. That prompted a conversation about what people ate for Easter dinner, and the methods of preparation. One lady talked about preparing the ham and that she did it the way her mother had taught her, this led to talk of family traditions. Just let the conversation flow and follow where it leads.

We had made Easter cakes and they were displayed on the table.

We also made a bunny patch display that got all of the residents involved. We placed a white picket fence around the edge of the table, placed Easter grass in the patch and displayed flowers the residents had made, or brought, to the party. We placed any additional stuffed bunnies and chickens in the patch. Everyone enjoyed this event.

Also, spend some time thinking back to old times. People might describe an Easter hat they wore.

One resident told about not liking the hat her mother had for her. It was pink (her least favorite color) and she didn't want to wear it, but she did to please her mother. She said when she grew up she never wore another hat!

If someone wears an Easter hat to the party have them come to the front and model their hat (residents enjoy the attention).

Many residents will contribute to the memories of Easter. Talk about family gatherings and Easter egg hunts. Many will remember the church activities.

We got the staff involved and had them do a "Bunny Hop" dance with the residents. You can have some staff members push the wheelchairs. Play some music like "Easter Parade" and "Here Comes Peter Cottontail". You can have residents pretend their hand is a bunny and make it hop to the beat of the music.

We served Bunny Cake and coffee and juice at the end of the party.

Easter Bunny Cake
Yield: One box mix will make two bunny cakes.

1   cake mix, flavor of your choice

3   cups of coconut ($1\frac{1}{2}$ cup per cake)

2   pounds of frosting (recipe follows)

Follow the preparation directions on the cake mix. Bake in two 8-inch round pans. Cool cakes and remove from the pan.

Cut a cardboard $9\frac{1}{2}$ x 12 inches and cover it with foil. (Tape the foil down on the backside so it doesn't shift.)

Cut each cake in half and frost one half, place the remaining half on top of the first frosted half. Place some frosting (to act as glue) on the middle of the cardboard base, now stand the two pieces of cake on the cut side with the hump up like a bunny's back. Cut a small chunk out up toward the top front of the cake to make the neck. Place this chunk at the bottom end of the back of the cake to form the tail.

Method One:

Frost both sides of the "bunny cake" using a #28 star tip. Pipe frosting on the entire body. Touch up any unfrosted parts of the cake and sprinkle coconut over the entire bunny (or use chocolate or colored frosting) to make the fur.

Method Two:

You can frost the "bunny cake" just like a normal cake instead of using the cake tube, if you prefer.

Make two bunny ears out of pink construction paper for each cake For whiskers use black licorice by cutting into shorter pieces (each bunny should have six whiskers). Use jellybeans for the bunny nose and eyes—be sure they are all the same color. You can use red licorice and color the coconut if you wish—pink and yellow make a cute bunny. Color some of the coconut green and place around the bunny for grass, and place some colored jelly beans in the grass

Refer to page 5 in color section of completed Bunny Cake.

Butter Cream Frosting

2	pounds powdered sugar
$1/4$ to $1/3$	cup water
1	cup white margarine, softened
1	cup shortening
$1/2$	teaspoon salt
2	teaspoons almond flavoring

Beat margarine and shortening until smooth, add the powdered sugar gradually, alternating with the water. Add the salt and flavoring. Continue beating until smooth and creamy.

Boil some water in a pan, when frosting the cake dip the spatula in the hot water to smooth the frosting for the crumb coat of frosting. Make swirls in the final frosting coat to make the bunny look fluffy.

Note: White margarine is getting hard to find in the stores. If it is not available in your area you can use regular margarine.

Easter Egg Hunt Party with Children

Contact a local nursery school, day care, or elementary school and invite them to participate in the egg hunt. You will need to have a correct number of children that will be attending, as they will need egg baskets. Have the residents make baskets for the children attending. Have the dietary department order eggs for the event. They will need to be hard cooked and colored. Some residents can help with the coloring. Purchase Easter candy and have the residents help put the baskets together.

I had resident's families and friends save round butter containers. Purchase Easter grass, pipe cleaners, and glue. The local wallpaper store may be able to contribute old wallpaper books, which will help with the cost. Start making the baskets two weeks in advance of the party. (See directions on following page.)

Have a staff member dress up like Mr. Bunny and be there to greet the children when they arrive. The residents should also be in the party room when the children arrive. Have each resident give a child a basket and direct the children to the area where the colored eggs are hidden. The residents can also help the children with directions. It's great to see the two generations interact.

Get the staff and resident's families involved if possible. Teach the children to do the Bunny Hop and get everyone involved in the dance. If you have a music therapist on staff they may have the music, or have "live music" if possible. It adds a festive note to the occasion. Maybe the children will like to sing a song for the residents, or they could bring Easter pictures they've colored at school for the residents.

The residents will enjoy the children and the extra attention. It takes so little to make residents happy, and the attention and time is valued by our elderly.

Supplies Needed for Easter Basket:

Margarine or cottage cheese container.
Construction paper or wallpaper to cover outside of container.
10-inch pipe cleaners.
Easter grass.
Candy.
Hole Punch.
Glue.

Directions for Easter Basket:

These directions are for containers $3^1/_2$ inches in diameter and $2^1/_2$ inches high. It's nice if all the containers are the same size so all the children have the same basket.

Cut strips of wallpaper or construction paper to fit the size of the container. Glue the paper to the container. Use a paper punch to make a hole on two sides of the container for the handle. Place a pipe cleaner in the holes and twist the ends to keep it in place for the handle. (Each pipe cleaner should be about 10 inches in length.) Fill each basket with individually wrapped Easter candy.

Egg Talk Game

Eggs are so versatile. Use the following list of multiple-choice options to see if you can identify the various ways eggs are used.

1. Eggs benedict are:
   a. Saintly eggs made by the clergy.
   b. Ham and poached eggs on a toasted muffin with white sauce.
   c. Fried eggs with a white sauce.
   d. Scrambled eggs with a white sauce.

2. Meringue is:
   a. Egg whites beaten with sugar and cream of tartar.
   b. Egg yolks beaten with sugar and cream of tartar.
   c. Egg whites and yolks beaten with sugar and cream of tartar.
   d. Egg whites and yolks made with brown sugar and cream of tartar.

3. Meringue is found on:
   a. Lemon pie.   b. Schaum torte.   c. None of the above.   d. a. and b.

4. An egg is added to meatloaf to:
   a. Binder.
   b. Decreases air in the meatloaf.
   c. Add flavor.
   d. None of the above.

5. A hard-cooked egg placed into beet juice is called:
   - a. Sugared red eggs.
   - b. Pickled eggs.
   - c. Extra-pickled eggs.
   - d. Double-dipped eggs.

   It is very popular in the Wooster/Akron, Ohio, area. These eggs can also be made and put into a brine of sugar, salt, mixed spices, and cider vinegar.

6. Beaten eggs with vegetables, cheese, and meat originating in France.
   - a. Scrambled eggs.
   - b. Vegetable eggs.
   - c. Omelet.
   - d. Puffy eggs.

   The mixture is placed into a 6-inch frying pan, cooked until egg begins to congeal, and then flipped over in the pan.

7. Shirred eggs are baked in what style of dish:
   - a. Lasagna pan.
   - b. Custard cup.
   - c. Microwave pan.
   - d. Frying pan.

8. Eggs Florentine is made with which of the following vegetables:
   - a. Carrots.
   - b. Zucchini.
   - c. Spinach.
   - d. Peas.

9. Hard-cooked eggs chopped with pickle relish, yellow mustard, onion, salt, pepper, and mayonnaise:
   - a. Egg salad.
   - b. Tuna salad.
   - c. Cream salad.
   - d. None of the above.

10. A hard-cooked egg with egg yolks scooped out and added to mayonnaise, yellow mustard, salt, pepper, Worcestershire sauce, and horseradish and served at picnics:
    - a. Romantic eggs.
    - b. Deviled eggs.
    - c. Summer eggs.
    - d. Winter eggs.

11. Eggs are found in which of the following dishes:
    - a. Custard.
    - b. Soufflé.
    - c. Salmon loaf.
    - d. All of the above.

12. This style of egg has a white sauce with seasonings. Egg whites are stiffly beaten. The mixture is poured into greased custard cups, and the cups are set into hot water and baked. These eggs also have cheese, green pepper, and pimentos in them. To serve them they are turned out onto platters and served with tomato sauce.
    - a. Timbales.
    - b. Creamed deviled eggs.
    - c. Stuffed eggs.
    - d. Cheesey eggs.

13. Eggs and milk are beaten together to brush on top of piecrust. It is called:
    a. Egg wash.
    b. Milk wash.
    c. Pie wash.
    d. None of the above.

14. Scottish egg meatloaf:
    a. Meatloaf with bacon and eggs.
    b. Meatloaf with hard-cooked eggs in the middle so when the loaf is sliced, you get a slice of egg also.
    c. Meatloaf with chopped hard-cooked eggs.
    d. All of the above.

15. An egg placed in a hole cut out of a slice of bread and then fried is:
    a. Fried egg and toast all in one.
    b. Egg in the nest.
    c. A dipping egg.
    d. Egg without much bread.

16. The egg yolk contains how many grams of fat:
    a. 5 fat grams.
    b. 10 fat grams.
    c. 2 fat grams.
    d. 12 fat grams.

17. Eggs goldenrod is hard-cooked eggs. The yolks are reserved for the top of the dish, while the whites are chopped and placed in a cream sauce. This mixture is placed on toast and the minced, cooked yolks are sprinkled on the top. Which country is known for this dish:
    a. England.
    b. Scotland.
    c. Ireland.
    d. France.

18. A style of cake that contains egg whites:
    a. Chiffon cake.
    b. Cream cake.
    c. Chocolate dream cake.
    d. Angel food cake.

19. This is a French-style, thin pancake and can be used as either dessert or main course:
    a. Lacey pancake.
    b. Potato pancake.
    c. Crepe.
    d. Swedish pancake.

20. An egg dish that contains chipped beef, butter, eggs, pepper, and milk is called:
    a. Egg frizzle.
    b. Egg drizzle.
    c. Egg chisel.
    d. None of the above.

21. A chiffon cake contains:
    a. Egg yolks only.
    b. Egg whites only.
    c. Egg whites and yolks, added to the cake separately.
    d. None of the above.

22. A style of single crust pie that uses eggs, syrup, vanilla, and a lot of sugar for the filling and is topped with nuts is called:
    a. Walnut pie. b. Pecan pie.
    c. Almond pie. d. Hazelnut pie.

23. A mousse contains egg white, sugar, evaporated milk, and vanilla and can be made into which of the following flavors:
    a. Strawberry. b. Vanilla.
    c. Brazil nut. d. All of the above.

24. Custard is served as a:
    a. Main course. b. Dessert.
    c. Appetizer. d. None of the above.

25. This type of breakfast food is considered in the pancake family. It must be baked in a special kind of iron. It has little square indentions throughout:
    a. Fancy crepe. b. Waffle.
    c. Swedish pancake. d. German pancake.

26. Eggs Au Gratin are made with:
    a. Cheese. b. Wine.
    c. Lemon juice. d. Potatoes.

27. A type of bread that contains eggs, but no yeast:
    a. Banana bread. b. Quick bread.
    c. Muffin. d. All of the above.

28. Cream puff dough contains:
    a. Egg whites. b. Egg yolks.
    c. The whole egg. d. No eggs.

29. Fritters can contain a fruit such as apple, or vegetables such as corn. Ingredients include: egg, sugar, flour, salt, milk, and oil. They are usually:
    a. Deep-fried. b. Broiled.
    c. Boiled. d. Baked.

30. A type of fish or meat that has egg, bread or cracker crumbs, and onion and is shaped into a log and rolled in crumbs, then in egg, and then again in crumbs and then fried in hot fat.
    a. Salmon croquette. b. Tuna croquette.
    c. Ham croquette. d. All of the above.

31. A food such as zucchini or eggplant that is dipped into egg is known as a:
    a. Binder.   b. Coating.   c. Cover.   d. None of the above.

32. A fish that is prepared by dipping into a mixture of flour, salt, egg, milk or beer is known as a...
    a. Batter.   b. Coating.   c. Topping.   d. All of the above.

33. A type of fish egg used for appetizer:
    a. Salmon eggs.   b. Caviar.   c. Frog eggs.   d. Octopus eggs.

34. A type of starch dish that contains egg, salt, and flour and is used in soups and casseroles—or can be served as a side dish:
    a. Shell pasta.   b. Bowties.   c. Noodles.   d. None of the above.

35. A type of food that contains flour, baking powder, butter, and milk. Egg can be added or left out. This food is often served on the farm for Sunday dinner with chicken.
    a. Potato pancakes.   b. Dumplings.   c. Potato pie.   d. Irish pie.

36. When you add an egg to a pudding it acts as what type of agent:
    a. Binder.   b. Thickener.   c. Extra flavor.   d. None of the above.

Egg Talk Answer Key:

1. b	10. b	19. c	28. c
2. a	11. d	20. a	29. a
3. d	12. a	21. a	30. d
4. a	13. a	22. b	31. b
5. b	14. b	23. d	32. a
6. c	15. b	24. b	33. b
7. b	16. a	25. b	34. c
8. c	17. d	26. a	35. b
9. a	18. d	27. d	36. b

Egg It Up Party

Dress up like a Chef and get the staff to help fry eggs to order for the residents.

Believe me, they are delighted! I turned the dining room into a short order restaurant once a month. They could order scrambled or fried eggs. The kitchen staff got the juice and toast, fruit cups, tea and coffee ready. We set the table with a chicken centerpiece.

At coffee time we gathered everyone together and did the Egg Word Search on the next page.

Egg Word Search

```
Q S H I R R E D N C Y I F Q U I C H E T Y
T E G G N O G S K Y R F R S E F E G G S T
E G T N C G O B I T F E I O P R P G B A I
G S I O V E R E A S Y A Z U P I C I P L S
G S B E N E D I C T I M Z F P E K A M A C
X T I M B A L E S K X E E L F P D L P D R
I O A P O A C H E F I D E L E L E Q U D A
O M E L E T E D I K U F U E I E D R S P M
P E E Q W D E F R I E D B V D P I O T C B
L G E A S T E R E G G I O T L D R A A Z L
H G P M E R I N G U E T A R T S B E R R E
S B E A T E R S P O D E V I L E X D M D D
```

Egg Words to Search for:

Quiche	Fried	Egg beaters	Meringue tarts
Eggnog	Poached	Timbales	Shirred
Custard	Deviled	Frizzle	Over easy
Easter egg	Scrambled	Eggs benedict	Pickled
Egg salad	Omelet	Creamed	Souffle

Egg Word Search Answer Key

```
Q S H I R R E D N C Y C F Q U I C H E T Y
T E G G N O G S K Y R R S E F E G G S T
E G T N C G O B I T F E I O P P P G B A I
G S I O V E R E A S Y A Z U P I C I P L S
G S B E N E D I C T I M Z F P C K A M A C
X T I M B A L E S K X E L F F K D L C D R
I O A P O A C H E D I D E L E L E Q U D A
O M E L E T E D I K U F U E I E D R S P M
P E E Q W D E F R I E D B V D D I O T C B
L G E A S T E R E G G I O T L D R A A Z L
H G P M E R I N G U E T A R T S B E R R E
S B E A T E R S P O D E V I L E D D D D D
```

Egg Words to Search for:

Quiche	Fried	Egg beaters	Meringue tarts
Eggnog	Poached	Timbales	Shirred
Custard	Deviled	Frizzle	Over easy
Easter egg	Scrambled	Eggs benedict	Pickled
Egg salad	Omelet	Creamed	Souffle

Song for the Egg Program

"I'm Putting All My Eggs in One Basket"
from *The Irving Berlin Collection* E-Z Play Today for Organs, Pianos, and Electronic Keyboards.

"I'm putting all my eggs in one basket.
I'm betting everything I've got on you.
I'm giving all my love to one baby.
Lord, help me if my baby don't come through.
I've got a great big amount saved up in my love account,
Honey, and I've decided love divided by two won't do.
So, I'm putting all my eggs in one basket—
I'm betting everything I've got on you."

Hawaiian Party

If your budget permits, purchase Hawaiian or tropical looking hats, decorations for the party room, two grass skirts, and a lei for each resident. You can find the items you need at any good party store, or activity purchasing catalog.

Each resident should receive a hat and lei to help create the proper mood.

Maybe you can find someone in the community (professional or volunteer) who can provide guitar music of Hawaiian songs, or someone to do Hawaiian dances. Pick a couple of the residents to join in doing the Hula dance. Even folks in wheelchairs can do the motions with their hands. Practice the hand motions before trying them to music:

Move their hands back and forth for birds flying.

Hands up and down for the rain.

A circle for the sun after the rain.

When they have mastered the motions, add the music.

The residents enjoy live dancing, if you can find some Hawaiian dancers, or a local dance studio, maybe they would like to perform for your facility. Many of your residents have been dancing all their lives and they will enjoy the music, dance motion, and reminiscing about dancing.

You may have a resident who is a "good sport" and who would enjoy wearing the grass skirt and doing the Hula dance.

It is fun to have each resident pick a Hawaiian name to go by during the party. They will enjoy knowing what their name sounds like in the Hawaiian version. See attached list of names on pages 133 to 139. Also talk about "Aloha" and that it means hello, goodbye, love, and affection.

Ask if any of the residents have traveled to Hawaii. Some may even have family or friends living in Hawaii.

Decorate a buffet table in a Hawaiian theme. Have the residents help with the decorations. You can make palm trees for your table (use a six-foot table). Place a fishing net on top of the tablecloth, covering two to three feet of the six-foot table. Scatter a variety of seashells around on the fish net. Make a pineapple centerpiece following the directions on page 208 of my book *Picnics, Catering on the Move*. Hang wall decorations. Just before the party place the food, plates, napkins, silverware, and cups on the table.

Supplies needed for Palm Tree decorations:

4   fat, long carrots.

4   potatoes.

4   green peppers.

4   toothpicks.

Wash the vegetables. With a sharp paring knife make cuts on the carrot to simulate a palm tree trunk. Do not peel the potato, but slice a thin piece across the bottom so it will be flat. Cut a round hole in the middle of the potato so you can see through to the bottom of the potato.

Leaving the green pepper whole, cut out the core and remove the seeds. With a sharp paring knife make "V" slits every inch or so around the entire pepper. Follow the diagram on page 206 in the *Picnics Catering on the Move* cookbook by Pat Nekola.

To assemble the palm tree, place the thick part of the circle of carrot
potato. Make sure the carrot fits. Stick a toothpick through the top center of the g.
into the top center of the carrot. It should stand up. The palm trees are then placed on u.
table.

Recipes:

Hawaiian Punch

Yield: 1 gallon.

2 quarts Hawaiian punch juice
2 quarts 7UP
1 orange with rind
1 ice ring

Mix the punch juice and 7UP together. Slice the orange and float the slices in the punch.
Fill a round jello mold with 7UP or water and freeze for 24 hours. Unmold the ice and float in the
punch.

Pineapple Cheese Ball

Yield: 50 servings, each ball will serve 25.

2 pounds cream cheese
1 teaspoon Worcestershire sauce
$1/3$ cup finely chopped pecans
1 can (16 ounce) crushed pineapple, drained well
$1/3$ cup chopped celery
$1/4$ teaspoon onion powder
$1/4$ teaspoon garlic powder

(You will need 1 cup chopped pecans to roll the ball in for a garnish.)

Blend the cheese, Worcestershire sauce, pecans, pineapple, celery, onion, and garlic powder, and beat until smooth. Form into 2 one-pound cheese balls. Roll the balls in chopped nuts.
Serve with crackers.

*Note: Check to make sure residents can have nuts before serving to them. Some people have
trouble swallowing and they should not have the nuts.*

Fresh Fruit Platter
Yield: 20 servings.
1 cantaloupe
1 pineapple
1 honeydew
1 pint strawberries
$1/2$ pound red grapes
$1/2$ pound green grapes

Clean and prepare fruit and arrange on a tray. Garnish with parsley. Some of the residents may enjoy cutting the fruit and getting the tray ready for the party—or your kitchen staff can prepare the fruit for you, or a local caterer may donate the fruit tray.

Hawaiian Luau

Residents will enjoy talking about the different foods grown and served in Hawaii. A luau can be an interesting activity. I was very surprised how many residents knew what poi was. Poi looks like cream of wheat. I was not fond of poi when I visited Hawaii.

The topic of roasting a pig and various food items to go with a roast pig is a good conversation starter. Refer to pages 77-78 in *Picnics Catering on the Move* for how to roast a pig. If you can raise the money, ask your local meat market or someone from your community who does this for parties, to roast a pig and serve it for your facility. This will be quite an exciting event for your residents.

The most popular meal on the islands is the luau. Most people attending one will eat light for the day before to save room for all the good things to eat.

It is very interesting to see how the pig is prepared. A pit is dug and the pig is seasoned and placed in the underground oven to cook. The oven is called an imu. It is a shallow hole lined with stones. A roaring fire is started in the hole and when it dies down the stones will be very hot. The ashes are swept away and the imu is ready for the pig. As the pig is cooked water is added through a long tube of bamboo sticks. It takes about four hours for the pig to be cooked completely.

Side dishes at a luau include: fish, chicken, poi, sweet potatoes, regular potatoes, bread fruit, bananas, pineapple, and coconut dishes.

There are many fruits and vegetables grown in the islands. They include: bananas, avocados, coconuts, breadfruit, papaya, passion fruit, and guava.

Macadamia nuts are very expensive in the states, however they are reasonably priced in Hawaii.

Litchi is a small fruit with a thin red shell; people call them nuts because they appear like a nut when dried. They have a sweet, juicy, white flesh when fresh.

Of course, pineapple is grown in Hawaii. When fresh-picked the pineapple is very sweet and many people add salt instead of sugar, it brings out the sweet taste.

Kona coffee is a famous Hawaiian coffee. It is grown on the big island.

A local beer is produced in Honolulu. It is Koolau Lager beer and is served at the luaus.

Additional Menu Items:

Spanfrukle
Roasted chickens
Poi
Parsley Potatoes
Rice Pilaf
Green Beans with Almonds
Fresh Fruit Platter
Raw Vegetables
Assorted Rolls and Butter
Pineapple Upside Down Cake
Coffee, Tea, Milk, Hawaiian Island Drinks (below)

Examples of Hawaiian Island Drinks: *Some of these can be served without liquor.*

Mai Tai

Mai Tai Mix
Light and dark rum
Orange juice or 7UP
Crushed ice
Residents enjoy this slushy drink!

Chi Chi

Vodka
Pineapple juice
Coconut syrup
This drink is like a milk shake and slides down easily. Don't be fooled by this drink!

Blue Hawaii

Vodka
Blue curacao
Planter's punch
Light rum
Grenadine
Bitters
Lemon juice
This is a wonderful thirst quencher.

Singapore Sling

Gin
Cherry brandy
Lemon juice
This is one drink you can't recreate without the liquor.

History of Foods in Hawaii

The Polynesians were the first group of people to settle in Hawaii. They grew bananas, taro, and coconuts. People from many other nations have also come to live in the islands, but there are many traditional Polynesian dishes served in Hawaii.

The Polynesian people enjoyed luaus and the hula dance for entertainment. They had baked most of their dishes in the underground oven called the imu.

Missionaries and sailors came and settled in Hawaii. A lot of these people carried ingredients with them to make puddings, pies, dumplings, gravies, and roasts.

The Chinese brought chop suey.

The Japanese brought in shoyu, sashimi boxed lunch, tempura, and filling noodle soups.

The people from the Mediterranean came with bean soups, sausages, and sweet breads.

The Koreans brought the idea of barbecue pits and fixed kimchi. This dish is beef cooked over an open fire.

The Filipinos made fish stew, and meat and chicken in a rich sauce of vinegar and garlic.

Fruits of Hawaii

Breadfruit is a large, round, yellow/green fruit grown on trees. You can spot this fruit while hiking in the islands. They ripen in August and September.

Coconuts are better when you pick one that looks green. It is much easier to spoon out the coconut meat. Most of the coconuts we see in the stores are brown with a hard shell that is hard to crack and dig out the coconut.

Guavas are green to yellow and are found along roadsides and trails. It is a thick-skinned fruit filled with seeds in a soft pinkish pulp. Guavas are used for jams, jellies, and juice.

Limes in Hawaii are more tangy, but are green and look like the ones sold in our stores.

Lychee is a grape-like fruit. It has a reddish shell and is in season in June and July. To eat this fruit you bite through the tough skin and suck out the juice. Open the shell and pop the entire morsel inside your mouth—but watch out for the seeds.

Lilikoi is also called passion fruit. This fruit is ripe in the summer. Passion fruit makes a great drink. Lilikoi and lychee are very much alike.

Mangos are very popular and grown on Kauai. They are in season in June and July. While there are several varieties, the most common mango is the color of a peach when peeled. Remember, there is a large pit in the center of each mango.

Mountain Apples are best in the early summer. They are pear-shaped, small, and tart. It is a very juicy red fruit found in the mountain valleys.

Methley Plum is bright red both inside and out. This fruit is found in the Kokee area and ripens in May and June.

Papaya The sunrise papaya is the most common variety. It has a yellowish-orange color. It is tasty when slightly soft. Some people like to squeeze a little lime on their papaya.

Pineapple is grown in many locals' backyards. There are many pineapple fields grown by the Dole

Corporation. The pineapple has green leaves at the top of the fruit and the body is a yellow-green color. If the leaves snap off the top easily, it is ripe.

Poha is a cape gooseberry. The poha has a lot of seeds and is often cooked for jam.

Soursop is a large, heart-shaped fruit with a thick, spiny skin. Usually juice and sherbets are made from soursop.

Starfruit is a yellow-green fruit with a thin-waxy skin. It has five prominent ribs. As the fruit is cut it has a star shape because of the ribs. It is used for decorative purposes for salads.

Tamarind has a brittle, brown pod and a sticky, slightly-acid tasting pulp around a black seed.

Hawaiian Food Terms and Meanings

It might be interesting and fun for your residents to see if they know any of the following food terms, or even interesting for them to learn some of them and try them out during your Hawaii Party.

Ahi is a yellow fin tuna.

Aku is a bonita tuna.

Alaea Salt is a coarse sea salt mixed with ocheous red earth.

Arma is mullet.

A'u is swordfish.

Hapu'upu'u is a sea bass.

Huli Huli Chicken is barbecued chicken.

Kaku is barracuda.

Kalua Pork is a pig roasted whole in an underground imu.

Limu is a variety of edible seaweed.

Mahi Mahi is a true dolphin.

Okolehao refers to liquor.

Ono Wahoo is a long, slender tuna-like fish.

Opae is shrimp.

Opakapaka is a pink snapper.

Opihi is a limpet mixed with seaweed and salt and is eaten raw.

Poi is served at very Hawaiian luau. It is a purplish paste made from pounding cooked taro roots. It has the consistency of cream of wheat.

Poke is a seafood salad with slices of raw fish or octopus mixed with kukui nut and seaweed.

Pupu is a small gastropod like a snail. Pupu is an appetizer.

Uku is a deep-sea grap snapper.

Ula'ula is a red snapper.

Ulua is the jackfish, also called the crevalle.

Hawaiian Birds

Researchers of bird life in Hawaii believe there are forty species on the islands. This includes seven species of geese; an unusual one-legged owl; hunting creepers; ibis; and lovebirds.

Unfortunately, many of the beautiful birds of Hawaii are gone due to several factors.

- The original Polynesians killed the unusual species.

- Farmers burned the forestland, this action hurt bird life the most.

- Many people made leis out of bird feathers.

- Disease was devastating to the bird population.

- The mongoose and rats preyed on the birds.

- In 1826, a boat brought mosquitoes to Hawaii. The larvae was found in the water barrels.

Through this unfortunate mishap the birds became infected and died.

It was Theodore Roosevelt in the 20th century who helped to preserve wildlife in the Hawaiian Islands. The Hawaiian Audubon Society and the University of Hawaii stays involved in helping to sustain the remaining birds in Hawaii. They stress to never disturb a bird nest if you are hiking.

Amakihi
See description under Hawaiian Honey Creepers.

Amakihi

Anianiau
This yellow-green bird is four inches in length and is found in Koke'e.

Crested Honey Creeper
This bird lives on Maui. It is about seven inches in length and mostly black. It has grey feathers and bright orange neck and underbelly. It has a distinctive fluff of feathers that form a crown.

Elepaio
This small brown bird's name comes from the sound of its song. This friendly bird will come to strangers if offered food.

Hawaiian Coot
This bird is also called the alae ke'oke'o in Hawaii. It is a web-footed water bird and looks like a duck. This bird lives on Maui and Kanai. It has dull grey feathers with a white bill and tail feathers. It is one of only two water birds found in Hawaii. The story goes that the Coot stole fire from heaven and that is why its forehead is red.

Hawaiian Gallnude or Alae ula
This duck-like bird is found in the Hanalei's taro patches. It has a red face tipped in yellow and huge chicken-like feet. It uses its feet to hop across floating vegetation.

Hawaiian Honey Creepers

There are about 40 varieties of Honey Creepers. Most of them are extinct. Some look like finches and others resemble blackbirds and parrots, or even woodpeckers. The majority of honey creepers live on Maui and Kauai. They have a white bill, white tail feathers and grey feathers. The two remaining species are the Amakihi and the Tiwi. The Amakihi is yellowish green and eats insects, fruit, or nectar. It is a small pretty bird. The Tiwi is bright red with a salmon-colored hooked bill. It has a harsh voice and feeds on a variety of flowers and insects.

Hawaiian Owl or Pueo

This owl is found on all of the main islands. It has a mixture of brown and white feathers and stands 15 inches tall. It has round, large, yellow eyes. The chicks are yellow.

Hawaiian Stilt or Ae'o

The stilt is primarily black and is 16 inches long. It is a very thin wading bird and has a white belly. The stick-like legs are pink. It lives on Maui on the Kaelia ponds. It is the other of the two water birds found on Maui. The other is the Hawaiian Coot.

Iwa or Frigate Bird

The Hawaiian name "Iwa" means thief. This bird cannot swim, stand, or walk but can live almost indefinitely in the air. It catches fish on the surface of the water. It is called a thief because it will steal food from other birds while flying. It will pick up a small object from the ground as it is flying down. It can pause over the object and rise up again. The female bird is larger than the male in this species.

The average frigate bird is $37^1/_2$ inches in height with a 7-foot wingspan. The male is black with metallic purple and green colors. The gular pouch is reddish yellow. The female is blackish-brown with a white breast and has scarlet around the eyes. The chicks are snow white.

Kauai Oo

Oo means dwarf or small in Hawaiian. The adult male has a black head with white lines. The upper surface is brown with rump and flanks russet in color. Each feather has some white and the center of the feather is grey. The wings and tail are black. This bird is active and quick when hunting for food.

Kauai Oo

Koloa Hawaiian Duck or Kola Mali

This particular duck survives by nesting on the twin islands of Mokulua off Lanikai. This duck returns to Oahu by swimming or flying and carrying the chicks between its feet. The head is blackish with upper back brown. The speculum is deep purple bordered with white.

Laysan Duck or Laysan Teal in Hawaii

This duck is very much like the Koloa. It has an irregular white ring around the eye. It doesn't swim well, but has strong feet.

Lesser Snow Goose

This is a large goose measuring 27 inches in length. It has a pure white body with black flight feathers and a reddish bill and feet.

Lovebird

The lovebird is also known as the shell parakeet. The head and wings are yellow and the body is green. This bird comes in several different colors and is a favorite bird for a cage.

Maui Parrotbill

The Maui Parrotbill has an olive green back and a yellow body. It has a parrot-like bill and uses it to crack branches and pry out larvae. It is only found on the slopes of Haleakala, about 5,000 feet above sea level.

Moli

This is a water bird. It has an eleven-foot wingspan, nests along the baraking sands, and has little fear of man.

Nene or Hawaiian Goose

This goose is special because it is Hawaii's state bird. They are found on the slopes of Mauna Loa, Hualaiai, and Mauna Kea. This bird can be raised in captivity. The nene symbolizes Hawaii with the following words, "let it be, and it will live". The adult male is black on the neck, head, cheeks, chin, and throat. The remainder of the neck and sides of the head are brown. The underside is white and the bill and feet are black. They eat berries, and rich soft plants.

Nene or Hawaiian Goose

Nukupu'u

This drab green bird with a bright yellow chest is five inches in length. Very few are found on Maui. They are found in Kauai's upper forests and alkaline swamps.

O'o'a'a'

Hunters captured this bird for its yellow leg feathers, which they used for capes and helmets. It is a black bird, eight inches in length.

O'u

The chubby bird's song ranges for half an octave. It is green with a yellow head and is seven inches in length.

Pintail Duck or Napu

The male's head and upper neck is brown. It has some green and purple and white stripes on the sides of the head. The female is gray and has yellowish brown streaks. They migrate to Hawaii in the fall and leave in the spring. This duck also goes by the name of Sprig.

Pouli

This bird is five inches in length and is dark brown. It also has dark brown feet, a short tail, and a conical bill. They survive in the deep forests of Maui. A Pouli Owl has a heart-shaped face, and that is how to distinguish them from a Pueo Owl.

Puaiohi

This is a rare bird. It is dark brown with a white belly and is seven inches in length.

Red-Footed Booby
This is a water bird. It is white with a blue bill and three-foot wingspan.

Shoveller Duck or Moba
This duck has a shiny green head and breast. The outer scalpulars are white, underparts are chestnut and dark bluish green. It has orange feet. It is also known as the spoonbill.

Tiwi
See description under Hawaiian Honey Creeprs.

Turkey or Palahu
The Hawaiian name of this bird refers to the soft, elastic bare red skin about the head and neck. The body is shiny bronze, copper, and green. Turkeys are easy to catch.

Tiwi

White-Faced Glossy Ibis
This bird appears to be black, but has a bright iridescent chestnut-colored plumage. It has long legs and flies in orderly diagonal lines with legs and neck extended. It is approximately 24 inches in length.

White-Tailed Tripic
This water bird is snow white with a kite-like tail. It has a three-foot wingspan.

Seashell Program

The Hawaiian Islands located in the Central Pacific has unique cowrie and cone shells. There are many varieties of shells found not only in the Hawaiian Islands, but all over the world.

The Murex snail was used for making deep purple dye in the days of the Phoenicians, Greeks, and Romans. They boiled and treated this yellowish fluid from the snail to make the purple dye. The wool and cotton from royal Tyrian purple brought very high prices. This was the official color for Cardinals in the Christian Church.

- Shells were used for jewelry. Cowries were worn by Roman women. Many times, the cowries were consecrated to Venus and often given as bridal gifts. Mother-of-pearl is still very popular today.
- The scallop is the emblem of Saint James. In past history pilgrims visited the shrine. They brought back a shell to prove they were there.
- The chank shell is sacred to the Hindu god Vishnu.
- Food was, and still is, a big source coming from shells.
- The cowrie shells were used for currency and trade in Asia, Central Africa, and the Malaysian islands.
- North American Indians strung certain clamshells. They especially prized the shells with a purple interior. Indian traders went from the coast to Abalones looking for tusk shells to trade for currency. They also looked for helmet, whelk, and Venus shells.
- Shells are very much a part of art and architecture.
- Leonardo da Vinci made drawings of spiral shells.
- Sailors would make shell collages as Valentines for their sweethearts.
- The Shell Oil Companies used the shell for their logo.

Seashells have such natural beauty and design. Collecting shells throughout the years has been a hobby of mine wherever I've traveled. While there are many shells from all over the world, Hawaii has many shells that are real beauties and make for great conversation when working with the elderly population.

A tip from the author: I carry my shell collection with me so the residents can see them and touch them.

Touching the shells is a great sensory exercise, especially for the lower functioning elderly person. It gives them a chance to feel from rough to smooth. If you do not have shells, use pictures or get slides from your local library. You may have a resident or family member who might have a shell collection you can borrow for the program. At our facility a family member came in and worked with me to discuss the various kinds of shells. We both had samples. The residents thoroughly enjoyed this activity.

Independent living residents could put a shell collection together with some help from staff members.

Suggestions: You can mount them on an 8 x 11-inch board for starters. This size is easy to pass for small group participants to visualize. Write a description by each shell. In an independent living facility a gentleman might be able to put a cabinet together for storage of a facility shell collection. It could have wooden drawers on simple runners. This would protect the shells from dust and careless handling. Possibly, the facility could supply the wood and supplies for such a project.

The purpose of the shell project is educational. The residents can learn about the shells and animals and where the animals live. Nature can come into the picture when talking about the shells. It is a project that will give the residents a sense of pride and satisfaction through their participation. You do not have to stick to just Hawaiian shells. You can expand the collection to include shells from all over the world.

Shell Examples:

Samples of Gastropods found in Hawaii are: chick pea cowrie, Hawaiian top, painted auger, banded miter, pink bubble, rough dog whelk, and Hawaiian tree snails.

Samples of major groups of marine bivalves are: clams, mussels, cockles, scallops, ark shells, and pearly oysters. Bivalves are also called pelecypods. Pelecypods are mollusks with two valves joined by a hinge. They have a horny ligament and one or two muscles. The majority of the 10,000 species are marine and the others are fresh water. The tree snail is found only in Hawaii.

Samples of Cephalopods are: octopus (has no shell), squids (thin internal shell) nautilus (smooth, chambered shell). The chambered nautilus is found in the southwestern Pacific Ocean.

Samples of Scaphopods are: tusk shells such as the Indian money tusk found in Alaska and ranging to Baja, California. The scaphopod is open at both ends and generally is curved. The shell covers the animal in this class of mollusks.

Samples of Chitons are: white chiton from San Diego, California, and conspicuous chiton found from California to Mexico. Chitons are primitive marine mollusks. This group is flattened mollusk and some are wormlike. They feed on algae. The giant chiton lives in deep waters, while the conspicuous Chilton lives under rocks between tides. The white chiton lives in moderately deep water.

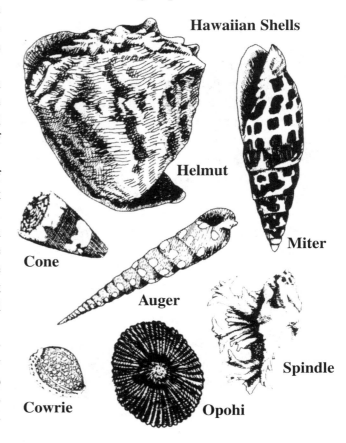

Hawaiian Shells

Helmut

Miter

Cone

Auger

Spindle

Cowrie

Opohi

The best shell work made in Hawaii comes from Niihau. The shells are very tiny and very rare. The white pupu shells are smooth small shells that are found along the rocky shoreline of the private island of Niihau.

They are abundant only in the deep waters off the windward coast. If the tides and winds are just right the shells are deposited on Nihau's beaches. The island folks will collect them and then sort them according to color and size. They keep only the finest shells and discard about 80 percent of those harvested. The most prize shells are so tiny that it takes a dozen to fit on a thimble. They make leis and jewelry from these tiny shells.

The women of Niihau take many hours to connect each shell by intricate and minute knots. They use the cowrie shell known only to the Hiihau to make the clasp. Each handmade necklace looks different in size, shape, and color. The Niihau shellwork is found in Kauai stores.

Shells of Hawaii

The word whorl will be used many times. Webster *states, "A whorl is one of the spiral turns of the univalve shell." An example of a univalve shell is the helmet shell. There are many univalve shells in the world.*

Information on Hawaiian Conch:
Bull Conch
Found in the coral reefs in the Central Pacific.
The shell is heavy.
It has two unique spins on the outer lip.
Found at depths of 20 to 50 feet.

Information on Cowries
Glossy, china-like shells.
Cowries have a shell, mantle, foot, siphon, tentacle, and snout.
Over 190 species are very common in the tropical seas.
Cowries feed on hydroids (polyps) and small marine creatures.
Primitive peoples used them for religious symbols and ornaments.
Shell collectors look for unusual cowries.
A cowrie starts with a cluster of egg capsules held by the female. Each capsule contains many eggs. As the eggs develop the veliger stage is free swimming. The cowrie species continue to develop to adulthood after six months to a year. Two other interesting cowries found in Hawaii are the tessellate cowrie and the rare spotted cowrie. The red cowrie is very common on many of the islands in the Pacific Ocean. Sometimes the shells are left in the sand and fade. The red color takes on a lavender color on the upper surface of the shell. The cowrie species are very common to the Hawaiian Islands. Cowries are from the gastropod family. The money cowrey is almost one-inch long. One hundred shells equaled one English penny. Tons of these shells were shipped to Africa in

Cowrie

early times where they were used for money. The cypaea tessellata cowrie is only found in the Hawaiian Islands. This cowrie is an uncommon species. Shell collectors search for this particular species. Uncommon cowries bring in thousands of dollars.

Uncommon Hawaiian Cowries:
Cypraea Tessellata
Common name is the checkerboard cowrie.
Size is one to one and one-half inches.
Difficult to obtain.
Distinctive dark brown dorsal.
Squares or brown blotches.
Lives in depths of water up to 43 feet.
Lives inside coral heads and crevices.
Cyraea Tigris
Common name is tiger cowrie.
Lives in moderately deep water off Hawaii.
Color is whitish to creamy whitish with irregular spots and blotches of black.
Aperture wide and curved.
Teeth robust.
Size is up to five inches.

Additional Names and Descriptions of Hawaiian Cowries
Sand Cowrie: sides are thick with a dusky top and transverse bands.
Calf Cowrie: large olive gray with white spots.
Mourning Cowrie: brown to black rim with pale spots on top.
Lynx Cowrie: shell is large with clouded brown and black spots.
Fringed Cowrie: brownish patch on top and sides of the shell.
Orange-banded Cowrie: dark transverse bars with fresh color.
Chick Pea Cowrie: yellowish in color and swollen with ends extended and top slightly grooved.
Ringed Cowrie: smoky white with orange or yellow ring.

Information on Helmet Shells
Helmet shells are large. They are found in tropical waters around the world. They live on sandy bottoms in shallow water and feed mostly on sea urchins.

Hawaiian Helmet Shells
Cassis Cornuta
Common name is Horned Helmet. Lives in moderately deep water on sandy bottoms.
It is 12 inches in height.
The shell is mainly made up of body whorls.
The surface of the shell has three rows of nodes.
The color is grayish white marked with brown. The lower surface is yellowish orange.
Helmet shells can be polished to a high sheen.

Helmut

Other Helmets:
Grooved Helmet: found in the sand in moderately deep water. It is creamy white with brown scattered dots.
White Helmet: found in moderately deep water and is 3 inches high, white color with pale orange streaks.

Information on Snails
Snails live in shallow water on rocky shores; in springs, swamps, and even in trees. The snail is a gastropod generally with a single shell that is coiled. The snail's head has tentacles and a rasping tongue. The majority of the 40,000 species have shells.
Trivia question:
That person is as slow as a _____ . (snail).

Tree snail

Hawaiian Tree Snails
Achatinella
Common name is Hawaiian tree snail.
Tree snails are found in bushes, vines, and trees only in the Hawaiian Islands.
Size is one inch high, with six rounded whorls.
The whorls produce a moderately tall spire.
The shell is smooth and polished.
The inner lip can be toothed or twisted.
The shell has many color combinations. Each valley seems to have its own colors and forms.
There are over 1,000 varieties of snails found in Hawaii. Most are not found anywhere else.
They are found on Oahu, Maui, Molokar, and Lanai—but are not found in Kauai.
Genus Coralliophila
The common name is Coral Snail.
They live in crevices of rocks and corals.
Size is one and one-half inch in height.
Rugged shell of up to six whorls.
Color of the aperture is often violet or rose.

Information on Auger Shells
Auger shells are long and brightly colored. Their size ranges from six to eight inches in length. Most of them dwell in the tropical sands.
The auger contains a poison gland that is much like the cone shells.

Hawaiian Augers
Terebra Dimidiata
Common name is divided auger.
Slender shell.
Five inches in height.
It is made up of about one and one-half whorls.
Spiral grooves are toward the bottom of

each whorl.

The color is reddish orange with streaks and bands of white.

There are many other Augers found in Hawaii such as:

Gould's Auger: narrow vertical ribs, distinct sutures, yellowish white.

Eyed Auger: large white spots with an orange/brown background.

Big Auger: vertical purplish streaks. It is heavy.

Shining Auger: slender, yellowish gray with vertical folds.

Painted Auger: yellowish gray with a spotted band at the suture. It has weak vertical grooves.

Spotted Auger: large chocolate spots; slender shape.

Information on Cone Shells

There are about 400 species of cone shells in the tropics. Cone shells are heavy with broad spires and tapering whorls. Cones feed on worms and small fish, and they can sting their victim. Cones like the shallow water in coral reefs and under rocks. This shell is more common to the southwestern Pacific, not in Hawaii. It is a rarity and collectors seek this particular cone. It is very capable of inflicting a serious sting. It has a beautiful shiny bronze crackled look, highly colored. These shells can sell for hundreds of dollars.

Hawaiian Cone Shells
Rhododendron Cone Shell
Pinkish color mixed with pearl white.
The tip is pearl white.
It is very rare in Hawaii.
Conus Abbreviatus

Auger

Common name is cone shell.
The size is one and one-fourth inches.
It is short and stocky.
Almost flat in shape.
Coronated sprie.
Slightly convex body.
The color is pale lavender with light gray bands and tiny rich brown dots.
This shell is found in the Ala Moana Reef in Oahu.

Samples and Descriptions of Other Hawaiian Cone Shells

Pearled Cone: orange to brown in color with a moderate spire.

Soldier Cone: large and heavy, yellowish brown in color with thin vertical lines.

Cloth of Gold Cone: yellowish brown with a well-developed spire and web-like markings.

Worm Cone: mostly black with vertical grooves on the surface.

Flag Cone: chestnut brown, heavy, with blotched shoulders and center of body whorl.

Cat Cone: bluish gray with brown patches. Small in size.

Oak Cone: lemon yellow to white with a pointed spire and smooth surface.

Calf Cone: olive to tan color with a low spire and an encircling band.

Marbled Cone: dark brown color with whiteish or pinkish triangles.

Imperial Cone: light brownish bands with knobby shoulders and a low spire.

Rat Cone: yellowish brown with flat top and smooth shoulders.

Knobby Cone: yellowish gray with shoulders with small knobs.

Hebrew Cone: banded with heavy black blotches.

Spiteful Cone: olive to tan in color with knobby shoulders.

Cone

Information on Miters

The miter shells are from the mitridae family and are found in shallow seas. There are 600 species in sizes from 0.3 to 6 inches in length. Miters use their long snout to feed on worms and clams found in the sand. They are usually found in rocky areas.

Miter

Hawaiian Miters

Mitra Cononata
Common name is crowned miter.
Lives in moderately shallow water.
Has a stocky shell.
The size is about one-inch high.
Orange brown in color flecked with white.
Usually has five or six whorls.

Mitra Astricta
The common name is smooth miter.
Size is one-inch in height.
Has six sloping whorls.
The surface is very smooth.
Olive gray in color.
Sometimes the shell will have narrow, encircling lines of brown.

Other Hawaiian Miters
Banded Miter: smooth with fine lines, sturdy with small shoulders.
Brown Miter: smooth, white aperture with no shoulders.
Ridged Miter: strong with encircling ridges and is yellowish orange in color.
Lettered Miter: an irregular white body with dark scrawls.
Nodular Miter: a small shell with encircling nodes.

Information on Bubble Shells

Bubble shells have external plume-like gills. Bubble shells are found mostly in the tropics. They lay eggs in long gelatinous strands. It is called "bubble" due to the shape of the creature inside the shell.

Hawaiian Bubble Shells
Haminoea Crocata
Common name is paper bubble.
Size is one-half inch in height.
It is a glossy, tiny shell—and very thin.
The color is translucent yellowish.
It has a smooth, glassy appearance.
The animal inside is too large for its shell.

Hydantina Albocincta
Common name is clown bubble.
It is thin and fragile.
The top is a small, sunken spiral.
Polished surface.
Pale brown in color.
There are sharply defined bands of white on the body whorl.

Hydatina Amplustre
Common name is pink bubble.
When mature it is one-inch in height.
Polished surface.
Rich pink color.

Hydtina Physis
Common name is striped bubble.
This shell lives in shallow water.
Yellowish gray in color.
Smooth, polished surface.

Information on Olive Shells

Olive shells live on sandy bottoms and feed on smaller mollusks. You can collect olives at night at a low tide. The living animal is shaped like an olive. The Hawaiian Olive shell varies in color.

Hawaiian Olive
Olive Sandwichensis
Common name is Hawaiian olive.
This shell lives in sandflats at low tides.
One inch in height.
Has four to five whorls.
It has a short spire and a long body whorl.
The long body whorl is cylindrical in shape.
Surface is smooth and polished.
Yellowish white with brown spots.
The brown spots are in three irregular bands.

Hawaiian Whelks
Pisania Billetheusti
Common name is marbled whelk.
Lives in moderately deep water.
A very slender shell about one inch in height.
It has eight whorls.
White in color with reddish brown.
Pisania Tritnoides
Common name is pisa whelk.
Lives in moderately deep water.
It is a small elongate shell.
Contains seven whorls.
One inch in height.
Yellowish white with mottled pale orange.
Nassarius Papillosus
The common name is dog whelk.
It lives in shallow water.
Measures from one to two inches in height.
Has six or seven whorls.
White in color sometimes tinged with yellow.

Hawaiian Drupes
Drupa Grossularia
Common name is finger drupe.
Lives in moderately shallow water.
One inch in height.
Has four whorls.
The surface has revolving lines.
The aperture is narrow and strongly toothed.
Whitish with a bright orange aperture.

Drupa Morum
Common name is the mulberry drupe.
Lives in moderately shallow water.
Height is one to one and one-half inches.
A very sturdy shell.
Squat in shape.
Three or four whorls.
The last whorl is very large.
Rough and spiny surface.
Strongly toothed purple aperture.
Drupa Ricina
Common name is spotted drupe.
Lives in moderately shallow water.
Outer lip has spines.
Squarish black nodes.
Color is whitish with black nodes.
The aperture is small and narrow.
Four whorls encircle the body whorl.
The long, narrow aperture is closed by the teeth of the outer lip.

Hawaiian Horn Shells
Cerithium Baeticum
Common name is banded horn shell.
Lives in weedy, shallow water.
A pretty shell about one-half inch in height.
Has eight well-rounded whorls.
The body consists of low vertical ribs.
There are encircling rows of tiny beads.
White to yellowish in color.
There is a band of chocolate brown on each volition.
Cerithium Nassoides
Common name is spotted horn shell.
This shell lives in shallow water.
Shape is short and stout and only one-third inch in height.
Has vertical ridges and knobby spiral bands on the shoulders.
There are six whorls.
The aperture is oval.
Yellowish white with spots of brown.
Cerithium Columna
Common name is columnar horn shell.

Lives in weedy, shallow water.

One to one and one-half inches in height.

Stout and elongated.

Approximately nine whorls and indistinct sutures.

There are small notch-like canals at both ends of the aperture.

Grayish white and sometimes mottled with brown.

Note: The Obelisk horn shell and the Thaanum's horn shell both live in weedy, shallow water. The horn shell, in general, is rugged. The Thaanum horn shell is whitish and sometimes spotted with reddish brown; where as the Obelish horn shell is yellowish white and is spotted with purplish brown.

Hawaiian Sundial
Torinia Variegata

Common name is variegated sundial.

Whitish with numerous streaks of brown.

Adorned with strongly-cut revolving lines.

Distinct vertical lines.

Hawaiian Stromb
Strombus Hawaiensis

Common name is the Hawaiian stromb.

Large and solid.

Yellowish white color

Outer lip is expanded and thick.

Hawaiian Harp Shell
Harpa Conoidalis

Common name is harp shell.

Lives in moderately deep water.

One of the most attractive of marine shells.

Up to two inches in height.

Pinkish grey to bluish white.

Contains squarish spots of violet on the ribs.

The spaces between the spots are marked with brown and lavender.

Inner lip has two strong patches of chocolate brown.

Hawaiian Pearly-Top Shells
Trochus Intxtus

Common name is Hawaiian top.

Conical in shape.

Pinkish white color.

Bands commonly covering the upper half of whorls.

Information on Jewel Boxes

There are about 20 species of jewel boxes. They live attached to rocks and wrecks. Jewel boxes are tropical shells with brilliant colors.

Hawaiian Jewel Box
Chama Hendersoni

Common name is Henderson's jewel box.

Small shell.

Often twisted.

Chama Iostoma

Common name is violet-mouthed jewel box.

The valves are solid and unequal.

The interior has a violet border.

Umbrella Shell
Umbraculum Sinicum

Common name is umbrella shell.

It is white with a dark brown center.

Oval, flat shape.

Three inches in length.

Hawaiian Pelecypods
Pinna Semicostata

Common name is costate pen.

Lives in moderately shallow water.

This is a bivalve and ranges from six to ten inches in length.

An elongated triangular shape.

The surface has a series of folds radiating from the tip of the triangle.

Yellowish tan color.

Information on Oysters

Many of the tropical species have pearly white interiors.

They have a hinge and the shells are very fragile. Oysters are from the pelecypod family.

Hawaiian Oyster

Pteria Nebulosa

Common name is the little pearl oyster.

A thin shell.

Radiating bands of brown.

Pearly appearance on inside.

Yellowish green with broad radiating bands of brown.

Lives in shallow water.

Three inches in length.

Pinctada Galtsoffi

Common name is black-lipped pearl oyster.

Lives in moderately deep water.

Heavy and solid.

Pearly interior.

Large muscle scar.

Eight inches in length.

Valuable pearls are sometimes found under the mantle of the bivalve.

Ostrea Sanwichensis

Common name is Hawaiian oyster.

Irregular shape.

Wavy surface.

Yellowish gray color.

Spondylus Hawaiensis

Common name is Hawaiian spiny oyster.

Interlocking hinge.

Whitish and interior is white.

Porcelain-like appearance.

Information on Scallops

The edible part of the scallop is the muscle. Do you know that the scallop has a heart, foot, rectum, tentacles, eyes, top valve, gills, and mantle? Scallops are from the pelecypod family.

Hawaiian scallops.

Hawaiian Scallops

Haumea Juddi

Common name is Judd's scallop.

Round shape.

Small wings.

Coarse ribs.

Mottled white.

Chalamys Cookei

Common name is Cooke's scallop.

Unequal wings.

Finely ribbed.

Yellowish to orange in color.

Isognomon Costellate

Common name is little purshe shell.

Radiating lines.

The hinge has vertical grooves.

Yellowish gray in color.

Nodipecten Langfordi

Common name is Langford's scallop.

Lives in moderately deep water.

Contains a solid shell about one and one-half inches in length.

There are about eight ribs that are nodular.

Colors are red or orange.

Interior is deep rose.

Information on Clams

There are many species of clams. They dwell in the sand in the tropics.

Venus clams are from the pelecypod family.

Hawaiian Clams

Rocellaria Hawaiensis

Common name is gaping clam.

Is considered to be a boring mollusk.

Lives in coral.

One-half inch in length.

The oval shell gapes.

Yellowish white in color.

Periglypta Edmondsoni

Common name is reticulate venues.

Lives in moderately shallow water.

The exterior is yellowish gray with scattered spots of pale orange.

The interior is white stained with salmon pink on the teeth of the hinge.

Has a short, rounded anterior end.

Information on Mussels

Mussels are from the mytilidae group. They are the most abundant of all the mollusk. Mussels feed on snails, worms, and crabs and live on rocky shores.

Hawaiian Mussels

Modiolus Matris

Common name is smooth mussel.

Lives in moderately deep water.

Has a short interior end.

Small beaks.

Yellowish brown in color.

Brachidontes Crebristriatus

Common name is striate mussel.

Lives in shallow water.

The shell has a bent look, as it slopes from point to point.

Purplish gray in color with a dark interior.

One inch in length.

Information on Cockles

There are cockles in western Europe, West Africa, Asia, and the Indo-Pacific. The heart shape and half-heart cockle are found in the Indo-Pacific. Cockles are active animals. They can jump several inches. Cockles are food for fishes and man. They come in all shapes and all types of degree of sculpturing. Cockles are very colorful and have various textures. Water enters through the inhalant-siphon to bring food and oxygen to the cockle. They are from the pelecypod family.

Hawaiian Cockle

Trachycardium Hawiensis

Common name is Hawaiian cockle.

Lives in moderately shallow water.

Oval in shape.

Has radiating ribs that are marked with numerous evenly-spaced curning schales.

A large strong shell about three inches long.

Yellowish white with blotched chestnut brown.

Interior is shiny white with a purple rim at the scalloped margin.

Fragum Thurstoni

Common name is blunt cockle.

Lives in moderately deep water.

It is very small at one-half inch.

Yellowish white in color.

Information on Ark Shells

The ark shell is called arcidae. There are 200 species, with the majority in the tropics.

The ark is in the pelecypod family.

Hawaiian Ark Shell

Acar Hawaiensis

Common name is reticulate ark.

Lives in shallow water.

Has a cross-barred pattern and is about one inch in length.

It has a square-like appearance.

Yellowish white in color.

Arca Ventricosa

Common name is bentricose ark.

An elongated shell with a broad hinge area and a gaping base.

There are radiant lines that are fine at the center and coarser at the ends.

The hinge area is streaked with chocolate color.

Yellowish brown with wavy streaks of reddish brown.

Information on Limpets

All 400 species of limpets are vegetarians, some living on seaweeds.

The limpets are from the gastropod family.

There is also a black limpet shell with a silvery lead interior colored with dark ribs. There is a central patch of black or purplish blue.

This animal is found at Hawaiian fish markets and is called opihi.

Note: The gastropods are also called univalves. Gastropods are single-shelled mollusks. Examples of gastropods are snails, conch, periwinkle, and whelks. There are 40,000 species in the gastropod family. About half of them are marine. The rest are terrestrial and fresh water. Most gastropods live five to six years, but some survive up to thirty years. Eggs are laid in the water or in capsules.

Hawaiian Limpets

Cellana Agentata

Common name is kneecap shell.

Lives near shore rocks.

Fine, large shell four inches in length.

Interior is white with a border of dull lustrous white, part of the interior also shines with a silvery sheen.

This is the largest Hawaiian species of the group.

Information on Periwinkles

Periwinkles live on rocky shores of most parts of the world.

They are small and drab in color. Their color protects them from predators.

Hawaiian Periwinkles

Littorina Picta

Common name is painted periwinkle.

Lives on rocks between the tides.

Only $^3/_4$ inch in height.

Has four or five whorls.

Brownish, spotted and marbled with white.

The aperture is purplish.

Littorina Pintadado

Common name is dotted periwinkle.

It lives on rocks between the tides.

Has five whorls.

Yellowish with brown dots

The aperture is reddish brown.

Littorina Scabra

Common name is variegated periwinkle.

Lives on the shoreline on rocks and vines.

Height is a little more than one inch.

Gray, reddish/yellow, or purple variegated with dark oblique markings.

This particular periwinkle is found all over the Pacific Ocean area and also in the Atlantic Ocean.

Trivia Questions about Hawaii

1. The big island is _____. (Hawaii)

2. Honolulu is found on the island of _____. (Oahu)

3. _____ is the island used for a military target. (Kahoolawe)

4. _____ is the island known for lush vegetation. (Kaui)

5. _____ was the island that housed the people with leprosy. (Malolkai)

6. The privately owned island used for growing pineapples is _____. (Lunai)

7. _____ islands make up Hawaii. (130) They spread about 1,600 miles across the mid-_____ Ocean. (Pacific)

8. Only _____ of the 130 islands are inhabited. (Seven)

9. Most of the islands were formed due to _____ action. (Volcanic)

10. Captain James _____ and his crew were the first Europeans to visit the Hawaiian Islands. (Cook)

11. _____ Harbor was bombed in World War ___ by the _____. (Pearl) (II) (Japanese)

12. Hawaii became the _____ state on August 21, _____. (50th) (1959)

13. The eight larger islands are located in the _____ area of Hawaii. (southeastern)

14. The island of _____ has one of the world's largest extinct volcanic craters. (Haleakala)

15. Seventy-five percent of the population lives on the island of _____. (Oahu)

16. The U.S.S. _____ Memorial at Pearl Harbor remembers crewmembers of the ship sunk by the _____. (Arizona) (Japanese)

17. The U.S. Missionaries in the early 19th century established the first formal _____. (schools)

18. A little more than forty percent of Hawaii is covered with _____. (forest)

19. A common tree grown in Hawaii is the screw _____. (pine)

20. There are _____ species of flowering _____. (1,400) (plants)

21. Name five flowering plants grown in Hawaii. _____, _____, _____, _____, _____. (orchid, hibiscus, gardenia, poinsettia, antherium)

22. The _____ or _____ _____ is the state bird. (Nene) (Hawaiian goose)

23. The Hawaiian Islands are approximately _____ miles away from San Francisco. (2,000)

24. The two agricultural products that are grown in Hawaii are _____ and _____ _____. (pineapple) (sugar cane)

25. Between 400 and 900 AD, the _____ from the islands of Tahiti and Marguesas settled some of the Hawaiian Islands. (Polynesians)

26. Captain Cook named the Hawaiian Islands the _____ Islands. (Sandwich)

27. The _____ industry is the leading private segment of the Hawaiian economy. (tourism)

28. The largest city in Hawaii is _____. (Honolulu)

29. Hawaii is the _____ smallest state in the United States. (fourth)

Hawaiian Shell Word Search

```
C O N E T R E W W T Y I D R U P E S K H E
A R I T H E L M E T H J K L J Y U H O O W
V F O G F B E R W C L A M S N O P O T R S
S U U M B R E L L A D A D F I N D W E N Q
O N L E R T S G D E R S P I O D K E S B C
P A A F W D C C V B J K U R T A R R X V X
O U M I E T A Y U P E R I W I N K L E S A
L G N D L D L D A F T E R C O W R I E Y H
I E S F S S L T R R Y U I O H F G M T N N
V R A D E F O I G J K U S O C D T T L R S
E K F P D D P O F M H Y U I O P D H K D T
Y M A H O R D L H N E T N J C O X K U G R
U E T A E H X P J T R R D U K T C N H F O
Q D E R F G I O E Y F T I Y L R P E V D M
A S D P D J X F W U D U A T E L E E W D B
S A A F E K Z R E J G K L R M K A C F S C
I T T E R L C E L B O X G E N Z R A A V V
J H E B U B B L E R H J F H J E L P C N M
R A G G H J K L Y T E W R E O P Y T O P F
G S O X O Y S T E R W E Y B T X S L O W R
F T R B N J K L O N E E M U S S E L S E T
T Y K K I T M O P E T T U I L Q W F V B N
```

Hawaiian Shells to Search for:

Auger	Apohi	Mussels	Periwinkles	Harp
Helmet	Clams	Kneecap	Stromb	Bubble
Cone	Oyster	Snails	Scallop	Drupes
Cowrie	Cockle	Ark	Umbrella	Olive
Pearly Top	Jewel Box	Horn	Sundial	

Hawaiian Shell Word Search Answer Key

```
C O N E T R E W W T Y I D R U P E S K H E
A R I T H E L M E T H J K L J Y U H O O W
V F O G F B E R W C L A M S N O P O T R S
S U U M B R E L L A D A D F I N D W E N Q
O N L E R T S G D E R S P I O D K E S B C
P A A F W D C C V B J K U R T A R R X V X
O U M I E T A Y U P E R I W I N K L E S A
L G N D L D L D A F T E R C O W R I E Y H
I E S F S S L T R R Y U I O H F G M T N N
V R A D E F O I G J K U S O C D T T L R S
E K F P D D P O F M H Y U I O P D H K D T
Y M A H O R D L H N E T N J C O X K U G R
U E T A E H X P J T R R D U K T C N H F O
Q D E R F G I O E Y F T I Y L R P E V D M
A S D P D J X F W U D U A T E L E E W D B
S A A F E K Z R E J G K L R M K A C F S C
I T T E R L C E L B O X G E N Z R A A V V
J H E B U B B L E R H J F H J E L P C N M
R A G G H J K L Y T E W R E O P Y T O P F
G S O X O Y S T E R W E Y B T X S L O W R
F T R B N J K L O N E E M U S S E L S E T
T Y K K I T M O P E T T U I L Q W F V B N
```

Hawaiian Shells to Search for:

Auger	Apohi	Mussels	Periwinkles	Harp
Helmet	Clams	Kneecap	Stromb	Bubble
Cone	Oyster	Snails	Scallop	Drupes
Cowrie	Cockle	Ark	Umbrella	Olive
Pearly Top	Jewel Box	Horn	Sundial	

Hawaiian Word Search

```
A S T P O I H J Z D A P O Y P E A R L S A
S D L I O T H A W A I I A N L U A U G U I
S F E T Y I L P U Y R W E P A R A D I S E
C R I T O H J L H U L A O P R W S Q S D R
R H G H U U I O L O J F D C V B N U W R T
E O Q S D T R H J E Q A L O H A D X R G H
W N P E R G B I J K B W Z X C F Z X P F K
P O E A C R T Y S D V B I O G R A S S S Y
I L A M B O J H L M K S Z P X A X C M K R
N U R K M F R U N L W S U G A R C S N I D
E L L O A T J C M I E X X W A C V D V R X
X U H L U L M J H R R C C S Q A B Y O T C
C C A F I N A U E I P M E C W N M U L U W
Y X R D S F B V Q G D W A X B E W J C Y Q
I R B H J O T H A V P S B L M Q E E A F E
O H O L E T K G P I N E A P P L E D N H W
Y J R F Z R I T Y T P Q G F U A X W O B R
P A C I F I C O C E A N R X O P C Q B V T
Q B I G I S L A N D Z A W T V R Q G T R Y
Z Z C B H J I T E R S C V U I O E L U T U
U N U S U A L B I R D S G J K Z X S W E O
I E F L O W E R I N G P L A N T S U T I O
```

Hawaiian Words to Search for:

Surf	Pacific Ocean	Pearls	Big Island
Poi	Flowering Plants	Honolulu	Tourism
Hula	Screw Pine	Sugar Cane	Paradise
Aloha	Pearl Harbor	Volcano	Pineapple
Lei	Hawaiian Luau	Orchids	Maui
Lava	Unusual Birds	Forest	Grass Skirt

Hawaiian Word Search Answer Key

```
A S T P O I H J Z D A P O Y P E A R L S A
S D L I O T H A W A I I A N L U A U G U I
S F E T Y I L P U Y R W E P A R A D I S E
C R I T O H J L H U L A O P R W S Q S D R
R H G H U U I O L O J F D C V B N U W R T
E O Q S D T R H J E Q A L O H A D X R G H
W N P E R G B I J K B W Z X C F Z X P F K
P O E A C R T Y S D V B I O G R A S S Y
I L A M B O J H L M K S Z P X A X C M K R
N U R K M F R U N L W S U G A R C S N I D
E L L O A T J C M I E X X W A C V D V R X
X U H L U L M J H R R C C S Q A B Y O T C
C C A F I N A U E I P M E C W N M U L U W
Y X R D S F B V Q G D W A X B E W J C Y Q
I R B H J O T H A V P S B L M Q E E A F E
O H O L E T K G P I N E A P P L E D N H W
Y J R F Z R I T Y T P Q G F U A X W O B R
P A C I F I C O C E A N R X O P C Q B V T
Q B I G I S L A N D Z A W T V R Q G T R Y
Z Z C B H J I T E R S C V U I O E L U T U
U N U S U A L B I R D S G J K Z X S W E O
I E F L O W E R I N G P L A N T S U T I O
```

Hawaiian Words to Search for:

Surf	Pacific Ocean	Pearls	Big Island
Poi	Flowering Plants	Honolulu	Tourism
Hula	Screw Pine	Sugar Cane	Paradise
Aloha	Pearl Harbor	Volcano	Pineapple
Lei	Hawaiian Luau	Orchids	Maui
Lava	Unusual Birds	Forest	Grass Skirt

A Fish Talk Mens' Program
Hawaiian Game Fish

A'u
- Island delicacy.
- Broadbill swordfish.
- Also called marlin.
- Expensive because it is hard to catch.
- The meat is white and moist.

Mahimahi
- Very common fish.
- Least expensive in Hawaii
- Weighs 10 to 65 pounds.
- Flesh is light and most.
- Broadest at the head.
- Serve as a main course or a fish patty.

Manini
- A favorite with the local people.
- Not served on the menu very often.
- This fish will school.
- Won't bite on fish.
- Can be taken with a net or spear.
- Is about five inches in size.
- Abundant in Hawaii
- They live in ten feet of water.

Ono
- Means "delicious" in Hawaii.
- Tastes like king mackerel.
- White, flaky meat.
- One of the finest in the ocean.

Uku
- Firm-fleshed fish.
- Gray snapper.
- A favorite of the local people.
- Grills well.
- Meat is light and firm.

Ulua
- Weighs 15 to 100 pounds.
- White flesh.
- Steak-like texture.
- Found on menus on all the islands.

Ahi
- Yellow-fin tuna.
- Distinctive pinkish meat.
- Cooked or uncooked in sushi bars.

Moi
- Hawaiian word for "king".
- Large eyes and shark-like head.
- Popular in the summer months.
- Finest eating fishes in Hawaii.

Other Island Seafood Found on Menus
- Crawfish.
- Aloalo (tiny lobsters).
- Albacore tuna.
- Octopus (squid or calamari).
- Shark of various types.

Trivia: A delicacy known in Hawaii is Limu. This is an edible seaweed. The locals enjoy this treat very much.

Reef Fish
Painted Triggerfish
- Official state fish.
- Nose like a pig.
- Black painted stripes.
- Brown wedge to the rear.
- Eyes in the center of the nine-inch body.
- Rows of black spines near the tail.
- Can attack spiny sea urchins with its sharp teeth.

Butterflyfish
- Six inches in length.
- Bright color.
- Dainty.
- Body is short and narrow.

This fish became popular from the song "My Little Grass Shake".

Long Nose Butterflyfish
- Bright gold body.
- Topped with 12 dorsal spines.
- Long nose.
- Black head and tail.
- Black circle beneath the tail.

Bluestripe Butterflyfish
- Horizontal blue stripes.
- Gold body.
- No vertical black bar through the eye.

Scorpionfish
- Perch in reefs.
- Snatches small fish.
- Ten inches in length.
- Has spots and stripes.
- Long, spindly fins.
- Their camouflage makes them difficult to see.
- Weird-looking fish.
- Carries venom in the following parts of its body: anal, dorsal, ventral fine spines.

Hawaiian Scorpionfish
- It's a mass of black.
- Brown and white stripes and spots.

This fish is a popular aquarium fish. It should not be handled. Also, note the Scorpionfish goes by other names such as: dragonfish, tiger fish, lion fish, and turkey fish. If you receive a puncture wound from this fish it will be painful—but not fatal. There is also a stone fish found in the Indo-Pacific with fatal venom. None of them are found in Hawaiian waters.

Goatfish
- 16 inches in length.
- These fish are gaudy.
- They have double whiskers under the mouth.
- Used for food.

Whitespot Goatfish
- Orange in color with a white tail.
- Black horizontal stripe through the eye.
- A tasty fish often caught with a spear.

Red or Yellowstripe Goatfish
- Called the weke.
- Bright pink body.
- Horizontal yellow stripe with a blue back.
- They swim in school in large circles near reefs.

White Goatfish
- Pure white.
- Do not eat this fish during the summer months, it is believed it will cause nightmares.

Parrotfish
- Grows to two feet in length.
- Adult males are brightly colored.
- Females are red, grey, and brown.
- Named because of their beak-like mouths.
- The beaks help bite off coral for the algae.
- They are capable of crushing the coral with their teeth.
- The teeth are in the back of the throat.
- The rubble passes through the digestive tract and is ejected.

Blue-mottled Parrotfish
- Also called uhu.
- Males have yellow scales with bright blue edges.
- Pink and blue dorsal fins and tails.

Red-lipped Parrotfish
- Has a chartreuse green head, back, and dorsal fin.
- Light blue underside.

If a person has a chance to go snorkeling you will see many colorful fish. It's a great experience!

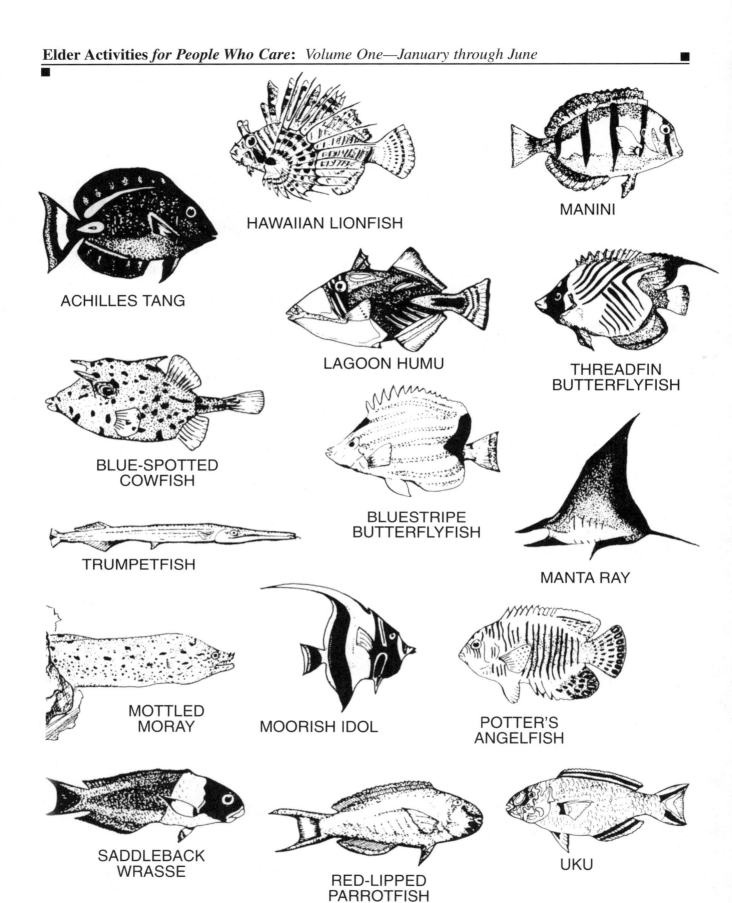

HAWAIIAN LIONFISH

MANINI

ACHILLES TANG

LAGOON HUMU

THREADFIN
BUTTERFLYFISH

BLUE-SPOTTED
COWFISH

BLUESTRIPE
BUTTERFLYFISH

TRUMPETFISH

MANTA RAY

MOTTLED
MORAY

MOORISH IDOL

POTTER'S
ANGELFISH

SADDLEBACK
WRASSE

RED-LIPPED
PARROTFISH

UKU

Hawaiian Reef and Game Fish Word Search

```
B D U L U A A C H I L L E S G J Z C O N O
L C M A N I N I E Q W D A T G H J K L G B
U G H R R R T H M K L M H A S R M Y J O L
E H A N G O A T F I S H I N W F A B M L U
S Y W I P R B N K L O P E G O S N A I O E
T H A S C R T B N M O I M J R Y T W E F S
R J I C K V B N U I O W E R D F A V B M P
I K I O H U L U A S E R T N F J R K L E O
P L A R G A S V B N M I T S I W A F G H T
E S N P M A H I M A H I Y U S T Y E R S T
D T L I Z X U R E R G H I O H M S R Y H E
B B I O C E J T B N M O P M R O T E S A D
U N O N V Q M O T T L E D O K I T T E N C
T W N F B Z N H R T Y U M I Q A J I D F O
T A F I N O U H U I T R O K I T E Z X F W
E I I S M L M M A M I U R E R G U K U B F
R O S H W E S D S E T S A D F L Y I P N S
F L H E E T F H F O E U Y A W A S Y B M H
L P Q T A N G E L F I S H D X E Y O N J Q
Y R E D L I P P E D P A R R O T F I S H W
F I S H G O T R U M P E T F I S H T R A Y
```

Reef and Game Fish to Search for:

Hawaiian Lionfish	Trumpetfish	Goatfish	Manta Ray
Blue-spotted Cowfish	Angelfish	Ahi	Ulua
Mottled Moray	Achilles Tang	Ono	Swordfish
Bluestripe Butterflyfish	Scorpionfish	Uku	Moi
Red-lipped Parrotfish	Mahimahi	Manini	

Hawaiian Reef and Game Fish Word Search Answer Key

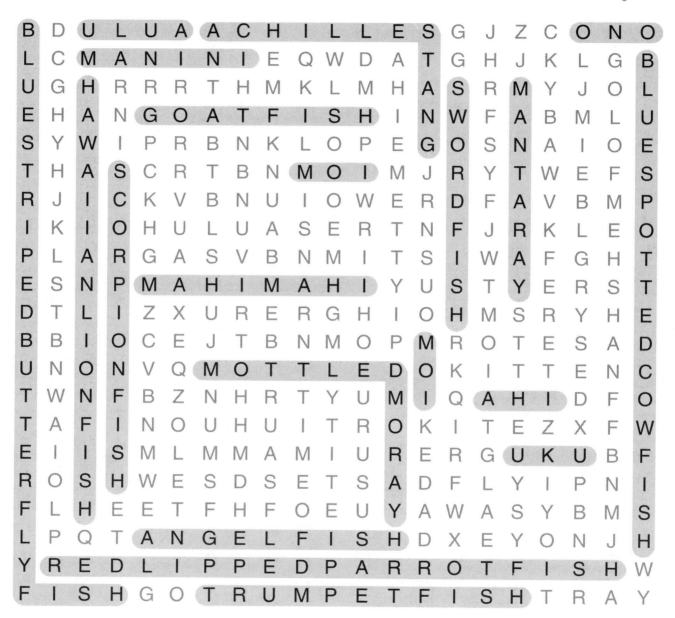

Reef and Game Fish to Search for:

Hawaiian Lionfish	Trumpetfish	Goatfish	Manta Ray
Blue-spotted Cowfish	Angelfish	Ahi	Ulua
Mottled Moray	Achilles Tang	Ono	Swordfish
Bluestripe Butterflyfish	Scorpionfish	Uku	Moi
Red-lipped Parrotfish	Mahimahi	Manini	

Whales in Hawaii

Humpback Whales

The Humpback whale gets its name because while in drive movement it appears to be humped. It has to do with how they expose their dorsal fin. There is a tape featuring the humpback whale songs. Your residents will enjoy hearing the sounds of the whales. The sounds imitate grunting, shrieking, and moaning. The singer is the male whale as it accompanies the mother whale and calf. They will repeat the same 20-minute ritual over and over. The notes will carry underwater for at least 100 miles. The singing can be heard both above and under the water.

A full-grown adult humpback is 45 feet long and weighs 40 tons. The whale travels from Alaska to Hawaii to give birth to her 2,000-pound calf. The humpback nurses its baby for about one year, when she will become pregnant again. The whales usually don't eat while living near Hawaii, they wait until they return to Alaska where they gorge themselves on krill. The whale creates a giant bubble net that helps them catch the krill (a small, shrimp-like crustacean).

The whale has a 15-foot flipper and this helps to make it very aquabatic. It is very exciting to witness a humpback whale leap from the water and perform. Whales are in Naui from November through May. Visitors there can take a whale-watching ship out in the harbor to watch the whales perform.

In the 1800s, whales were used for blubber, meat, bone, whale oil, and lighting fuel. In today's market we do not need to kill whales for these items.

Other whales in Hawaii are the sperm whale, killer whale, piolet whale, and the culver's beaked whale.

All whales, dolphins, and porpoises are cetaceans. These creatures can be distinguished by their length. Dolpins are from six to thirty feet, while porpoises are less than six feet long. The whale is the largest, measuring thirty feet and longer.

The killer whale is a toothed whale. It has black and white markings, and lives a long life. Sperm whales have as many as fifty teeth. Each tooth can be from four to twelve inches and weigh up to two pounds.

Some people confuse the mahi-mahi as a dolphin. The mahi-mahi is a true fish, and is a favorite on many restaurant menus. Mahi-mahi is found in most restaurants in Hawaii.

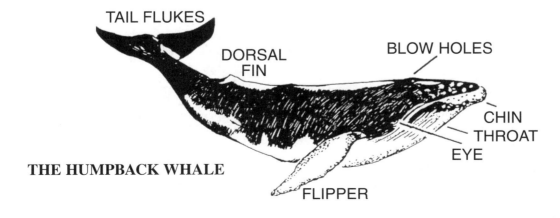

THE HUMPBACK WHALE

Hawaiian Names
Men's Names

American Name	Hawaiian Name	Pronunciation
Adam	Akamu	ah.KAH.moo
Alan, Allen	Alena	ah.LEH.nuh
Albert	Alapake	AH.luh.PAH.keh
Alec, Alexander	Alika	ah.LEE.kuh
Alfred	Alapai	AH.luh.PAHēe
Alvin	Alewina	AH.leh.VEE.nuh
Andrew	Analū	AH.nuh.LOO
Anthony	Akoni	ah.KOH.nee
Archie, Archibald	Ake	AH.keh
Arthur	Aka	AH.kuh
Ben	Beni	PEH.neh
Benjamin	Peniamina	PEH.nee.uh.MEE.nuh
Bernard	Pelenalako	PEH.leh.nuh.LAH.koh
Bert, Burt	Peka	PEH.kuh
Bill	Pila	PEE.luh
Bob	Lopaka	loh.PAH.kuh
Brian, Bryan	Palaina	puh.LAHēe.nuh
Bruce	Puluke	poo.LOO.keh
Calvin	Kalawina	KAH.luh.VEE.nuh
Carl, Karl	Kala	KAH.luh
Cecil	Kekila	keh.KEE.luh
Charles	Kale	KAH.leh
Christopher	Kilikikopa	KEE.lee.kee.KOH.puh
Clarence	Kalalena	KAH.luh.LEH.nuh
Dale	Kaela	KAHēh.luh
Dan, Dana	Kana	KAH.nuh
Daniel	Kanaiela	kuh.NAHēe.EH.luh
David	Kāwika	KAH.VEE.kuh
Dennis	Kenika	keh.NEE.kuh
Dick	Likeke	lee.KEH.keh
Don	Kona	KOH.nuh
Donald	Konala	koh.NAH.luh
Douglas	Koukalaka	KOHōo.kuh.LAH.kuh
Dwight	Kuaika	koo.AHēe.kuh
Earl, Earle	Ele	EH.leh
Edgar	Ekeka	eh.KEH.kuh
Edmond	Ekemona	EH.keh.MOH.nuh
Edward	Ekewaka	EH.keh.WAH.uh
Edwin	Eluene	EH.loo.EH.neh
Elmer	Elema	eh.LEH.muh
Eric, Erik	Elika	eh.LEE.kuh
Ernest	Eleneki	EH.leh.NEH.kee
Eugene	Iukini	EE.oo.KEE.nee

Floyd	Poloika	poh.LOHēe.kuh
Francis	Palakiko	PAH.luh.KEE.koh
Frank	Palani	puh.LAH.nee
Fred	Peleke	peh.LEH.keh
Gary	Kali	KAH.lee
Gene	Kini	KEE.nee
George	Keoki	keh.OH.kee
Gerald	Kelala	keh.LAH.luh
Gilbert	Kilipaki	KEE.lee.PAH.kee
Glenn	Kelena	keh.LEH.nuh
Gordon	Kolekona	KOH.leh.KOH.nuh
Gregory	Kelekolio	keh.LEH.koh.LEE.oh
Hank, Hans	Haneke	han.NEH.keh
Harold	Halola	hah.LOH.luh
Harry	Hale	HAH.leh
Harvey	Halewe	hah.LEH.veh
Henry	Hanalē	HAH.nuh.LAY
Herbert	Hapaki	hah.Pah.kee
Herman	Helemano	HEH.leh.MAH.noh
Howard	Haoa	HAHōo.uh
Hubert	Hupeka	hoo.PEH.kuh
Hugh	Hiu	HEE.oo
Jack, Jacques	Keaka	keh.AH.kuh
James, Jim	Kimo	KEE.moh
Jay	Kē	KAY
Jeffrey, Geoffrey	Keopele	KEH.oh.PEH.leh
Jerome	Ielome	EE.eh.LOH.mah
Jerry	Kele	Keh.leh
John, Jon	Keoni	keh.OH.nee
Jonathan	Ionakana	EE.oh.nuh.Kah.nuh
Joseph	Iokepa	EE.oh.KEH.puh
Keith	Kika	KEE.kuh
Kenneth	Keneke	keh.NEH.keh
Lawrence	Lauleneke	LAHōo.leh.NEH.keh
Leo	Lio	LEE.oh
Leonard	Leonaka	LEH.oh.NAH.kuh
Lloyd	Loeka	loh.EH.kuh
Louis, Lewis	Lui	LOO.ee
Malcom	Malakoma	MAH.luh.KOH.muh
Marc, Mark	Maleko	mah.LEH.koh
Martin	Makini	mah.KEE.nee
Matthew	Makaio	mah.KAHēe.oh
Melvin	Melewina	MAH.leh.VEE.nuh
Michael, Mike	Mika'ele	MEE.kuh.'EH.lah
Ned	Neki	NEH.kee
Nicholas	Nikolao	NEE.koh.LAHōh
Noel	Noela	noh.EH.luh
Norman	Nōmana	NOH.MAH.nuh

Oliver	Oliwa	oh.LEE.vuh
Oscar	Oka	OH.kuh
Oswald	Okewoleka	OH.keh.who.LEH.kuh
Otto	Oko	OH.koh
Owen	Owene	oh.WEH.neh
Patrick	Pakelika	PAH.keh.LEE.kuh
Paul	Paulo	PAHōo.loh
Peter	Pekelo	peh.KEH.loh
Philip	Pilipo	pee.LEE.poh
Ralph	Lalepa	lah.LEH.puh
Ray	Lei	LEHēe
Raymond	Leimana	LEHēe.MAH.nuh
Rex	Leke	LEH.keh
Richard	Likeke	lee.KEH.keh
Robert	Lopaka	loh.PAH.kuh
Robin	Lopine	loh.PEE.neh
Rodney	Lokenē	LOH.keh.NAY
Roger	Lōkela	LOH.KEH.luh
Roland	Lolana	loh.LAH.nuh
Ronald	Lonala	loh.NAH.lah
Roy	Loe	LOH.eh
Russell	Lūkela	LOO.KEH.luh
Samuel	Kamuela	KAH.moo.EH.luh
Scott	Koka	Koh.kuh
Sidney	Kikinē	KEE.kee.NAY
Stanley	Kānalē	Kah.nuh.LAY
Stephen, Steven	Kiwini	kee.VEE.nee
Terry	Keil	KEH.lee
Theodore, Ted	Keokulo	KEH.oh.KOH.loh
Timothy	Kimokeo	KEE.moh.KEH.oh
Thomas, Tom	Koma	KOH.muh
Vernon	Wenona	veh.NOH.nuh
Victor	Wikoli	vee.KOH.lee
Walter	Walaka	wah.Lah.kuh
Warren	Walena	wah.LEH.nuh
Wayne	Wene	WEH.neh
William	Williama	WEE.lee.AH.muh
Willie, Willy	Wile	Wee.leh

Women's Names

American Name	Hawaiian Name	Pronunciation
Abigail	Apikalia	AH.pee.kuh.LEE.uh
Ada	Aka	AH.kuh
Agnes	Akeneki	AH.keh.NEH.kee
Alberta	Alepeka	AH.leh.PEH.kuh
Alice	Aleka	ah.KEH.kuh
Alma	Alema	ah.LEH.muh

Amy	Eme	EH.meh
Angela, Angie	Anakela	AH.nuh.KEH.luh
Anita	Anika	uh.NEE.kuh
Ann, Anna, Anne	Ana	AH.nuh
Annette	Aneka	uh.NEH.kuh
Annie	Ane	AH.neh
Arleen	Alina	uh.LEE.nuh
Audrey	Aukele	AHōo.KEH.leh
Barbara	Palapala	PAH.luh.PAH.luh
Beatrice	Peakalika	PEH.uh.kuh.LEE.kuh
Becky	Peke	PEH.keh
Bernice	Pelenike	PEH.leh.NEE.keh
Bertha	Peleka	puh.KAH.keh
Bessie	Pakake	phu.KAH.keh
Betsy, Betty, Bette	Peke	PEH.keh
Beverly	Pēweli	PAY.VEH.lee
Blanche	Palaneke	PAH.luh.NEH.keh
Bonnie	Poni	POH.nee
Brenda	Palēnaka	phu.LAY.NAH.kuh
Bridget	Pilikika	PEE.lee.KEE.kuh
Carlotta	Koloka	kuh.LOH.kuh
Carmen	Kalamela	KAH.luh.MEH.luh
Carol	Kālola	KAH.LOH.luh
Caroline	Kalolaina	KAH.loh.LAHēe.nuh
Cecelia, Cecilia	Kikilia	kee.KEE.LEE.uh
Charlotte, Sharlot	Halaki	hah.LAH.kee
Cheryl	Kelela	keh.LEH.luh
Christina, Christine	Kilikina	KEE.lee.KEE.nuh
Claire	Kalea	kuh.LEH.uh
Clara	Kalala	kuh.LAH.luh
Claudia	Kalaukia	kuh.LAHōo.KEE.uh
Connie, Conny	Kani	KAH.nee
Cynthia	Kinikia	KEE.nee.KEE.uh
Daisy	Kaeki	KAHēh.kee
Deborah	Kepola	keh.POH.luh
Diana, Diane	Kiana	kee.AH.nuh
Dinah	Kina	KEE.nuh
Dolores	Kololeke	KOH.loh.LEH.keh
Donna	Kona	KOH.nuh
Dora	Kola	KOH.luh
Doris	Kolika	koh.LEE.kuh
Dorothy	Kōleka	KOH.LEH.kuh
Edith	Ekika	eh.KEE.kuh
Edna	Ekena	eh.KEH.nuh
Eileen	Ailina	AHēe.LEE.nuh
Elaine, Elayne	Ileina	ee.LEHēe.nuh
Eleanor, Elinor	Elenola	EH.leh.NOH.loh
Elizabeth	Elikapeka	eh.LEE.kuh.PEH.kuh

Ella	Ela	EH.luh
Ellen	Elena	eh.LEH.nuh
Eloise	Eloika	eh.LOHēe.kuh
Elsie	Eleki	eh.LEH.kee
Emily, Emilie	Emelē	EH.meh.LAY
Emma	Ema	EH.muh
Erica, Erika	Elika	eh.LEE.kuh
Estelle, Esther	Ekekela	eh.Keh.KEH.luh
Ethel	Ekela	eh.KEH.luh
Eunice	Eunike	EH˘oo.NEE.keh
Eve, Eva	Iwa	EE.vuh
Evelyn	Ewalina	EH.vuh.LEE.nuh
Faith	Mana'o'i'o	MAH.nuh.'oh.'EE.'oh
Fannie, Fanny	Pane	PAH.neh
Florence	Pololena	POH.loh.LEH.nuh
Frances	Palakika	PAH.luh.KEE.kuh
Gail, Gale	Kaila	KAHēe.luh
Georgia	Keokia	KEH.oh.KEE.uh
Gertrude	Kekaluka	KEH.kuh.LOO.kuh
Gladis, Gladys	Kalākeke	kuh.LAH.KEH.keh
Gloria	Kololia	KOH.loh.LEE.uh
Grace	Kaleki	kuh.LEH.kee
Hannah	Hana	HAH.nuh
Harriet	Haliaka	HAH.lee.AH.kuh
Hazel	Hakela	huh.Keh.luh
Helen	Helena	heh.LEH.nuh
Henrietta	Heneliaka	HEH.neh.lee.AH.kuh
Hester	Kekala	keh.KAH.luh
Hilda	Hileka	hee.LEH.kuh
Hope	Mana'olana	MAH.nuh.'oh.LAH.nuh
Ida	Aika	AHēe.kuh
Ingrid	Inakika	EE.nuh.KEE.kuh
Irene	Ailina	AHēe.LEE.nuh
Isabel	Ikapela	EE.kuh.PEH.luh
Jacqueline	Keakalina	KEH.ah.kuh.LEE.nuh
Jane, Jean, Jenny	Kini	KEE.nee
Janet, Janette	Ianeke	EE.uh.NEH.keh
Janice	Kānike	Kah.NEE.keh
Jessie	Ieke	ee.EH.keh
Jill	Kila	KEE.luh
Joan, Joanne	Iō'ana	ee.OH.'AH.nuh
Josephine	Iokepine	EE.oh.keh.PEE.neh
Joy	Ioi	ee.OHēe
Joyce	Ioke	ee.OH.keh
Juanita	Wanika	wuh.NEE.kuh
Judy	Iuki	ee.OO.kee
Julia, Julie	Iulia	EE.oo.LEE.uh
June	Iune	ee.OO.neh

Karen	Kālena	KAH.LEH.nuh
Kate, Katie	Keke	KEH.keh
Katherine	Kakalina	KAH.kuh.Lee.nuh
Kathleen	Kakaline	KAH.kuh.LEE.neh
Kay, Kaye	Kei	KEHẽe
Laura	Lala	LAH.luh
Leonora	Leonola	LEH.oh.NOH.luh
Libby	Lipi	LEE.pee
Linda	Līnaka	LEE.NAH.kuh
Lillian	Liliana	LEE.lee.AH.nuh
Lily, Lilly	Lilia	lee.LEE.uh
Lois	Loika	loh.EE.kuh
Loretta	Loleka	loh.LEH.kuh
Lorraine	Loleina	loh.LEHẽe.nuh
Louisa, Louise	Luika	loo.EE.kuh
Lucille	Lukila	loo.KEE.luh
Lucy	Luke	LOO.keh
Lydia	Lukia	loo.KEE.uh
Lynn	Lina	LEE.nuh
Mabel	Meipala	MEHẽe.PAH.luh
Madeline	Makelina	MAH.keh.LEE.nuh
Marcia	Malakia	MAH.luh.KEE.uh
Margaret	Makaleka	MAH.kuh.LEH.kuh
Marianne, Marion	Meleana	MEH.leh.AH.nuh
Marie	Malia	muh.LEE.uh
Marilyn	Melelina	MEH.leh.LEE.nuh
Marjorie	Makoli	muh.KOH.lee
Marlene	Malina	muh.LEE.nuh
Marsha, Martha	Māleka	Mah.LEH.kuh
Mary	Malia	muh.LEE.uh
May, Mae	Mei	MEHẽe
Michael, Michelle	Mikala	mee.KAH.luh
Mildred	Milikeleka	MEE.lee.keh.LEH.kuh
Millie, Milly	Mile	MEE.leh
Minnie	Mine	MEE.neh
Miriam	Miliama	MEE.lee.AH.muh
Muriel	Miuliela	MEE.oo.lee.EH.luh
Myrna	Milena	mee.LEH.nuh
Myrtle	Makala	muh.KAH.luh
Nancy	Naneki	nuh.NEH.kee
Natalie	Nakeli	nuh.KEH.lee
Nell, Nellie	Nele	NEH.leh
Noreen	Nolina	noh.LEE.nuh
Norma	Noma	NOH.muh
Olga	Oleka	oh.LEH.kuh
Olive	Oliwa	oh.LEE.vuh
Olivia	Olīwia	oh.LEE.Vee.uh
Pamela	Pāmila	PAH.MEE.luh

Patricia	Pakelekia	puh.KEH.leh.KEE.uh
Paulette	Poleke	poh.LEH.keh
Pauline	Polina	poh.LEE.nuh
Pearl	Momi	MOH.mee
Peggy	Peki	PEH.kee
Penny	Peni	PEH.nee
Phyllis	Piliki	pee.LEE.kee
Polly	Pole	POH.leh
Priscilla	Pelekila	PEH.leh.KEE.luh
Rachel	Lāhela	LAH.HEH.luh
Ramona	Lamona	luh.MOH.nuh
Rebecca	Lepeka	leh.PEH.kuh
Roberta	Lopeka	loh.PEH.kuh
Robin	Lōpine	LOH.PEE.neh
Rosalie	Lōkālia	LOH.KAH.LEE.uh
Rose	Loke	LOH.keh
Rosemary	Lokemele	LOH.keh.MEH.leh
Roxanna, Roxane	Lokana	loh.KAH.nuh
Ruby	Lupe	LOO.peh
Ruth	Luka	LOO.kuh
Sally	Kale	KAH.leh
Sandra	Kānela	KAH.NEH.luh
Sara, Sarah	Kala	KAH.luh
Sharon	Kālona	KAH.LOH.nuh
Sheila, Shelagh	Kalia	KAHēe.luh
Shirley	Kele	Keh.leh
Sophia	Kopia	koh.PEE.uh
Stephanie	Kekepania	KEH.keh.puh.NEE.uh
Susan, Susannah	Kukana	koo.KAH.nuh
Susie	Kuke	KOO.keh
Sylvia, Cylvia	Killwia	KEE.lee.VEE.uh
Thelma	Kama	KAH.muh
Theresa, Teresa	Keleka	keh.LEH.kuh
Valerie, Valery	Wālelia	VAH.leh.LEE.uh
Vera	Wila	VEE.luh
Vicky	Wiki	VEE.kee
Victoria	Wikōlia	vee.KOH.LEE.uh
Viola	Waiola	VAHēe.OH.luh
Violet	Waioleka	VAHēe.oh.LEH.kuh
Virginia	Wilikīnia	VEE.lee.KEE.NEE.uh
Vivian	Wiwiana	VEE.vee.AH.nuh
Wanda	Wanaka	wah.NAH.kuh
Wilma	Wilima	wee.LEE.muh
Winifred	Winipeleke	WEE.nee.peh.LEH.keh
Yvonne	Iwone	ee.VOH.neh

Weather Watch Party

Weather is a common subject that is discussed by everyone on a daily basis. Weather is a good "ice-breaker" (pardon the pun!) in any group of people.

Most residents don't get out as often as they would like, therefore when a health aide, nurse, activity director, or visitor comes in to see them it is nice for them to be told what the day is like (hot, cold, sunny, foggy). As Activity Director, you can make the weather a part of every gathering you have with your residents. Tell them what the temperature is today, and maybe what it was last year, or what the record temperature is for that day.

A weather watch party is a fun thing to do, and also informative.

Use pictures of rain, lightening, tornadoes, hurricanes, weather vane, lightening rod, etc. to get the conversation going.

Invite a local meteorologist from your radio or television station to come and talk about the weather and their job. Most of the elderly will not be aware of all the things a meteorologist does besides talk on the TV. Meteorologists are very busy people, so set up the appointment before you plan the time for your weather party.

A movie called "Storm Watch" may be interesting to your higher functioning residents. It shows tornadoes.

You can also sing weather songs. Ask your residents to think of songs and then the group can sing them. (See pages 148-150 for suggestions.)

At our party, we served Hurricane Matilda Shakes and Sunshine Cake to carry out the weather theme.

Beginning and second-stage Alzheimer's patients helped make the cake. The aroma of the cake baking is good for sensory exercise and the stirring is good physical exercise. One lady in our group could still read, so she read each step as we made the cake. *Of course, I acted like I needed a lot of their help.* These residents *need* to be needed and loved. These are sometimes the ingredients to help fuel the resident to keep on trying.

Advertise your weather party with flyers in the hallway and send invitations to family members, they will also enjoy the meteorologist.

Clock Party

Note: I did the clock party for the mens' luncheon, and they enjoyed it greatly.

Bring in a variety of clocks and set up a display. Some of the residents may have clocks in their rooms to contribute to the display. One of my residents was a clock collector. His daughter brought in his clocks, which was a great conversation piece. Maybe you, or someone you know, has a bird clock from the National Audubon Society. There are different birds pictured and they sing their songs. This is also a great conversation piece. It is a great tool to get into a conversation about birds that your residents may know. Refer to page 5 in colored section for picture of bird clock.

Many of the elderly have been feeding the birds all of their lives. Talk about the different species, when you can expect to see them (time of year, time of day), and the habits of different birds. Does anyone know where the saying, "He/she is such a night owl," came from? Talk about sighting the first Robin of spring, and how you can tell the season by the birds and their actions.

Since April is when Daylight Savings Time starts, bring that into the converstation about spring (and also fall). Ask your residents what time means to them; how they liked to spend their leisure time; and how some people are always late to everything (doesn't every family have someone like that?).

At any rate, get the residents into conversations about birds, time, and clocks. Maybe your town has a town or church clock that chimes on the hour, or is there an old public clock in your town square or on Main Street? There are many avenues this conversation can take, and everyone will have something to share with the group. Visual aids are also handy for different avenues of the conversation.

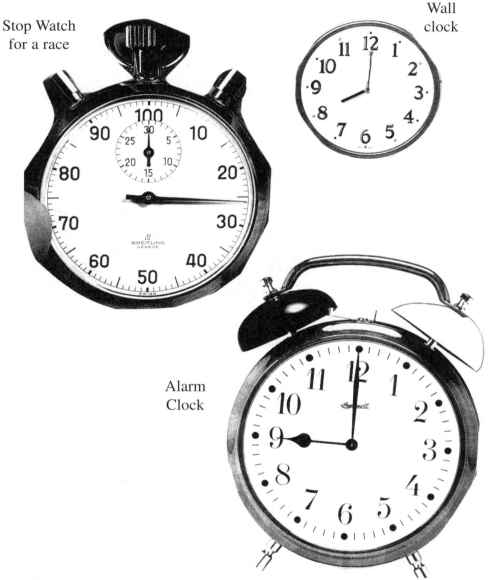

Stop Watch for a race

Wall clock

Alarm Clock

A clock showing that the short hand is on the eight and the long hand is on the 12. The long hand moves by the minute and touches each number every five minutes. Refer to pages 5 and 6 in colored section for more pictures of clocks.

Recipes:

Hurricane Matilda Shakes
Yield: 4 to 6 shakes, depending on the glass size.
  1 cup milk
  2 cups orange juice
  4 scoops vanilla ice cream

Blend ingredients in the blender until smooth and creamy.

Note: For diabetics substitute sugar free ice cream and orange juice with no sugar added.

Sunshine Cake
Yield: one-half sheet cake.
  1 package (18.25 ounces) Yellow Cake mix
  1 package (18.25 ounces) Butter Cake mix
$2\frac{2}{3}$ cups water
$\frac{1}{3}$ cup oil
$\frac{1}{2}$ cup margarine
  6 large eggs

Review package directions. In a five-quart mixing bowl add water, oil, margarine, and eggs and beat until smooth. Pour the batter into a 11 x 17 x 1-inch greased pan. Bake at 350 degrees for 30 to 35 minutes. Cool. Yield: One-half sheet cake.

Topping for Sunshine Cake
  1 pound non-dairy whipped topping, thawed
  1 can (20 ounces) crushed pineapple, drained well

Garnish for Sunshine Cake
  1 can (15 ounces) mandarin oranges, drained well
 20 whole maraschino cherries

Fold crushed pineapple into whipped topping and frost cake. Arrange cherries and oranges in alternate rows, so each cut piece will have a piece of fruit. Refrigerate cake—it will keep for up to three days. Do not freeze with topping or garnish.

Weather Chitchat Spelling Bee

The residents can spell the words and talk about the meaning, or use the words in sentences while they have their refreshments. The food will get the residents to come out to your activities!

Easy Words:

Dew	Mist	Frost	Dog Days	Flood	Hot
Fog	Storm	Wind	Sunshine	Cloudy	Cold
Snow	Rain	Rainbow	Muggy	Heat	Warm

Advanced Words:

Tornado	Hurricane	Hygrometer	Meteorologist
Sleet	Weather Watch	Blizzard	Thermometer
Barometric Pressure	Thermal	Lightening	Thunder
Breeze	Hailstones	Heat Wave	Weather Vane

Weather Chitchat Word Game

There are four words and definitions in each group. Draw a line from the word to the correct definition.

1. Drizzle   a. Fine particles of water held in the lower atmosphere.
2. Dew   b. Relative humidity.
3. Fog   c. Moisture that condenses on the ground.
4. Hygrometer   d. Rain in very small drops.

******

5. Showers   a. Very hot days in July and August.
6. Dog Days   b. A loud sound following a flash of lightning.
7. Snow   c. A very short fall of rain.
8. Thunder   d. Crystals of ice formed from water vapor in the air.

******

9. Frost   a. A grounded metallic rod set up on the roof to protect the building from lightning.
10. Lightning Rod b. A covering of ice crystals on a cold surface.
11. Wind Sock   c. Movement of the air.
12. Wind   d. Shows the direction of the wind and is also used for decoration.

******

13. Mist   a. A light spray of water falling in the air.
14. Storm   b. Rain coming down quickly in a short amount of time.
15. Breeze   c. A heavy fall of rain or snow.
16. Flash Floods d. A light wind.

******

17. Blizzard
18. Temperature
19. Rainbow
20. Tornado

a. Degree of hotness or coldness.
b. A long harsh snowstorm.
c. A violent destructive whirling wind in a funnel-shaped cloud.
d. An arch of colors formed by reflection of the sun's rays in the rain.

******

21. Ozone
22. Thermal
23. Barometer
24. Sunshine

a. A bluish gaseous reactive form of oxygen that is formed naturally in the atmosphere.
b. Caused by heat.
c. Direct light of the sun.
d. An instrument for measuring atmospheric pressure.

******

25. Sleet
26. Muggy
27. Hurricane
28. Heat Wave

a. Warm and humid.
b. Freezing rain.
c. Long period of days with hot weather.
d. A tropical cyclone with high winds.

******

29. Rain
30. Weather

31. Weather Vane
32. Humidity

a. The atmosphere pertaining to hot or cold, moist or dry, clear or cloudy.
b. Shows the direction of the wind and is placed on top of buildings. A rooster with an arrow with north, south, east, or west.
c. The amount of atmospheric moisture.
d. Water falling in drops from the clouds.

Answer Key:

1. d.	8. b.	15. d.	22. b.	29. d.
2. c.	9. b.	16. b.	23. d.	30. a.
3. a.	10. a.	17. b.	24. c.	31. b.
4. b.	11. d.	18. a.	25. b.	32. c.
5. c.	12. c.	19. d.	26. a.	
6. a.	13. a.	20. c.	27. d.	
7. d.	14. c.	21. a.	28. c.	

Weather Word Search

```
S I Y H U C V J K S D S M J D A Z X Y U W
U Y P E R E W Z X B M L T H U N D E R H I
N K L A N B G F S F D E T H J M Q W E S N
S Z X T W A V E V T Y E J I O P T R U I D
H F E C O L D F G B M T R T U O H L L M C
I N E R F O Z O N E B V C X Z B E N I O H
N I P R T R E W Q J R A I N Q E R D G S I
E Q H E A C L O U D Y X W E A O M L H P L
S D A A Z C X V N J K J L O P H A R T H L
E R I N H Y G R O M E T E R T O L U E U O
W Q L S T O N E S T U Y G M H T D F N A S
B A R O M E T R I C U Y R U E W D F I H J
W B V A S M Y U O P W I R G E F G V N D E
Z X L W E T U G H R E W R G T B N M G T Y
Q J O I R V R L T E A M N Y U Z X C V B N
A K L J Z A D G K S T T E W R A I N B O W
Z L K F T Z H L W S H Q H U R R I C A N E
W G J L Y S A Z B U E S E R I Y H G F S D
R H G A J D J R N R R W A T C H S D F N K
F N H S B I Z T D E A S D F G H J L L Z X
H U I H F L O O D S A S D T O R N A D O G
J R M B M O X U J Q W E R N M R E S X A W
K T E M P E R A T U R E C V T Y U L I P O
L U N T N T H E R M O M E T E R C F H Z W
F Y U P V U C B N K L P Q Z X C V E R I T
```

Weather Words to Search for:

Tornado	Sunshine	Cold	Flash floods
Rain	Rainbow	Hot	Wind chill
Blizzard	Hailstones	Temperature	Barometric pressure
Hurricane	Sleet	Weather watch	Thermal
Thunder	Heat wave	Ozone	Hygrometer
Lightning	Muggy	Cloudy	Thermometer

Weather Word Search Answer Key

```
S I Y H U C V J K S D S M J D A Z X Y U W
U Y P E R E W Z X B M L T H U N D E R H I
N K L A N B G F S F D E T H J M Q W E S N
S Z X T W A V E V T Y E J I O P T R U I D
H F E C O L D F G B M T R T U O H L M C
I N E R F O Z O N E B V C X Z B E N D H H
N I P R T R E W Q J R A I N Q E O M L S I
E Q H E A C L O U D Y X W E A R A R H L
S D A A Z C X V N J K J L O P H O A E H L
E R I N H Y G R O M E T E R T O T R U U L
W Q L S T O N E S T U Y G M H T D F N A S
B A R O M E T R I C U Y R U E W D F I H J
W B V A S M Y U O P W I R G E F G V N H E
Z X L W E T U G H R E W R G T B N M G T Y
Q J O I R V R L T E A M N Y U Z X C V B N
A K L J Z A D G K S T T E W R A I N B O W
Z L K F T Z H L W S H Q H U R R I C A N E
W G J L Y S A Z B U E S E R I Y H G F S D
R H G A J D J R N R R W A T C H S D F N K
F N H S B I Z T D E A S D F G H J L L Z X
H U I H F L O O D S A S D T O R N A D O G
J R M B M O X U J Q W E R N M R E S X A W
K T E M P E R A T U R E C V T Y U L I P O
L U N T N T H E R M O M E T E R C F H Z W
F Y U P V U C B N K L P Q Z X C V E R I T
```

Weather Words to Search for:

Tornado	Sunshine	Cold	Flash floods
Rain	Rainbow	Hot	Wind chill
Blizzard	Hailstones	Temperature	Barometric pressure
Hurricane	Sleet	Weather watch	Thermal
Thunder	Heat wave	Ozone	Hygrometer
Lightning	Muggy	Cloudy	Thermometer

Songs Related to the Weather

Songs to sing to jog memories related to words about the weather.

"You Are My Sunshine"

The other night, dear, as I was sleeping,
I dreamed I held you in my arms.
When I awoke, dear, I was mistaken
And I hung my head and cried.
You are my **sunshine**, my only **sunshine**.
You make my happy when skies are grey.
You'll never know, dear, how much I love you.
Please don't take my **sunshine** away.

"Oh Suzanna"

I came from Alabama with a banjo on my knee,
I'm going to Louisiana my true love for to see.
It **rained** all night, the day I left,
The **weather** it was **dry**.
The **sun** so **hot** I **froze** to death,
Suzanna, don't you cry.
Oh! Susanna, Oh don't you cry for me,
I came from Alabama,
With a banjo on my knee.

"Smiles"

There are smiles that make us happy.
There are smiles that make us blue.
There are smiles that steal away the teardrops,
As the **sunbeams** steal away the **dew**.
There are smiles that have a tender meaning
That the eyes of love alone may see,
But the smiles that fill my life with **sunshine**,
Are the smiles you give to me.

"Home on the Range"

Oh, give me a home where the buffalo roam,
Where the deer and the antelope play.
Where seldom is heard a discouraging word,
And the skies are not **cloudy** all day.
Home, Home on the range,
Where the deer and the antelope play,
Where seldom is heard a discouraging word,
And the skies are not **cloudy** all day.

"On a Clear Day"

On a **clear** day,
Rise and look around you,
And you'll see who you are.
On a **clear** day,
How it will astound you,
That the glow of your being
Outshines every star.
You feel part of
Every mountain, sea, and shore.
You can hear, from far and near,
A world you've never heard before.
And on a **clear** day, On that **clear** day,
You can see forever, and ever
And ever, and ever more!

"He's Got the Whole World in His Hands"

He's got the whole world in His hands,
He's got the whole world in His hands.
He's got the whole world in His hands,
He's got the whole world in His hands.
He's got the **wind** and the **rain** in His hands,
He's got the **wind** and the **rain** in His hands,
He's got the **wind** and the **rain** in His hands,
He's got the whole world in His hands.

"Whispering Hope"

Soft as the voice of an angel,
Breathing a lesson unheard,
Hope, with a gentle persuasion,
Whispers a comforting word.
Wait till the **darkness** is over,
Wait, till the tempest is done.
Hope for the **sunshine** tomorrow
After the **shower** is gone.
Whispering hope,
Oh, how welcome thy voice,
Making my heart in its sorrow, rejoice.

"Amazing Grace"

Amazing Grace! How Sweet the sound,
That saved a wretch like me!
I once was lost, but now am found,
Was blind, but now I see.

'Twas grace that taught my heart to fear,
And grace my fears relieved;
How precious did that grace appear,
The hour I first believed!

Through many dangers, toils, and snares,
I have already come;
'Tis grace hath brought me safe thus far,
And grace will lead me home.

When we've been there ten thousand years,
Bright shining as the **sun**,
We've no less days to sing God's praise,
Than when we first begun.

"Edelweiss"

Edelweiss, Edelweiss, Ev'ry morning you greet me.
Small and white, clean and bright,
You look happy to meet me.
Blossom of **snow**, may you bloom and grow,
Bloom and grow forever.
Edelweiss, Edelweiss,
Bless my homeland forever.

"Shine on Harvest Moon"

Shine on, harvest **moon** up in the sky,
I ain't had no lovin' since,
January, February, June or July,
Snow time ain't no time to stay
Outdoors and spoon,
So shine on, shine on, harvest **moon**,
For me and my gal.

"I Found a Million Dollar Baby"
(In a Five and Ten Cent Store)

It was a lucky April **shower**,
It was the most convenient door.
I found a million dollar baby,
In a five and ten cent store.
The **rain** continued for an hour,
I hung around for three or four,
Around a million dollar baby,
In a five and ten cent store.
She was selling china,
And when she rolled those eyes,
I kept buying china,
Until the crowd got wise.
Incidentally, if you should run into a **shower**,
Just step inside my cottage door,
And meet the million dollar baby,
From the five and ten cent store.

"When the Lights Go On Again"
(All Over the World)

When the lights go on again,
All over the world,
And the boys come home again,
All over the world,
And the **rain** or **snow** is all,
That may fall from skies above.
A kiss won't mean Goodbye,
But hello to love.
When the lights go on again,
All over the world,
And the ships will sail again,
All over the world.
Then we'll have time for things
Like wedding rings,
And free hearts will sing.
When the lights go on again,
All over the world.

"Blue Skies"

Blue skies, smiling at me,
Nothing but **blue skies**,
Do I see.
Bluebirds, singing a song,
Nothing by bluebirds,
All day long.
Never saw the **sun shining** so bright,
Never saw things going so right,
Noticing the days hurrying by.
When you're in love,
My! How they fly.
Blue days,
All of them gone,
Nothing but **blue skies**,
From now on!

"The Birth of the Blues"

They heard the **breeze**,
In the trees,
Singing weird melodies,
And they made that
The start of the blues.
And from a jail,
Came the wail,

Of a down-hearted frail,
And they played that,
As part of the blues.

From a whippoorwill,
High on a hill,
They took a new note,
Pushed it through a horn,
Till it was worn,
Into a new note!
Then they nursed it,
Rehearsed it,
And gave out the news,
That the southland
Gave birth to the blues!

"Emilia Polka"

There's a girl, There's a girl that I keep thinking of,
Emilia, my love, Emilia my love.
And the **stars** fill the sky,
and the **moon** shines above.
Because my Emilia has given me her love.
My Emilia is never tempermental.
She is sweet and gentle, and so very sentimental.
So we kiss and we kiss, and what a thrill I get,
When my Emilia tells me of her love.
Laugh with me Emilia, Ha, Ha, Ha.
Laugh with me Emilia, Ha, Ha, Ha.
We can laugh at **rainy weather**, Ha, Ha, Ha
1. long as we're together.
2. fun to be in love.

"Just Because Polka"

Just because you think you're so pretty.
Just because you think you're so **hot**,
Just because you think you've got something,
Nobody else has got.
Though you made me spend all my money,
You laughed and called my old Santa Claus,
But I'm telling you, honey,
I'm through with you,
Because, just because.

Volunteer Appreciation Party

Each year facilities should try to have a volunteer appreciation party. To show your volunteers your appreciation for their countless hours of dedicated work. The residents gain a great deal from the work of these dedicated people.

Some facilities go to a restaurant while others have a party in the evening or on the weekend at their facility so that families of both the residents and volunteers can attend. There is some expense involved in the activity, but it is a very necessary part of the whole program. Where would you be without the volunteers?

Because I was a professional caterer for 18 years, I chose to get the residents involved in the planning and work. They enjoyed helping prepare the food and decorate the room. Everyone has a different talent and situation, so do what is best for your facility.

We chose to have our party in April. It is far enough along in the year, and everyone is wanting to get out after the winter season, so many people responded and attended this special time.

Written invitations should be sent to each volunteer. Keep a record of all the people who have volunteered during the year. Some large facilities could end up with from 20 to 100 people. When the numbers are that large, it is best to have the dietary staff, a restaurant, or a professional caterer take care of the food. Be sure to involve your administrator in the planning for this event. He/she knows where funds may be available for this special occasion. Reserve the room for the evening by marking it on the facility's calendar of events.

Pick a theme for your party, and carry it throughout the meal and the program and decorations. Purchase blank Appreciation Certificates and complete one for each of your volunteers. Present them to the recipients as part of the evening's entertainment. Call them to the front to honor them and say something about each person's particular accomplishment.

This whole event is a great experience for everyone involved, and your residents will be particularly proud of helping with the planning. It is also great for the residents to interact with volunteers they haven't seen recently.

These are just some of my suggestions. You may have many other ideas for entertainment or games. The important thing is to have fun and honor your volunteers.

The payback, of course, is seeing how much everyone enjoys the event!

NAME OF FACILITY
DAY, MONTH, YEAR OF AWARD

Certificate of Appreciation

This award is presented to:

In Appreciation of

Congratulations on a Job Well Done

Granny's Soup Kitchen

This is a great time for the ladies to get together and socialize. They can cut the vegetables and prepare the soup and egg salad sandwiches. On the day of the soup party the ladies can decorate the tables. The staff can heat the soup and the residents can make the sandwiches. Cut sandwiches into four sections. Use wheat, white, or sour dough bread for the sandwiches.

Cabbage Soup

Yield: 24 one-cup servings.

2 cans (49-ounces each) chicken broth (use 99% fat free)
2 cups sliced mushrooms
1 can (15 ounces) whole kernel corn
2 cups julienne carrots (from your local grocery store produce department)
1 cup diced celery
1 cup diced red pepper
1 package (14 ounces) beef smoked sausage (cut into circles about $1/8$-inch thick)
1 (2 pound) head green cabbage, chopped finely (about 7 cups)
1 teaspoon granulated onion powder
1 teaspoon garlic flakes (dehydrated)
1 teaspoon dried parsley flakes
2 teaspoons pepper
2 teaspoons bouquet garni seasoning

In a large crockpot combine the broth, vegetables, sausage, and seasonings. Cook on low for about 6 hours or until the vegetables are tender.

Note: The core of a two-pound head of cabbage weighs about four ounces, so take that into consideration when buying your cabbage.
You can add cooked, cubed potatoes to the soup when it has finished cooking. Microwave four potatoes for 15-18 minutes, peel, and dice small before adding to soup.

Egg Salad for Sandwiches

Yield: 17 whole sandwiches, 34 half sandwiches.

18 eggs

$^1/_4$ cup lemon juice

1 teaspoon salt

Place eggs in a pot and cover with cold water. Add the lemon juice and salt and bring to a boil. Boil for 5 to 10 minutes. Remove pot from heat and let stand for 25 to 30 minutes.

To test an egg for doneness, spin it on the countertop. If the egg wobbles, it is still uncooked.

Rinse cooked eggs under cold water to prevent the egg yolk from becoming green. To peel an egg, tap the nose of the egg to break the shell. Remove the membrane with the shell to avoid gouges in the egg.

Add to the peeled eggs:

1 tablespoon yellow mustard

2 tablespoons pickle relish

1 tablespoon chopped onion

$^1/_2$ teaspoon pepper

$^1/_2$ teaspoon salt

$^1/_2$ cup light mayonnaise

Chop the eggs medium fine. Add mustard, relish, onion, and salt and pepper. Mix together and then add the mayonnaise and mix well.

Place three ounces, or three tablespoons of egg salad per sandwich. Cut sandwiches in half.

Note: You can use either sweet or dill pickle relish, but dill is best for diabetics. If you are dealing with high cholesterol use the egg whites only. For the low salt diets, omit the salt. You may want to divide your recipe to suit the various dietary needs.

May Activities

Cinco de Mao Celebration

Cinco de Mao is celebrated on May 5th each year in Mexico. It is their Independence Day celebration. They dress up in costume, play music, and dance. Their dress is usually red, white, and green, the same colors as found in the Mexican flag.

Mexico won their independence from Spain in 1821 after 12 years of fighting for their freedom.

Father Miguel Hidalgo was a Catholic priest at that time. He helped the Mexican people learn to read and write. He also showed them how to set up businesses to earn a living. But, the Spaniards wouldn't let the Mexicans have businesses and closed them down. One day Father Miguel Hidalgo rang the church bells and got the Mexican people to gather at the church. He shouted, "Long live our Lady of Guadalupe! Down with the bad government! Death to all Spaniards!" He convinced the Mexican people to fight the Spaniards, which led the people of Mexico to fight for independence.

My library supplied me with a videotape on Cinco de Mao, check with your library for such a resource. Play the video, give some information on the Mexican culture and play music from Mexico. Use the Mexican flag as the theme for your decorations for the event.

Some of the facility staff may have Mexican decorations they can bring to help with the décor. You can also use pictures of the ancient ruins and talk about them. Residents seem to enjoy hearing about personal experiences so if you, or someone on the staff, have traveled to Mexico talk about the trip.

I made up Churros and served them at mid-morning with coffee. For the afternoon snack I made non-alcoholic Margariettas and Chili Go Rounds (recipe on page 15 of *The Best of Mexican Cooking*). Also include salsa and taco chips or popcorn for snacking.

Recipes:

Churros

Yield: 20.

Cooking oil, such as peanut or sunflower oil

2	cups water
1	cup margarine or butter
$1/4$	teaspoon salt
2	cups all-purpose flour
6	eggs
$1/2$	cup sugar
$1/2$	teaspoon cinnamon

Place the oil in a frying pan and, using a thermometer, heat to 360 degrees F.

Heat water, margarine, and salt to a rolling boil in a 6-quart saucepan. Stir in the flour and mix vigorously over low heat until the mixture forms a ball (about 1 minute), then remove pan from the heat. Beat the eggs all at once until smooth and add to saucepan mixture while continuing to stir.

Place the mixture into a cake decorators' tube that has a large star tip. Squeeze 4 to 6 strips of dough into the hot oil. Fry until golden brown, turning once (about 2 minutes per side). Drain on paper towel. Mix the sugar and cinnamon together and roll the churros in the mixture. Serve with coffee.

Yum! I can taste them already.

Chili Go Rounds

Yield: 8 dozen.

2	cups finely chopped smoked sausage, fully cooked
$1/4$	cup chili sauce
2	tablespoons shredded Mexican cheese
2	tablespoons grated Parmesan cheese
$1/2$	teaspoon dried and crushed thyme leaves
$1/2$	teaspoon cilantro
	dash of cinnamon
2	packages refrigerated crescent dinner rolls

In a medium-size bowl, combine sausage, chili sauce, cheeses, and spices. Remove half of the roll dough from the package, unroll and place between two sheets of wax paper. Roll the dough between the paper until it measures 13 x 5 x $1/8$-inch thick.

Spread half of the sausage mixture over the dough, and roll jellyroll fashion starting at the long end. Cut into $1/2$-inch slices with a sharp knife and place cut side down on a baking sheet. Do this with the remaining dough. Bake at 375 degrees for 12 to 15 minutes.

Mexican Maracas Art Project

Note: You may be able to invite children from a preschool or elementary school class to join you for the celebration. Include them in the snack time and they can also help the residents with this art project.

Supplies needed:

1	12-ounce juice can.
	Colorful paper or plain colored wallpaper $9^1/_4$ x $4^7/_8$ inches.
1	pencil, unsharpened or a 7-inch wooden dowel, $1^3/_4$ inch in diameter.
75	sequins (per maraca) I use 10 mm multi-color, 120 count.
100	dry pinto beans (per maraca).
	Multi-color glitter.
	Glue.
	Hammer, punch, screwdriver.

Make a hole in the top center of the lid with the hammer and punch or screwdriver. You will insert the pencil, or wooden dowel, in this hole to act as the handle of the maraca. Remove the bottom lid. Cover and glue colorful strips of paper on the can, gluing sequins at random for decoration. Place a handful of pinto beans in the can, and glue the bottom lid back on the can. (Don't use too many beans—fewer beans will make more sound.)

When finished you can play the "Mexican Hat Dance" and have the children shake their maracas in rhythm with the music.

Just measure around your juice can and its height.
Draw it out on your colored paper or wallpaper and cut!
Refer to page 7 in color section for picture of finished maraca project.

$4^7/_8$"

$9^1/_4$"

Various Activities for the Cinco de Mao Celebration

Obtain prizes (sometimes local merchants will contribute items) for a fish pond. Pair up a resident and child as a team. This is a fun event for all!

A great sensory activity for the lower-functioning residents is a sand box. If you can obtain sand, make a sand box using a child's swimming pool. Both the children and adults can remove their shoes and socks and enjoy the feel of the sand.

You can also do a Penny Scramble with the children (the adults will enjoy watching). Bring in a small amount of straw and scatter the pennies in it.

Other activities to do with the children is a dart game, with suction cups on the darts—not sharp points. If you have a children's bowling game, it is also fun for all. Give a quarter to anyone that gets a strike, and let some of the children be the pinsetters.

If your high school has a dance team, or if there is a dance studio in your area, ask if someone (or a group) would like to dress up in peasant clothes and do the Mexican Hat Dance. Include castanets in the costuming—the dancers will also learn something new and everyone will enjoy the presentation.

Kentucky Derby Party

The Kentucky Derby is a big event held each year on the first Saturday in May at Louisville, Kentucky, at the Churchill Downs racetrack.

If you want to learn more facts about the Derby go online to: info@derbymuseum.org. There are many items such as the Breeder's Cup trivia contest, Derby history, fun facts, Derby merchandise, Derby party, and Churchill Downs.

Note: When planning the party get the residents involved. Let them decide which of the recipes they want at their buffet. They enjoy the party more if they are involved in the decision-making.

On the day before the party involve the residents in the Derby Madness exercise.

On the day of your party do the Kentucky Derby Word Search (see page 168) and lead into talk about the Derby.

Outline of the Derby Party

- Plan to hand out Derby hats for the residents to wear.
- Display a United States map and point out where the state of Kentucky is located. Then point out where Churchill Downs, the home of the Derby ("Run for the Roses") is located.
- Hand out song sheets and play songs like "My Old Kentucky Home" and "Camptown Races." Before your 'pretend' race play the "Derby Charge" (see page 165). Divide the residents and guests into groups and see who can yell the loudest for their chosen horse.

Note: When I did this I invited school children to join us for the beginning of the party. They joined in the singing and out-yelled the residents. The residents got to giggling like school kids and really got a charge out of the kids' response. The residents talked about this for two days after the party. It is the little things that make the residents happy!

- Discuss Derby Fever and show Derby decorations. Derby Fever involves filling a silver wine cooler with long-stemmed red roses as a centerpiece and surrounding it with silver julep cups filled with fresh mint.
- Use grapevine and straw wreaths decorated with betting tickets, racing forms, miniature horses, roses, and ribbons.
- Cover an 8-foot table with a lace cloth with red taffeta underlining and use the centerpiece of roses and mint. If you have the mint juleps in a punch bowl, place it on this table.
- Talk about the foods on your Derby buffet.
- Have the children visit with the residents about the different hats they are wearing. You will get some great interaction between the ages.
- Tell a couple of stories about the Derby.

Note: Did you know that waiters and waitresses at area restaurants compete by racing around an obstacle course balancing six full glasses of wine on a tray?

Another stories goes: Members of the clergy were looking for a horse on which to place a wager—they went with a horse named Pulpit, whose Mother was named Preach.

Recipes:

Mock Mint Juleps

Let the residents know they will have mock mint juleps at your Derby party.

Ginger ale

Springs of fresh mint

Place the ale and mint in a punch bowl. Serve with Kentucky Derby Pie and coffee.

Cucumber Finger Sandwiches

2	packages (8-ounces each) cream cheese, softened
1/4	teaspoon garlic powder
1	teaspoon Worcestershire sauce
1/4	teaspoon onion powder
1/4	cup finely chopped celery
1	cup finely chopped cucumber

Garnish:

Black olives

Cherry tomatoes

Beat the cream cheese and add the seasonings and celery.

Remove the seeds from the cucumber and chop. Add to the cream cheese mixture, beating until smooth and creamy.

On the day before the party use a shot glass to cut out bread rounds. Butter the rounds, wrap and refrigerate. On party day spread the filling on the rounds, garnish with parsley and one small piece of black olive or cherry tomato cut into a thin, small petal and placed on the sandwich so it stands up like a rose petal. In Kentucky the sandwiches are garnished with a REAL rose petal.

Horseshoe Liver Pate Dip

Yield: 35 to 40 servings.

1	package (8 ounces) cream cheese
1	pound liverwurst
1	teaspoon Worcestershire sauce
1	tablespoon yellow mustard
1	teaspoon onion powder
$1/2$	teaspoon garlic powder

Blend all ingredients until smooth and shape into a horseshoe shape on your serving plate.

Garnish:

1	package (8 ounces) cream cheese
$1/2$	teaspoon Worcestershire sauce
$1/4$	teaspoon onion powder

Blend until smooth and place in a cake tube bag using a number 28 star tip. Pipe a border on the inside and outside of the horseshoe-shaped liver pate. Decorate with radish roses and fresh mint sprigs or fresh parsley.

Horseshoe Cheese Spread

Yield: 25 servings.

1	pound sharp cheddar cheese spread, softened
1	package (8 ounces) cream cheese
1	teaspoon Worcestershire sauce
$1/4$	teaspoon garlic powder
$1/4$	teaspoon onion powder

Blend until smooth and shape into a horseshoe on your serving plate.

Garnish:

1 package (8 ounces) cream cheese

1 teaspoon Worcestershire sauce

dash onion powder

Blend until smooth and place into a cake tube bag using a number 28 star tip. Pipe a border on both inside and outside of the horseshoe and garnish with dehydrated parsley flakes and radish roses.

Kentucky Derby Pie

Note: Buy convenience pie shells in the freezer department of your grocery store. This pie tastes just like eating a chocolate chip cookie.

Yield: 2 pies.

2	sticks butter
2	cups sugar
4	eggs, beaten
1	cup flour
$1/8$	teaspoon salt
2	teaspoons pure vanilla
2	cups chocolate chips
2	cups chopped pecans
2	9-inch pie shells

Cream butter and sugar together and add the eggs, flour, salt, and vanilla. Stir in the chocolate chips and pecans. Pour into pie shells and bake for 30 minutes at 350 degrees, or until the center is set. Serve with vanilla ice cream or whipped cream. Yield: 2 pies.

Other famous Derby entrées include:

Benedictine, which is cucumbers, onion, and cream cheese with a few drops of green food coloring. You can serve it as a sandwich spread or dip.

Dead Heat Kentucky Burgoo, which consists of hen chicken, beef, veal, and lamb. It has black and cayenne pepper, tomatoes, potatoes, onions, cabbage, corn, carrots, and Worcestershire sauce. You can also add butter beans, green peppers, and okra if desired. Actually, this is a southern stew and is very tasty.

Kentucky Trout is rainbow trout with crabmeat, delicious apple, country ham, walnuts, eggs, pepper, and bacon. You stuff the trout and wrap tightly with bacon. You grill the fish on medium heat until the bacon is brown and crisp. Then you bake it in a 325-degree oven until done. The mesquite wood used for grilling gives it a great taste.

Beef Brisket Barbecue is brisket, liquid smoke, ground celery seed, seasoned salt, fresh garlic, onion juice, paprika, and barbecue sauce. You rub the meat with the seasonings and wrap the meat in foil and refrigerate overnight. Bake at 250 degrees for 5 hours. You can cook this in a crockpot. Once it is cooked, slice the meat very thinly, pour the barbecue sauce mixed with the meat juices over the brisket and bake another half hour at 350 degrees. Serve on buns.

Kentucky Derby Trivia

Note: When I presented this activity to the residents, I got many comments about the amounts of refreshments needed for Derby Day. They were almost in disbelief at how much it took to serve the people attending the event.

1. What seven states surround Kentucky?
   a. Illinois (southern)   b. Indiana (southern)   c. Ohio (southern)   d. West Virginia
   e. Virginia   f. Tennessee   g. Missouri   h. All answers are correct

2. Kentucky is in what region of the United States?
   a. South   b. North   c. East   d. West

3. What is the name of the facility where the Derby is held?
   a. Brewers   b. Lombardi Field   c. Churchill Downs

4. How many years has the Kentucky Derby been in existence?
   a. 25 years   b. 75 years   c. over 100 years

5. The Kentucky Derby is known as the race for:
   a. Run for the Daisies   b. Run for the Roses   c. Run for the Sunflowers

6. How many times a year is the Kentucky Derby held?
   a. 4 times.   b. 3 times.   c. 1 time.

7. In what month is the Kentucky Derby held?
   a. 1st Saturday in May.   b. 2nd Saturday in June.   c. 1st Saturday in July.

8. What is the name of the million-dollar horse that won the race in May of 1997?
   a. Grey Fox   b. Silver Lining   c. Whiskey   d. Sunny Hello

9, How many hot dogs are sold the at Churchill Downs on Derby day?
   a. 25,000   b. 50,000   c. 75,000

10. How many mint juleps are sold on Derby day to the 130,000 people in attendance:
    a. 25,000   b. 40,000   c. 80,000

11. How many kegs of beer are sold to the 130,000 people on Derby day?
    a. 100 kegs   b. 2,000 kegs (110 beers per keg=220,000 beers a day)   c. 1,000 kegs

12. How many souvenirs are sold to the 130,000 people?
   a. 10,000   b. 40,000   c. 50,000

13. How many gallons of soft drinks are sold to the 130,000 people?
   a. 1,000   b. 2,000   c. 4,000

14. How many bushels of mint does it take to make 80,000 mint juleps?
   a. 100 bushels   b. 135 bushels   c. 150 bushels

15. How many quarts of julep mix does it take to mix 80,000 mint juleps?
   a. 8,000   b. 4,000   c. 3,000

16. What word pertains to horses?
   a. equestrian   b. equalize   c. equalquest

17. Name of the person that rides a horse in a horse race is?
   a. horse runner   b. jockey   c. horse rider

Key for the Kentucky Derby Trivia Game

1. h.	9. c.
2. a.	10. c.
3. c.	11. b.
4. c.	12. c.
5. b.	13. c.
6. c.	14. c.
7. a.	15. a.
8. b.	16. a.
	17. b.

Horse Race Game

Write the name of six horses on a blackboard. (You can pick any names you like.) Let each resident pick a horse from the list and place a bet on their horse. Beforehand you should place the horse names on a spinning wheel.

Divide the residents as evenly as possible at tables. Play the Derby Charge tune to signal the race is starting. Let each team member spin the wheel and someone should keep track of the score. The table with the most wins is the winner, and let each winning resident pick a prize from a cart you have prepared ahead of time.

Serve snacks from the suggested recipes and let the residents have some visiting time.

You can end the Derby party by reciting the "Pledge of Allegiance," or singing "My Old Kentucky Home," which is the theme song for the Derby.

Don't forget to thank the residents for coming at the conclusion!

Derby Charge Song

"And they're off!"

Stephan Foster Music

"My Old Kentucky Home"
by Stephen Foster

The sun shines bright on my old Kentucky home,
'Tis summer, the people are gay.
The corntop's ripe and the meadow's in the bloom,
While the birds make music all the day.

The young folks roll on the little cabin floor,
All merry, all happy and bright.
Bye 'n bye hard times come a knocking at the door,
Then my old Kentucky home, Good night!

Weep no more my lady, Oh weep no more I say,
We will sing one song for my old Kentucky home,
For my old Kentucky home, far away.

Note: Stephen Foster songs are some of the residents' favorite songs. I played my accordion for the residents while they sang. But you can accompany with a piano, or any other instrument you wish. Or, have a student or community person join the group to accompany the singing.

Stephen Foster songs:

"Beautiful Dreamer"	"Camptown Races"
"Come Where My Love Lies Dreaming"	"Gentle Annie"
"Jeannie with the Light Brown Hair"	"Laura Lee"
"My Old Kentucky Home"	"Nelly Bly"
"Oh! Susanna"	"Old Dog Tray"
"Old Folks at Home"	"Ring the Banjo"

Stephen Foster was born in 1826 in Pittsburgh, Pennsylvania. All of these melodies go back to the nineteenth century. He wrote over 200 songs. His music has been adapted with a variety of tempo marks, accompaniment patterns, and phrase groups. A good reference book on Stephen Foster is *Stephen Foster Favorites* by Wesley Schaum.

Note; You might want to do a music appreciation hour (or half-hour) featuring Stephen Foster music. The residents will enjoy the tunes.

Stephen Foster Music Bingo

Note: This is Two-For-One Bingo. Players will get two placements for each song!

B	I	N	G	O
Beautiful Dreamer	Old Folks At Home	My Old Kentucky	Ring the Banjo	Laura Lee
Come Where My Love Lies Dreaming	Old Dog Tray	Nelly Bly	Oh! Susanna	Jeannie with the Light Brown Hair
Gentle Annie	Camptown Races	**FREE**	Old Folks At Home	Beautiful Dreamer
Oh! Susanna	Ring the Banjo	Laura Lee	Gentle Annie	Come Where My Love Lies Dreaming
My Old Kentucky Home	Old Dog Tray	Camptown Races	Nelly Bly	Jeannie with the Light Brown Hair

Kentucky Derby Word Search

```
C P Y D B E N E D I C T I N E M U S I L C
H S X E Z C J O C K E Y E B Q I W P R R A
U E U R O L M N C X Q W R E Y N L O A J M
R H D B T M A Y U K H F V T M T P R C K I
C A I Y D E R B Y P I E H T G J V T I F N
H T T S K L P B U R E G U I P U O I N C Q
I S X P R R G R T F U M I N O L P N G P L
L A Z I B A O E O I P K J G Y E I G F N X
L W D R G C A E K R M B F G Y P E E O K N
D S F I H E R D N E M K Z I E R Q V R Y U
O R Y T U K A E N W B K P M L R H E M B E
W Q Z D G H M R R O V H K Q W L R N N U N
N W I N N E R S P R T L H E G F I T B N T
S R T H B K C C Z K F O B M N K P E T V E
E E R I U Q L U R S L U U M W T X C S P R
Z D O K R W A P U U J Z R T A R U K P P T
A T P G G D S E N F O R T H E E Y C J L A
Q O H V O T S M Q J R P Y P R I E I K O I
H H Y N O I I W Y K T L I Y O Z R P M Y N
M O U B A K C R A C E T M Z S T G D H T M
V T R I P L E C R O W N C S E B U S I R E
B A L L O O N R A C E S Z Y S S H Z O O N
Z C R I V E R B A N K P I C N I C S P U T
S D F G H J K T H O R O U G H B R E D T U
```

Kentucky Derby Words to Search for:

Entertainment	Hats	Race	Derby Spirit
Betting	Fillies	Jockey	Classic Race
Kentucky Trout	Trophy	Tout	Thoroughbred
Run For the Roses	May	Winner	Derby Pie
Churchill Downs	Triple Crown	Mint Julep	Burgoo
Benedictine	Fireworks	Racing Form	Sporting Event
Riverbank Picnics	Balloon Races	Breeders Cup	

Kentucky Derby Word Search Answer Key

```
C P Y D B E N E D I C T I N E M U S I L C
H S X E Z C J O C K E Y E B Q I W P R R A
U E U R O L M N C X Q W R E Y N L P O R J M
R H D B T M A Y U K H F V T M T P R A C I I
C A I Y D E R B Y P I E H T G J V O I N C N
H T S K L P B U R E G U I P U O P N G P L Q
I S X P R R G R F U M I N L P P E F O X L
L A Z I B A O E O I P K J G Y E I G R N X
L W D R G C A E K R M B F G Y P E E O K N
D S F I H E R D E N E M K Z I E R Q V R Y N
O R Y T U K A E N B K P M L R H E M B U
W Q Z D G H M R R O V H K Q W L R N N U E
N W I N N E R S P R K T L H E G F I T B N T
S R T H B K C C Z K F O B M N K P E T V E
E E R I U Q L U R S L U U M W T X C S P R
Z D O K R W A A P U U J Z R T A R U K P P T
A T P G G D S E N F O R T H E E Y C J L A
Q O H V O T S M Q J R P Y P R I E I K O I
H H Y N O I I W Y K T L I Y O Z R P M Y N
M O U B A K C R A C E T M Z S T G D H O T M
V T R I P L E C R O W N C S E B U S I R E
B A L L O O N R A C E S Z Y S S H Z O U N
Z C R I V E R B A N K P I C N I C S P U T
S D F G H J K T H O R O U G H B R E D T U
```

Kentucky Derby Words to Search for:

Entertainment	Hats	Race	Derby Spirit
Betting	Fillies	Jockey	Classic Race
Kentucky Trout	Trophy	Tout	Thoroughbred
Run For the Roses	May	Winner	Derby Pie
Churchill Downs	Triple Crown	Mint Julep	Burgoo
Benedictine	Fireworks	Racing Form	Sporting Event
Riverbank Picnics	Balloon Races	Breeders Cup	

Derby Fever Madness

There are four sets of words and definitions. Draw a line to match the meaning of the word with the correct definition and place the correct letter in front of the number.

1. Jockey	a. A popular drink served at the Kentucky Derby.
2. Derby pie	b. A popular chicken dish in Kentucky. Also known as Dirty Rice in Louisiana and Bog in South Carolina.
3. Burgoo	c. A dessert with pecans and chocolate chips.
4. Mint Julep	d. A person that rides racehorses.

5. Benedictine	a. Gambling on a winning horse.
6. Kentucky Trout	b. A valued horse that wins all three races: Kentucky Derby, Preakness, and Belmont Stakes.
7. Triple Crown	c. A fish served with bourbon and applesauce.
8. Betting	d. Fancy cucumber sandwiches.

9. Run for the Roses	a. The Kentucky Derby is held at this racetrack.
10. May	b. Female horse.
11. Churchill Downs	c. A name of flower associated with the Kentucky Derby.
12. Filly	d. The month of the Kentucky Derby.

13. Thoroughbred	a. A type of attire worn at the race.
14. Tout	b. Enthusiasm revealed at the race.
15. Hats	c. To watch racehorses in training to get betting information.
16. Derby Spirit	d. A kind of horse that races.

Key for Derby Fever Madness

1. d.	9. c.
2. c.	10. d.
3. b.	11. a.
4. a.	12. b.
5. d.	13. d.
6. c.	14. c.
7. b.	15. a.
8. a.	16. b.

A Mother's Day Party

Give a Pose and a Rose

Grandmothers like to show off pictures of their grandchildren and to also tell how many times they are Great Grandmothers. For Mother's Day we had school children come to visit. In advance we gathered pictures from the residents of their grandchildren. The visiting children framed the pictures. Some of the children also gave a picture (pose) to a resident.

Supplies needed:
Cardboard.
Wallpaper.
Glue stick.
Scissors.

Cut cardboard to desired shape for the picture you're framing. Select a style of wallpaper and cut it to fit the cardboard. Glue the paper on the cardboard. Center the picture and glue onto the wallpaper. Decorate the outer part of the picture with leaves, or flowers, or another type of decoration of your choice. Cut a one-inch strip of cardboard and glue to the back of the picture as a leg that will enable your picture to stand up. The resident can place this picture on their nightstand or dresser.

Refer to page 7 in color section for picture of completed project in color.

My Fair Lady Mother's Day Lunch

The purpose of the luncheon is to get Mothers, Daughters, and Family Members together to share stories and pay tribute to Mothers. Invite guests to share with the group a story about their mom or grandmother.

Meet with the residents and staff of your facility to plan a My Fair Lady Mother's Day observance. It is important to include the residents in the planning. It makes them feel important and needed—after all, it is *their* party! Don't forget to also include your dietician in the menu planning.

Take a tally of the residents to get a total number of residents, daughters, and granddaughters that will be attending. Maybe you want to help the residents make R.S.V.P. invitations for them to give to their family members. However, plan enough time to get the invitations back so you know the number that will be in attendance.

I've included some sample menus and recipes. Of course, you can mix and match or add your own items. But work with your residents and kitchen in the planning, and maybe the residents can help with the decorating or some of the food preparation.

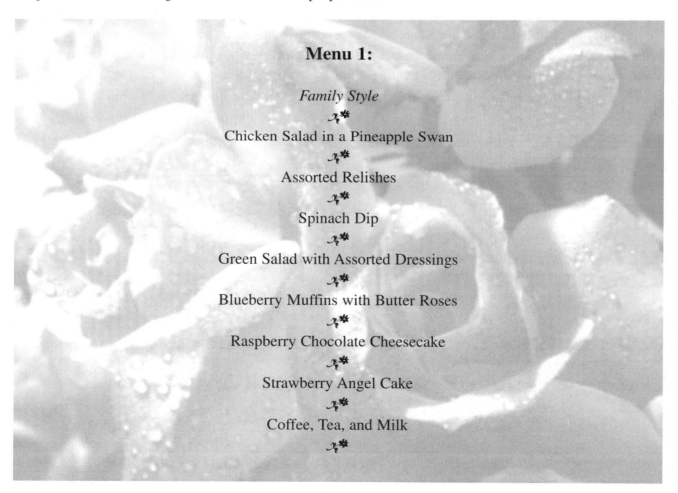

Menu 1:

Family Style

Chicken Salad in a Pineapple Swan

Assorted Relishes

Spinach Dip

Green Salad with Assorted Dressings

Blueberry Muffins with Butter Roses

Raspberry Chocolate Cheesecake

Strawberry Angel Cake

Coffee, Tea, and Milk

Chicken Salad Swans

Yield: 18 one-cup servings.

5	pounds chicken—boneless, skinless, chicken breast
1	can (14.5 ounces) chicken broth
2	cups celery
$1^1/_3$	cups green grapes, cut in half
$1^1/_3$	cups red grapes cut in half
1	cup silvered almonds
1	can (20 ounces) pineapple tidbits, drained
$1^1/_3$	cups finely diced red onion
$1^1/_2$	cups finely diced red pepper

Dressing:

3	cups mayonnaise
1	cup salad dressing
1	teaspoon granulated onion seasoning, or onion powder
1	teaspoon garlic pepper
4	teaspoons curry powder

Place the chicken breasts in a large pot, cover with broth and water. Bring to a boil and cook for 35-40 minutes or until the chicken is done. Drain. Place the meat on a cookie sheet and refrigerate to cool for at least two hours, or overnight. Dice the chicken. Add celery, grapes, almonds, pineapple, onion, and red pepper.

In a separate bowl combine mayonnaise, salad dressing, and seasonings. Mix thoroughly and stir the dressing into the chicken salad mixture.

Make a pineapple swan for each guest. Directions can be found on page 208, Chapter 7 of my cookbook entitled *Picnics, Catering on the Move.* If you don't want to make the swans, here's another pineapple suggestion.

Cut a pineapple in half lengthwise, cut out the fruit and core. Fill each pineapple with chopped lettuce and some of the pineapple you've just cut out of the pineapple. Top this mixture with chicken salad, and garnish with a red pepper circle, strawberry fan, and a sprig of fresh parsley. Of course, you can also serve the salad on a plate lined with lettuce and place assorted relishes on the same plate (carrot, celery, radish).

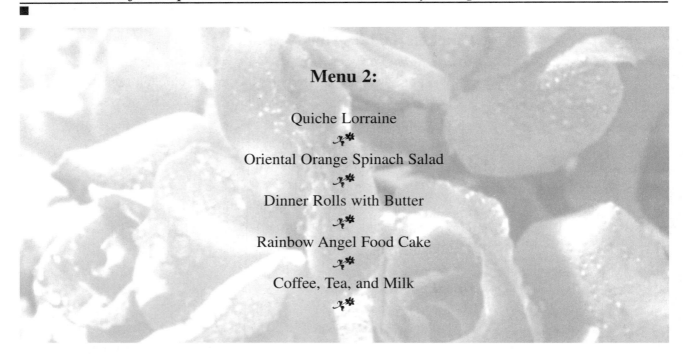

Menu 2:

Quiche Lorraine

Oriental Orange Spinach Salad

Dinner Rolls with Butter

Rainbow Angel Food Cake

Coffee, Tea, and Milk

Quiche Lorraine

Yield: 6 servings.

1	frozen 9-inch deep-dish pie shell
1	package (8 ounces) cream cheese
4	eggs
1	cup diced ham
1	tablespoon diced green onion
1/2	cup sliced mushrooms
2	tablespoons diced celery
2	tablespoons diced red pepper
1/2	cup diced broccoli flowerettes
1/2	teaspoon pepper
1 1/3	cups grated Parmesan cheese
1	cup shredded Mozzarella cheese

Preheat oven to 375 degrees. Beat the cream cheese to soften and smooth and add the eggs and continue to beat. Add the ham, onions, mushrooms, celery, red pepper, broccoli, and pepper and mix thoroughly. Pour the mixture into the unbaked pie shell and sprinkle with the Parmesan cheese and top with the Mozzarella cheese. Bake for 45 to 60 minutes, or until the filling is firm.

Oriental Orange Spinach Salad

Yield: 22-24 servings.

$^1/_2$ cup slivered almonds (optional)
2   cans (15-ounces each) mandarin orange segments, drained
2   cups fresh pea pods, whole
1   cup diced celery
1   small red onion, sliced
2   cans (8-ounces each) sliced water chestnuts
1   head Boston lettuce
1   head red leafy lettuce
1   package (10 ounces) fresh baby spinach
1   package (12 ounces) Chow Mien noodles (optional)

Clean and dry the pea pods, lettuce, and spinach. Add celery, water chestnuts, and onion. Divide the greens into salad bowls and top each salad with mandarin orange segments and Chow Mien noodles. Serve with Fat-Free Raspberry Vinaigrette dressing, or make a sweet and sour dressing.

Dressing:

Yield: 1 quart.

1   cup sugar
2   teaspoons paprika
1   cup honey
2   tablespoons grated onion
1   tablespoon celery seed or poppy seed
$^1/_2$ teaspoon salt
$1^1/_4$ cup vinegar
1   cup oil

Place all ingredients except the oil in a blender and blend well. Add the oil slowly through the top of the blender and mix well again. Chill for one hour.

For diabetics: Mix 1 tablespoon raspberry vinegar and 1 tablespoon juice from a fresh orange into plain yogurt.

Simple Broccoli Salad

One of my residents shared this simple recipe with me. I promised her I would include it in my book. Of course, this is a larger recipe than the original. This salad needs no salt or additional seasonings! Yield: 8-10 servings.

2	pounds broccoli flowerettes
1	pint grape tomatoes
1	medium red onion, sliced
1	8-ounce bottle Balsamic Vinaigrette

Clean the broccoli and cut into bite-size flowerettes. Rinse and dry the grape tomatoes. Peel and slice the red onion. Mix the vegetables together and toss with the dressing. Chill before serving.

Ripe Olive Quiche

This recipe makes an excellent appetizer.

Yield: 15 servings.

$1^3/_4$	sheets puff pastry
2	packages (8-ounces each) cream cheese softened
5	eggs
1	cup Parmesan cheese
3	cups sliced black olives
$1^1/_4$	cups Mozzarella cheese

Note: There are two ready-to-bake puff pastry sheets in a package (17.3 ounces).

Cover the bottom of a 9 x 13-inch pan with the pastry sheets to form the crust. Beat the cream cheese and eggs together and pour over the pastry. Sprinkle with the Parmesan cheese and then the olives. Top the whole quiche with Mozzarella cheese. Bake at 375 degrees for 35-45 minutes or until firm.

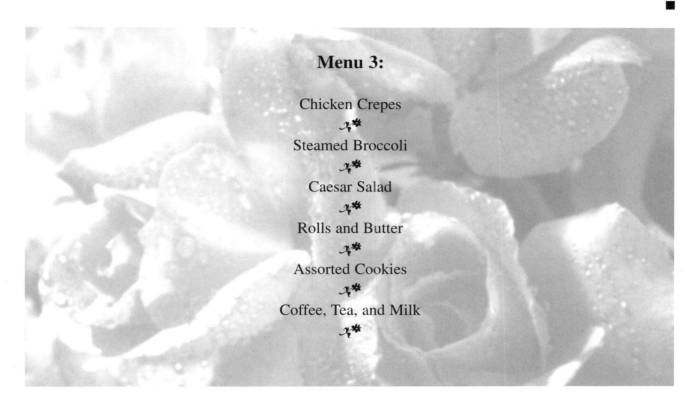

Menu 3:

Chicken Crepes

Steamed Broccoli

Caesar Salad

Rolls and Butter

Assorted Cookies

Coffee, Tea, and Milk

Chicken Crepes
Yield: 24-26 crepes.
Crepes:

$1^1/_2$	cup flour
$^3/_4$	teaspoon salt
6	eggs, well beaten
$1^2/_3$	cups milk
3	tablespoons melted shortening

Combine flour and salt. Combine eggs, milk, and shortening. Add flour mixture to egg mixture and beat until smooth. Pour enough batter onto a hot, lightly-greased griddle or crepe pan to make a crepe of 4-5 inches in diameter. Tip the pan to make the crepe as thin as possible. When one side is brown, flip the crepe to brown the other side. Cool.

Note: A Quick and Easy Caesar Salad—Purchase Caesar Salad mixture in a bag from your produce department. Each bag should serve 5 or 6 guests depending on the size of the serving. Top with dressing and sprinkle with croutons and garnish with grape tomatoes.

Chicken Filling for Crepes
Yield: Filling for 24-26 filled crepes.

4	(6-ounces each) cooked chicken breasts, boneless and skinless
1	tablespoon olive oil or butter
1	cup diced celery
1	cup diced red pepper
1	cup sliced mushrooms
1	bunch green onions with tops, chopped
2	teaspoons garlic
1	teaspoon Lawry's® seasoned salt
1	teaspoon Beau Monde
2	teaspoons dill weed
1	teaspoon white pepper
2	cans (14.5-ounces each) chicken broth
1	cup evaporated milk
$1^1/_4$	cups water
$^1/_2$	cup cornstarch
$^1/_4$	cup cooking wine

Note: Be sure to chill the chicken breasts after cooking.

Sauté celery, red pepper, mushrooms, onions, and garlic in olive oil. In a large saucepan mix the chicken broth and evaporated milk together and bring to a boil. Mix cornstarch and water and wire whip until smooth, and then add to the broth mixture and wire whip until the sauce is thickened to a nice consistency. Add the chicken, vegetables, and spices and heat thoroughly. Add the wine and cook for a few more minutes until the sauce is bubbly. Lay out the crepes on the countertop. Place 1/4 cup of the chicken mixture in the middle of each crepe and fold each side over to make a rolled crepe.

Gravy to serve with crepes:

2	cans (14.5-ounces each) chicken broth
1	cup evaporated milk
1	tablespoon butter or margarine
$1^1/_4$	cups water
$^1/_2$	cup cornstarch
1	teaspoon white pepper
2	teaspoons dill weed
1	teaspoon Beau Monde

1	diced red pepper
1	teaspoon Lawry's® seasoned salt
2	tablespoons white wine

Combine broth, milk, butter, and seasonings. Combine the water and cornstarch to a smooth consistency with a wire whip. Bring the broth mixture to a boil and slowly add the cornstarch mixture to thicken. Stir in the wine and simmer on low stirring constantly for a few minutes. Serve with the crepes.

Note: If you don't want to make the crepes, you can buy them from a wholesale food vendor. They come ready to use.

The chicken crepe filling makes excellent chicken a' la king. Serve it over rice or egg noodles. You can also serve it over biscuits, or puff pastry shells. Instructions for quick biscuits are found on page 138 of my Picnics, Catering on the Move *cookbook. Add only $^{1}/_{4}$ cup sugar to the pan biscuits instead of $^{3}/_{4}$ cup. You can do the chicken a' la king for the main entrée, and serve Crepe Suzettes for dessert.*

Crepe Suzette
Yield: 12 servings.

9	eggs, well beaten
6	tablespoons flour
1	teaspoon salt
3	tablespoons water
3	tablespoons milk
1	tablespoon grated orange rind

Combine all ingredients and mix well. Bake in thin cakes on a hot greased griddle, or crepe pan. Brown on both sides.

Sauce:

$^{1}/_{2}$	cup plus 1 tablespoon butter
$1^{1}/_{2}$	cups sugar
1	cup orange juice
$1^{1}/_{2}$	teaspoon grated orange rind

Cream the butter and sugar and add the orange juice and rind gradually. Spread on the cakes as they are baked and roll them up quickly. Generally, crepe suzettes have Curacao poured over and they are ignited at serving, and they are turned over as they are burning, and served as soon as the flame goes out.

Note: If you are not a chef, and are not experienced in flaming dishes, I urge you to skip this last step. Just pour the warmed sauce over the crepes and serve. If you have a chef on staff, or one in your community that will volunteer to serve the crepes, it is a great conversation piece for your residents.

Spinach Dip
Yield: 2 pounds.

1	package (16 ounces) frozen, cut, leaf spinach, thawed
2	cups mayonnaise
2	cups sour cream
1	teaspoon Beau Monde
1	teaspoon pepper
$^1/_2$	teaspoon garlic powder
$^1/_2$	teaspoon Lawry's® seasoned salt

You may substitute celery salt for Beau Monde. However, I do not like the flavor as well. If you want some 'crunch', add $^1/_2$ cup diced water chestnuts.

Rinse the spinach and squeeze very dry. In a medium bowl combine the spinach, mayonnaise, sour cream, and seasonings. Cover and chill. Serve with assorted relishes.

Blueberry and Cherry Muffins
Yield: 30 muffins.

4	cups flour
7	teaspoons baking powder
$^3/_4$	teaspoon salt
2	eggs, beaten
$^1/_2$	cup shortening, melted
1	cup sugar
2	cups milk
1	can (16 ounces) blueberries, drained
1	can (16 ounces) dark sweet cherries, drained

Note: This is one of my mother's recipes. I cherish it because it is a happy, comfortable memory. I think of Mother whenever I go to care facilities and serve her muffins. I use oil instead of shortening.

Many ladies in the facility probably used lard or shortening in their time.
If you know how to make butter roses, your residents will enjoy you showing how to do it. If you don't feel comfortable doing it find a volunteer from the community who would like to show your residents how it's done.

If you cut the recipe in half you will use 4 teaspoons baking powder, $^{1}/_{2}$ teaspoon salt. You can use 1 cup fresh blueberries instead of canned ones. You can also use tart cherries instead of the dark, sweet cherries.

In a medium bowl mix the flour, baking powder, salt, and sugar together. Mix the egg, milk, and shortening together. Make a well in the center of the dry ingredients and slowly add the wet mixture and mix until all are blended together. Divide the dough into two bowls. Fold blueberries into one bowl of dough and cherries into the other bowl of dough.

Place cupcake liners in your muffin pan. Fill the liners $^{2}/_{3}$ full. Bake 20 to 25 minutes or until a toothpick inserted in the muffin comes out clean. Serve with butter.

Raspberry Cheesecake
Yield: One 6-inch and one 10-inch cheesecake.
Crust:

3	cups chocolate cookie crumbs
6	tablespoons sugar
1	cup (2 sticks) butter, melted

Filling:

4	packages (8-ounces each) cream cheese, softened
1	cup sugar
2	teaspoons almond flavoring
1	pint whipping cream
6	eggs
2	cups *mini chocolate chips, melted
1	teaspoon water
1	cup flour

If you use regular chocolate chips, add 1 teaspoon of margarine or butter so they don't burn.

Topping:

3   cups sour cream at room temperature

5   tablespoons sugar

2   teaspoons almond flavoring

Garnish:

$1/2$ pint raspberries

48-50   whole pecans

$3/4$ cup mini chocolate chips

Fluffy Light Frosting:

5   tablespoons flour

1   cup half-and-half

1   cup (2 sticks) butter, softened

1   cup granulated sugar

$1/4$ teaspoon salt

1   teaspoon almond extract

Note: When I was in Mondovi, Wisconsin, I stopped at a specialty food store. I purchased raspberry chocolate chips. I used those on top of the following cheesecake. It was to die for! Raspberry chocolate chips are not easy to find—but very tasty!

Preheat oven to 300 degrees. In a bowl, combine cookie crumbs, sugar, and butter. Place 1 cup of the crumbs into a 6-inch spring-form pan and the remainder into a 10-inch spring-form pan.

In a separate bowl, beat the cream cheese until smooth, then, gradually add the sugar, beating until creamy. Add the flavoring and well beaten eggs. Add water to the chocolate chips and microwave in a 2-cup Pyrex measuring cup for about one minute and then stir. Cool the chocolate chip mixture slightly before adding it to the cheese mixture. Beat until smooth. Gradually blend in the flour mixing until smooth and creamy.

Fill the two spring-form pans $2/3$ full. Place each pan on a separate cookie sheet. Place the small cheesecake on the bottom rack and the large cheesecake on the top rack of your oven. Bake for 55-60 minutes, or until the center is firm. Shut off the oven.

Mix the sour cream topping and carefully spread over the warm cheesecake. Immediately return to the warm oven, leaving the oven door ajar for another 25 minutes. Cool thoroughly and refrigerate. Frost the sides of the cheesecake with Fluffy Light Frosting (recipe above and directions following).

Directions for frosting:

In a small saucepan, beat the flour and cream with a wire whisk until smooth. Cook the mixture until thick, and then refrigerate. (If the flour-cream mixture is added to the butter mixture before it has cooled, the butter will melt and curdle. Place the flour mixture bowl in some ice water to speed up the cooling process.)

Cream the butter, sugar, salt, and extract. Beat the cool flour-milk mixture into the butter-sugar mixture at high speed on your mixer or blender for about 10 minutes or until smooth and creamy.

Assembly:

Remove the cooled cheesecakes from the spring-form pans and place on cardboard circles. Place the circles on your serving plates and frost the sides.

With a star tip form a border on the top of the cake. Place a circle of raspberries on each frosting star. Garnish the top of the cakes with chocolate chips. Garnish the bottom border of the cakes with whole pecans.

Raspberry Refrigerator Cheesecake

Yield: One 9-inch pie.

Crust:

   1   prepared deep-dish 9-inch piecrust

Filling:

   3   packages (individual puddings) snack pack vanilla
           pudding—reserve 1 pack

   2   packages (8-ounces each) cream cheese, softened

 $1/4$ cup cold water

   1   envelope unflavored gelatin

   1   cup powdered sugar

   1   reserved pudding snack pack

   1   teaspoon almond flavoring

Topping:

   1   can (21 ounces) raspberry pie filling

With a fork, prick tiny holes into the bottom and sides of an unbaked pie shell to avoid blisters. Bake at 400 degrees for 8-10 minutes, or until golden brown. Cool.

Place 3 of the individual snack pack puddings into the bottom of the pie shell. Beat the cream cheese until smooth and then add powdered sugar, beating until smooth again. Add the unflavored gelatin to cold water and microwave for 25 seconds on medium high. Cool slightly before adding to the cream cheese mixture. Beat the cheese/gelatin mixture until smooth then add 1 pudding pack and the almond flavoring and beat until smooth. Pour into the pie shell, covering the bottom pudding layer. Top with the pie filling and refrigerate overnight.

Strawberry Angel Food Cake

1   ready-made angel food cake
1   quart frozen strawberries, thawed
1   pound non-dairy whipped topping, thawed

Note: This is such an easy dessert, and a favorite of the elderly.

Slice cake and place the slices on the serving plates. Spoon strawberries over the cake and place a spoonful of non-dairy whipped topping on top of the strawberries.

Rainbow Angel Food Cake

1   ready-made angel food cake
1   pint rainbow sherbet
1   pound non-dairy whipped topping, thawed

Slice the cake crosswise twice, making 3 layers. Place the bottom layer on your serving plate. Spread sherbet over the bottom layer. Place the second layer of cake over the layer of sherbet, and add a second layer of sherbet. Place the top cake layer on top of the sherbet and frost the cake with the topping and place in the freezer until serving time. Cut and serve on a pretty dessert plate.

So—now you have a variety of recipes to have a great Mother's Day lunch. Have fun and enjoy!

My Fair Lady

by Pat Nekola

In honor of my mother. I lost her to Alzheimer's Disease, and then to death.

You are the fairest lady of them all,
With your kind countenance and ever warm smile.
As a woman, in motherhood, you answered God's call.

You nurtured me well and helped me to grow,
Your hand in my hand and lighting life's path
With your beautiful, shining blue eyes, all aglow.

Each night you kissed me and gave me a hug;
Heard my prayers, and tucked me into my bed.
Then down into sleep I would drift, so safe and so snug.

Playing ball as a child I got hit in the head.
Your soothing words of comfort took the hurt away,
And you bore my pain with the tears you shed.

When I was ten, I tried to make the supper dish.
It turned out uneatable, but you encouraged me to try again,
And happily ate, in its place, my offering of tuna fish.

With your help and tutelage, I did learn to cook.
You taught me my way around the kitchen—and not to give up.
I became a teacher; then a caterer and wrote a *Picnics* book.

There are still so many words I would like to say,
Including a "Thank you" for all your good deeds,
And your inspirational strength that propels me on each day.

It is very clear that you loved me unconditionally from the start
And, although we are separated by my life here on earth,
Know that I love you, too, Mother dear—with all my heart.

Feel free to use my poem, and maybe you have someone on your staff, or a resident that is a poet.
Get them involved in your own Mother's Day program. Don't let them be shy!

My Fair Lady Music Bingo
Two for One

Instruct players to cover two squares of "FREE" at the beginning of the game. For every song the player guesses correctly they can cover another FREE square. When they cover the correct song title they can cover that square plus a "FREE" square.

B	I	N	G	O
Get Me to the Church on Time	I've Grown Accustomed to Your Face	I Could Have Danced All Night	**FREE**	With a Little Bit of Luck
On the Street Where You Live	**FREE**	I've Grown Accustomed to Your Face	Show Me	Wouldn't It Be Lovely
FREE	Show Me	**FREE**	I Could Have Danced All Night	**FREE**
With a Little Bit of Luck	I've Grown Accustomed to Your Face	Wouldn't It Be Lovely	**FREE**	Get Me to the Church on Time
Get Me to the Church on Time	I Could Have Danced All Night	Show Me	With a Little Bit of Luck	I've Grown Accustomed to Your Face

Tulip Flowerpot Centerpiece Art Project

Note: Make enough centerpieces so you have one for each table. When setting up the room, place a sticker under one chair seat at each table. When the luncheon is over tell people to check under their chair for the sticker. The one with the sticker is the winner of the centerpiece!

Supplies needed:
1 clay pot 4 inches tall and 12 inches in diameter.
Egg cartons.
1 Styrofoam ball per pot (6 inches in diameter and
    2 inches high).
Wire.
Florist tape.
Paper to make leaves.
Pink, yellow, red, purple paint.
Stamens for center of tulips.
Spanish moss filling for pot.
Felt.

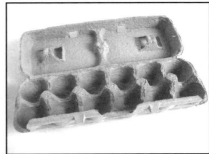

Directions:
1. Cut three pieces of wire $7^1/_2$ to 8 inches in length.
2. Wrap wire with tape, leaving one inch from the bottom bare.
3. Make six leaves, two for each flower. Put one leaf on each side of the wire, 3 inches from the bottom. The leaf size should be $5^1/_2$ to 6 inches.
4. Cut out the egg carton part that holds the egg.
5. Cut and shape into a tulip.
6. Paint each tulip a different color
7. Dry.
8. Hot glue the stamens to the center of the tulip.
9. Bend the top of the wire and hot glue it to the bottom of the tulip.
10. Stick the tulips into the Styrofoam ball.
11. Trace the bottom of the pot on a piece of felt. Cut out the circle and glue on the bottom of the pot. This prevents any scratches on the table.
12. Place ball with tulips in the pot.
13. Surround the ball and stems with filling.

Refer to page 8 in color section for a color picture of completed Tulip Flowerpot Centerpiece Art Project.

Gardening Club Gathering

One of the local facilities had a garden full of beautiful flowers. The residents enjoyed this greatly. My husband and family members of the residents came to help plant more flowers chosen by each resident. The Girl Scouts also came and helped. They donated not only their time, but also flowers.

Before the planting began we gathered interested residents. I brought in flowers and seeds, too. The residents identified the various flowers. They talked about their flower gardens. Each resident could have their name on the planted area with their favorite flowers. They felt they were important. They also got their families involved and they liked the families' participation. It was a beautiful day, and we all had fun. The garden became a conversation piece.

My husband worked with one of the residents. She had a huge flower garden when she was still in her home. She named every plant and flower. She also had her own idea about how things should be planted. My husband was great with her. He asked how many inches down, and how much water did they need. Little did she know that my husband is a gardener. He has our yard looking very sharp with many trees, shrubs, and flowers. He found the lady to be interesting, and he enjoyed pleasing her.

Note: I might also add that I made many visits to her when, six months later, she suffered from terminal cancer. I sat with her as she was dying. I learned much from her! She passed in her sleep. It is wonderful to comfort an elderly person as they are preparing for their final journey home.

Granny's Soup Kitchen

This soup is very tasty and unique. The mint adds an interesting flavor to the Cornish hen soup.

Cornish Hen Mint Soup

Yield: Serves 20.

1	can (49 ounces) chicken broth
1	cup white cooking wine
2	(18-24 ounces each) Cornish hens, skinned and left whole
1	package (18 ounces) mushrooms, sliced
1	package (1 pound) baby sweet peas, reserved
1	package (3.2 ounces) Shiitake mushrooms, sliced without stems
3	cloves fresh garlic, minced
1	cup diced red onion
1	bunch green onions, sliced with tops
2	tablespoons plus 2 teaspoons Greek or Italian seasoning
1	teaspoon thyme
$1/2$	teaspoon white pepper
3	packages (1-ounce each) fresh mint, finely diced (reserve 2 ounces for garnish)
2	cups uncooked garden harvest wild rice mix
1	red pepper for garnish

Place broth, wine, Cornish hens, mushrooms, garlic, red and green onion, seasonings, and 1 ounce of the fresh mint in a large crockpot. Cook for 6 to 8 hours on low. Reserve the peas and rice to add at the end of the cooking time.

Using an aspic cutter, or free hand, cut out 20 hearts from the red pepper for the garnish and reserve. Chop the reserved 2 ounces of fresh mint and set aside for the garnish.

Directions for cooking rice:

4 cups water
2 tablespoons oil

Place the water and oil into a large saucepan and bring to a boil. Add the rice to the boiling water and reduce heat so that the rice is cooking, but not boiling over. Stir occasionally to keep the rice from sticking to the bottom of the pan. The rice will be cooked when the water is absorbed. Rinse and set aside.

When the soup is cooked divide into three bowls to cool. Debone the Cornish hens and add the diced hens to the soup. Also add the peas and rice and mix into the soup. Just before serving place hot soup into individual serving bowls and garnish with the mint and red pepper heart. Serve with dill bread and/or plain bread, butter, and crackers.

Norwegian Independence Day, May 17th

Syttende Mai

Note: This program is especially for elder residents with a Norwegian background, but everyone will enjoy learning about Norway. It may give the residents a chance to speak about their ancestry and also have fun.

Each year Norway celebrates Independence Day on May 17, just like Americans celebrate the 4th of July. Don't forget to decorate your facility in the Norwegian theme for the day (or week).

- Tell Norway's story and also do the exercise with the material.
- Plan a dinner with the residents.
- Play folk music and have someone come in and do a folk dance in costume.
- Talk about the crafts and handi-work connected with Norwegians, such as: rosemaling, weaving, silver jewelry, and embroidery.
- A map of Norway and the surrounding countries is included below. Have a discussion about the Scandinavian countries.
- Make some Norwegian desserts such as rosettes and bakkels. Make sweet soup. You might have some Norwegian residents, ask them if they have memories of Norwegian dishes, or if they have Norwegian cookbooks. Maybe you can have a demonstration on preparing Norwegian foods.
- Show a travelogue on Norway including the beautiful scenery. Bring in a Norwegian flag and play the national anthem. (Lyrics on following page.)
- Practice some of the Norwegian words, such as "please," "thank you," "hello," "goodbye." Suggest that people try to use the Norwegian words in their conversations that day.
- Bring in a baker that can bake Scandinavian breads and have the baker talk about the favorite breads in Norway. Or get a Scandinavian bread cookbook and do a bread proj-

NORWAY, SWEDEN, FINLAND, & DENMARK

FINLAND

SWEDEN

Trondheim

Vaasa

NORWAY

Bergen

Turku   Helsinki

Oslo

Stockholm

Göteborg

DENMARK   Alborg

København   Malmö

Norway National Anthem

Words by Bjornst Jerne Biornson (1832-1910)
Music by: Rikard Nordraak (1842-1866)

Norwegian: **Ja, Vi Elsker Dette Landet**	**English Translation:** **Yes, We Love This Country**
Ja, vi elsker dette landet,	Yes, we love this country
Sopm det stiger frem,	Which rises up,
Furet, vaerbitt, over vannet,	Rugged and weathered, above the sea,
Med de tusen hjem.	With its thousands of homes.
Elsker, elsker det og tenker	Love it, love it, and think
Pa var far og mor	About our mothers and fathers
Og den saganatt som senker	And the saga of past ages
Dromme pa var jord,	That sends dreams to our earth,
Og den saganatt som senker	And the saga of past ages
Senker dromme pa var jord.	That sends dreams, sends dreams, to our earth.
Norske mann I hus og hytte,	Norseman, in house and cabin,
Takk din store Gud!	Thank your great God!
Landet ville han beskytte	It was His will to protect the country
Skjont det morkt sa ut.	Although things looked dark.
Alt hva federene har kjempet.	While fathers fought
Modrene har grett,	And mothers cried,
Har den Herre stille lempet,	Our Lord quietly opened the way
Sa vi vant var rett,	So that we won our right.
Har den Herre stille lempet,	Our Lord quietly opened the way
Sa vi vant, vi vant var rett.	So that we won, we won our right.
Ja, vi elsker dette landet,	Yes, we love this country
Som det stiger frem,	Which rises up,
Furet, vaerbitt over vannet,	Rugged and weathered, above the sea,
Med de tusen jhem!	With its thousands of homes.
Og som fedres kamp har hevet	And as our fathers' struggle has raised it
Det fra nod til seier	From distress to victory,
Ogsa vi nar det blir krevet,	We also, when called upon,
For dets fred slar leir,	Will strike a blow for its peace.
Ogsa vi nar det blir krevet,	We also, when called upon,
For dets fred, dets fred slar leir.	Will strike a blow for its peace, its peace.

I had the opportunity to visit New Glarus and Scandinavia, Wisconsin; and also Berne, Indiana. These communities are very Scandinavian. Also, Minnesota is heavily populated with descendants from Scandinavia. It is a great experience to visit these areas. The people are very friendly and willing to please their guests. My husband and I took friends from Mishawaka, Indiana, to Al Johnson's Swedish Restaurant and Butik in Sister Bay, Wisconsin. This is a *real* Scandinavian experience! They have goats grazing on top of their grass roof. The Butik is a beautiful gift shop, and the food at the restaurant is outstanding. I especially liked the thin Swedish pancakes with lingonberry jam. Waitresses are dressed in Norwegian costume.

The Vesterheim Norwegian-American Museum in Decorah, Iowa, has a collection dedicated to the Norwegian culture and folk arts. Decorah's Nordic Fest is held every July. (See the references on page 201 for address and telephone numbers.)

Flag of Norway

The Norwegian flag is red and white with a sideways blue cross, outlined in white.

History of Norway

Norway means "Northern Way".

Just about one-third of the country is north of the Arctic Circle. Norway has mountains and fjords, which are deep sea-filled canyons. These are long, narrow inlets of sea that cut into the coastline. Norway has 1,700 glaciers and the entire coastline has fjords.

There are thousands of beautiful waterfalls in Norway. There are 150,000 islands, but only 2,000 are inhabited.

There are about 160,000 lakes. The largest lake in Norway is the Mjosa, just north of the capital, Oslo.

Norway has vidders. A vidder is a flat plateau off the top of a mountain. A vidder is an open area. It is usually swampy. Throughout Norway the big boulders have layers of color on the rocks' surface. This is called lichen.

Norwegians think of their country in five parts: Northern (Nord-Norge), Mid-Norway (Trondelag), West Country (Vestlandet), East Country (Ostlandet), and very far Southern (Sorlandet).

The chief port of the North Sea oil industry is in Stavanger. This is found between Oslo and Stavanger. Fish found in abundance are: herring, cod, and mackerel.

The Langfjellet are called the long mountains and are found in the southern part of Norway.

Norway is cold in the winter and warm in the summer. This country covers 125,182 square miles. It is just a little larger than New Mexico, and has a population of 4.5 million.

Most of the population has a Scandinavian ancestry. The majority of Norwegians live within ten miles of the sea. It is the warm water of the Gulf Stream coming from the Caribbean Sea that keeps Norway warmer. This makes the climate mild. However, it does get cold in the winter. Because of the Gulf Stream waters the fjords do not freeze and the snow melts quickly. Harbor areas are free of ice.

Temperatures get as low as 5 degrees, and the weather is colder inland.

The northern portion of Norway is called "land of the midnight sun". From mid-May to the end of June the sun never sets. There is sunlight for the entire 24 hours of the day. It is dark from November through January. Norway is warmer than Alaska—even though both are in the far north.

Norwegians depend on hydroelectric power. This comes via dams on the rivers and fjords. If they do not get enough rain to keep the rivers full, they rely on neighboring countries for purchasing electric power.

People tend to think Norwegians are blue-eyed and blond. This is not necessarily so, they are tall with fair skin. There is a minority group in Norway called the Lapps; they live in a region called Lapland. It is very cold in this region. The majority of Lapps have high cheekbones and straight black hair. They are small in stature.

Most Norwegians are active in games and sports. Cross-country skiing is very popular and children start at a young age. People enjoy fishing and skating and summer sports such as soccer, hiking, and swimming. It is said that children in Norway are born with skis on their feet. Actually, it is a way to get around in the heavy snow. A yearly cross-country skiing race, which has been in existence for centuries, is called the Birkebeiner.

Norwegian Words with English Translation

Halo—Hello

Nigh—No

Takk or Tok—Thank you

Ja or yah—Yes

Var Soh Snill—Please

Ha duh—Goodbye

Du—You

Hva—What

God dag—Good day

Mor—Mother

Far—Father

The Vikings in Norway

The Vikings lived in Norway from the 700s through 1050, and were known as fierce warriors. By the 8th century the Vikings were setting out to explore the world and find treasure. They attacked Ireland and England, stealing possessions there. During their exploration they also found their way to North America. It is believed that Leif Ericson discovered North America in 1000 A.D. This was 492 years before Christopher Columbus came to the "new world".

The first King of Norway was King Harold in 872. In 1050 King Harald Hardrade founded Oslo as the capital city.

Christianity was established in Norway by King Olav II in 1013. This came about after the invasion of France. Olav demanded all Norwegians be baptized as Christians, or be killed. When he died, miracles began to happen and he was declared a saint in 1164. For several years the people were required to be married in the church and practice the Lutheran faith.

King Haakon IV came to power in 1217 and a time of peace and prosperity began. This is known as Norway's Golden Age.

In 1349 the Bubonic Plague known as the Black Death killed almost half of the Norwegian population.

Denmark gained control of Norway from 1381-1814, but then Norway was given to Sweden after the Napoleonic Wars. Norway disliked being ruled by others, so on May 17, 1814, they declared their independence, but it took 91 years to finally break away from Swedish rule. It was 1905 before Norway finally became officially independent of Sweden.

When World War I broke out, Norway, Sweden, and Denmark stated they would all remain neutral and not fight in the war. Norway also stayed neutral in World War II. Unfortunately, Germany attacked Norway in April 1940. Germany occupied Norway until 1945. During this time the King of Norway was safely exiled in England.

During World War II the resistance movement organized to fight against the Germans. They managed to ski softly past German troops and blow up the factory where Germans were making an atomic bomb.

Norwegian children learn to speak English in school at the age of seven or eight. The two official languages of the Norwegians are Boknal or "book language" and Nynorsk. The Sami speak Lappish. Eighty percent of the people speak Bokanl.

There are two big holidays in Norway—Christmas and Constitution or Independence Day (also known as Syttende Mai—May 17th). Religious holidays include: Epiphany-January 6; St. Canute Day-January 13; St Hans (John's) Day—June 24; and St. Olav's Day—July 29.

Important Dates in Norwegian History

1814: Norway declared their independence.

1854: First railroad completed.

1903: Bjonstjerne Bjornson was awarded the Nobel Prize for literature.

1905: Norway finally became independent of Sweden. Haakon VII became king.

1913: Women were given the right to vote.

1914-1918: Norway did not fight in World War I.

1940-1945: Germany occupied Norway.

1981: Gro Harlem Brundtland became the first female prime minister. She was very influential around the world. She resigned her office in 1994.

Norwegian Government

The country is a monarchy. The rank is: Statsrad, Prime Minister, and the Cabinet of Ministers. There is also a legislative branch with two houses: the lagting (law assembly) and the Odelsting (Heritage of the People Assembly). The judicial branch has three areas: Supreme Court, High Court (including courts of appeals), and District and City Courts.

Local government is divided into 19 provinces called fylkers. There are 435 municipalities, most are very small. The ten larger provinces have 50,000 or more residents.

You might want to purchase a map of Scandinavia and the Baltic states (or see if AAA will donate one). Post the map and use a yellow marker to mark different provinces and cities on the map. You might get the men residents into a discussion of the cities and provinces and then they can recognize locations and sizes from the map. You can discuss regions where the residents' ancestors may have immigrated from.

For instance: Oslo has a population of 480,000. It has a ski museum and is Norway's industrial and cultural center. People living in Oslo have a high standard of living and many have vacation homes in other regions. Only 15 percent of the population is over 65, 20 percent of the population is aged from 0-14, and ages 15-24 make up the other 65 percent.

People pay taxes in Norway, but the health care and education is paid for by the government. Workers have excellent retirement benefits. Taxes in Norway are one of the highest in the world.

Children in Norway start school at the age of six. At thirteen they go to secondary school for three years. Norwegian children play a game called stikka. They toss a coin against a wall, the child with the coin closest to the wall wins all the coins.

People travel mostly by car in Norway, but gasoline is very expensive. There are busses, airplanes, boats, trains, snowmobiles, skiing, and ferries. Oslo has a subway system.

The Norwegian currency is known as the Kroner (Nok)

The largest religion in Norway is Evangelical Lutheran, with 86 percent of the people following this religion. Roman Catholics make up three percent, and eleven percent makes up all the others.

Animals of Norway

Norway's largest mammal is the elk, also known as the European Moose. Other animals native to the country are the white-coated arctic fox, reindeer, the Fjord horse, elkhound hunting dog, the off-white snowy owl, seals, polar bears, grouse, and eagles.

Cod is the most important fish; they can weigh up to 100 pounds.

Lemming is an unwelcome furry rodent. Some Norwegians think the lemming goes toward the sea and drowns, but lemmings are afraid of water. They can swim if they are in the water, but prefer to stay on dry land. Large fish will feed on the lemmings, as well as birds. Refer to page 9 in color section for Animals of Norway.

Forests and Christmas in Norway

Norway is covered with forest and pine trees. The most famous pine is the Norway spruce. Norwegian families cut down the spruce for Christmas trees. They decorate the trees with straw ornaments, strings of lights, and tiny strings of Norwegian flags.

Some families prepare trout and salmon for their holiday feast. Christmas is celebrated through January 6 (Epiphany a religious holiday).

Resources

Norway's natural resources include: petroleum, natural gas, iron, titanium, copper, zinc, and lead. Iron ore, copper, and ilmenite-titanium are mined in Norway.

Norway is the second-largest oil exporter in the world (Saudi Arabia is first). They also make chemicals and metals such as aluminum magnesium.

With the forests, there is production of paper products and shipbuilding.

Agriculture

Each farmer in Norway usually owns no more than ten acres of land. Only three percent of the land in Norway is farmland. Because Norway is cool and damp during the growing season, vegetables such as potatoes, carrots, cauliflower, peas, and rutabagas do quite well. Norway also grows strawberries, blueberries, lingonberries (mountainberries), and cloudberries. Cloudberries grow in clusters and are orange-yellow raspberries. They are native to the mountains of southern Norway.

Famous Norwegian People

Henrik Isben (1828-1906). He was known as one of the greatest playwrights in the world. He wrote "A Doll's House", "The Wild Duck", and "Gabler".

Edvard Grieg (1843-1907). A well-known composer.

Gustav Vigeland (1869-1943). Famous sculptor.

Vidkun Quisling (1887-1945). Traitor.

Sonja Henie (1912-1969). Figure skater.

Edvard Munch (1861-1930). Painter.

Other Trivia about Norway

- A Norwegian invention is the cheese slicer (osthovel).
- Norway was one of the first countries to allow women to vote.
- If you go to a Norwegian home, please take off your shoes.
- Forty-five percent of the women in Norway are employed.
- John Vaaler, invented the paper clip in 1899.
- Norway is a leader in contributing money to help poorer countries in the world.
- The Nobel Peace Prize is sponsored by Norway.

Norwegian Music

The hardanger fiddle is the official folk instrument of Norway. It looks like a violin in many respects. You play on four strings and the other four vibrate in response to the strings actually being played. This gives the sound like the drone of a bagpipe.

Edvard Grieg wrote folk songs honoring Norway.

Here are some references for music:

- *Norwegian Fiddle Fantasia* by AnnBjorg Lien Felefeber. She is very talented on the hardanger fiddle. This CD is produced by Shanachie Entertainment Corporation.
- *Folk Music from Norway* by Leif Sorbye and a variety of other artists. The producer is ARC Music Productions Int. Ltd., P.O. Box 111, East Grinstead, West Susses, RH19 4FZ Great Britain. Email: info@arcmusic.co.uk. Arc Music, Eiffeste, 422, 20537, Hamburg, Germany

  Arc Music, Inc., P.O. Box 2453, Clearwater, FL 33757-2453

Norwegian Food

There are quite a number of good Scandinavian cookbooks at your local library. Remember, you can also discuss ethnic foods with your residents. Some of them will undoubtedly have their family recipes committed to memory, or be able to bring their own family cookbooks to your discussion. Get your residents personally involved—everyone will have a great time!

Here are some good cookbooks I've found useful.

A Little Scandinavian Cookbook by Janet Laurence.

Classic Scandinavian Cooking by Nika Hazelton. The recipe on page 15 for Norwegian Lamb and Cabbage casserole is interesting. When making this dish the whole peppercorns must be removed before serving. On page 24 there is a recipe for Norwegian Fish Mousse. On page 50 is Spinatsuppe or spinach soup. Norwegian Corned Trout is on page 69, it is also a national dish. Norwegian Cold Cauliflower with Shrimp is on page 133. On page 161 is a recipe for Eggedosis. This dish is also made for the Independence Day celebration. Norwegian King Haakon's Cake on page 192 was used to celebrate the first Independence day.

Cooking the Norwegian Way by Sylvia Munsen. A typical Norwegian menu is listed on pages 14-15. Rice pudding or Rispudding is listed on page 10-11. On page 30 is Baked Cod or Ovnstekt Torsk.

Scandinavian Feasts by Beatrice Ojakangas. Pages 70-95 list picnic menus. Using this book you could plan a wonderful Norwegian picnic for the residents. Get the kitchen staff and dietician involved.

Notably Norwegian by Louise Roalson. On page 79 is the delicious Fruit Soup or Sotsuppe. This book contains recipes, festivals, and folk arts. There are many pictures showing rosemaling, Norwegian dolls, costumes, and Christmas trees taken in Decorah, Iowa; New Glarus, Wisconsin; Minnesota; and New York. The spritz cookie recipe is in this book.

Best of Scandinavian Cooking by Shirley Sarvis and Barbara Scott O'Niel has a wonderful Lamb Chop and Mushroom Stew on page 96. There are some great breakfast recipes in this book, as well as the Norwegian Cream Cake on page 122. The Rosettes recipe is on page 47.

Time-Honored Norwegian Recipes tells a family story. It tells of cooking in Norway where the measurements are according to the metric system (everything is weighed rather than measured in spoons and cups).

A Few Norwegian Food Facts

The story goes that sunshine makes Norwegians smile. If porridge is served for breakfast the Norwegian is extra happy. The legend says that trolls lived in the mountains. They were small creatures that were very mean spirited, but they were all smiles when able to cook and eat porridge at breakfast time.

Norwegian women are expected to know how to make a good porridge. If she could not produce a good porridge she was not welcome in the household!

When the cook has the table all set and the food prepared she will say "Vaer sa god", meaning, "come on", or "here it is".

"Julebrod" is a Christmas bread. This bread can be tricky to make. It is filled with candied fruit and green and red cherries, raisins, and almonds.

Norwegians enjoy "open-faced" sandwiches for lunch or a snack.

Norwegians cook with buttermilk, almond extract, allspice, cardamon seed, cornmeal, cornstarch, dill, gelatin, nutmeg, sorghum (a dark-colored syrup), wheat flour, white pepper, and yeast.

Norwegians enjoy Gjetost Cheese (goat cheese). They also smoke, freeze, and pickle fish. Of course, lutefisk is a Norwegian favorite served at Christmastime.

Rice Pudding or Rispudding is another Christmastime favorite.

Norwegians are known for starting the smorgasbord.

For lower-functioning residents the Activity Director could bring in some of the foods ready-to-eat. The residents will enjoy the aromas, visual stimulation, and, of course, the good tastes!

A Brain Tickler on Norway

There are four answers to each set (a-d). Connect the arrow between each letter that best matches the statement.

1. Description of the Norwegian flag
2. Patron Saint of Norway
3. Official Religion

4. Chief of State

   a. St. Olaf
   b. King
   c. Blue Cross with white outline and red background
   d. Evangelical Lutheran

5. Average temperature in Southern Norway in July
6. Average temperature in the inlands in January
7. Lowest elevation
8. Countries near Norway

   a. Sweden, Finland, Russia
   b. 14 degrees F.
   c. 63 degrees F.
   d. Sea level along the coast

9. Latitude and Longitude of the geographic center
10. Highest elevation is 8,100 feet in the Jotunheimen National Park
11. Names of cities in Norway with the largest populations
12. Capital of Norway
**

   a. Oslo, Bergen, Stavanger, Troridheim
   b. 62 degrees North 10 East
   c. Oslo
   d. Galdhopiggen is the highest peak in Scandinavia

13. Head of government
14. Norwegian Independence Day
15. U.S. Independence Day
16. The Norwegian name for Independence Day

   a. May 17th
   b. Prime Minister
   c. July 4th
   d. Syttende Mai

17. Official name of Norway
18. Official language of Norway

19. National Anthem
20. The men that invaded Norway in the 700s

   a. Vikings
   b. "Yes, we love this land" "Ja, Vi elsker dette landet"
   c. Bokmal
   d. Kingdom of Norway

21. Currency of Norway   a. Krones

22. Plural of Currency in Norway   b. Henrik Isben

23. A famous Norwegian poet (1896-1968)   c. Gro Harlen Brundtland

24. A woman Prime Minister in Norway   d. Krone
    born in 1939

25. A famous Norwegian writer who   a. Thor Heyerdahl
    won the Nobel Prize (1882-1949)

26. Norwegian scientist   b. Sonja Henie

27. Norwegian painter   c. Sigrid Undset

28. Norwegian figure skater   d. Edvard Munch

29. Lutefisk   a. Salmon soaked in a seasoned salt
                                   for a long time

30. Gravlaks

31. Lefse   b. Dried cod, soaked in lye and served

32. Torsk   at Christmastime

                                     c. Cod

                                     d. Norwegian potato pancake

33. A variety of fruit called   a. Sweet soup
    "Sotsuppe" in Norwegian

34. A simple porridge   b. Stew

35. A pickled fish   c. Grot

36. A dish served at a picnic in Norway d. Herring

37. A winter sport in Norway   a. Birkebeiner

38. A summer sport in Norway   b. Downhill

39. Cross-country ski race held   c. Skiing
    for centuries   d. Swimming

40. Skiing on the mountains

**Note the names of the larger cities in Norway on your map to help the residents visualize their locations.*

Brain Tickler on Norway Answer Key:

1. c.   2. a.   3. d.   4. b.   5. c.   6. b.   7. d.   8. a.   9. b.   10. d.   11. a.   12. c   13. b.
14. a.   15. c.   16. d.   17. d.   18. c.   19. b.   20. a.   21. d.   22. a.   23. b.   24. c.   25. c.   26. d.
27. a.   28. b.   29. b.   30. a.   31. d.   32. c.   33. a.   34. c.   35. d.   36. b.   37. c.   38. d.   39. a.   40. b.

References:

"Scandinavia: Denmark, Sweden, and Norway" Travel the World by Rick Steves. Questar, Inc., P.O. Box 11345, Chicago, IL 60611

"The Wonders of Norway" by Ed Lark. Traveloguer Collection, 3301 W. Hampden Avenue, Suite N., Englewood, CO 80110.

"Norway" a 50-minute video on Norway from Lonely Planet Publications, 150 Linden Street, Oakland, CA 94607 1-800-275-8555.

Decorah, Iowa, Nordic Fest 1-800-382-3378 www.nordicfest.com

The Vesterheim Norwegian-American Museum, Decorah, IA 52101
(563) 382-9681 www.vesterheim.org

The Genealogical Center and Naeseth Library, 415 W. Main, Madison, WI 53714 (608) 255-2224

My friend's dad's mother grew up in Norway, Michigan. Each summer they would drive back to visit relatives there.

One day, while attending school in Milwaukee, the teacher announced they were going to be talking about Norway. He proudly raised his hand and said, "I have been to Norway many times."

The teacher asked, "What means of transportation did you use to get there? Did you fly, or go by boat?"

He nicely replied, "No, we drove."

The teacher immediately told him to sit down.

Later he told her his mother's family was from Norway, Michigan!

The Date Game

I went to a facility to play my date game with the residents. (These residents were in the 1st Stage Alzheimer's, or had some form of dementia.) The activity assistant and volunteers were assisting the residents as they came to the activity. I had a large board on an 8-foot table and I wrote on the board "The Date Game".

Two ladies were in the front row waiting for the activity to begin. One lady said loudly, "The date game!"

The other lady said, "Maybell, you don't suppose we are going to be required to tell about our first date, do you?"

"I sure hope not! If that's the case, I'm just going to say I don't remember. That will fix her for asking such a thing."

The buzz was on in the room.

When every resident was finally settled, I introduced myself and said, "Thanks to God we have dates in our life to produce beautiful memories." I continued, "Thank God, you don't have to tell about your first date—or maybe it would be good to talk about your first date—I understand that someone in this room fell in love on her first date and was married 50 years before he went to heaven."

You should have seen Maybell's face! (I had a hard time keeping a straight face.)

"Today we will think of dates from each month to make you smile about the 'good old days'."

I had brought props to help jog the resident's memories. I had a turkey for Thanksgiving, a soldier for November 11, a Christmas tree, and a bell for New Year's. I also had a dog for Dog Days, a birthday cake, a Mother and Father for Mother's and Father's Days, and a picture of the Nina, Pinta, and Santa Maria. All of these things get their minds working to get into conversation about the "Date Game".

I asked who would like to be first, a lady named Bea volunteered.

"What is your favorite holiday?"

"Christmas," was the answer.

"What is the date of Christmas? What special person was born on Christmas? What is the real meaning of Christmas? What did you do on Christmas Day?," were all questions I asked Bea to get her memory going. She went on to tell about Christmas dinner, what they had to eat and who made which dish. Then I played some Christmas music and everyone joined in singing along. Other residents joined in with their memories of Christmas.

Then I asked who has a birthday throughout the year, and of course, everyone raised their hand. They took turns telling about their birthday parties through the years.

I asked if anyone knew a summer holiday, and we discussed the 4th of July celebrations the residents had attended or hosted. We sang, "You're a Grand Old Flag" and "America the Beautiful".

I brought up holidays in November and one gentleman piped up and said Veteran's Day. He told his story about being in World War II. We played "Anchors Away", and recited the "Pledge of Allegiance". We also talked about Thanksgiving, and I read my history of Thanksgiving. (It is printed in the book *An Alzheimer's Guide, Activities and Issues for People Who Care* pages 278-282.)

We discussed the Dog Days of August and how hot it is then. I played "How Much is that Doggy in the Window".

I'm sure by now, you have ideas of your own to use in the "Date Game" activity. This can last as long a time as you have available, and you can always continue it to another "date" if you don't get around to everyone. It was fun and everyone left with a smile on their face!

Hot Air Balloon Party
Taking a Balloon Ride

During the Kentucky Derby they have ballooning as one of their events. It is held on the first Saturday of May in Louisville, Kentucky.

A cluster of hot air balloons are ever so beautiful and fascinating. The weather must be good to take a balloon ride. You must make sure there isn't a thunderstorm in sight, or gusting winds. It is very important for the pilot to check the balloon for any tears, and any other safety issues.

A hot air balloon is like a giant parachute. It weighs 120 pounds. Even though the balloon is bulky, when it lays flat it can be packed into a three-foot canvas bag.

Students can begin training to be a balloon pilot at the age of 14, and can be eligible to get their license at age 16. Students must pass a test by the Federal Avaiation Administration (FAA). The FAA also inspects all balloons for safety before anyone can fly.

The student is required to learn every part of the balloon and all the different weather conditions. No on should fly a balloon in bad weather. They will also learn how to inflate and anchor a balloon. Balloons come in all sizes, shapes, and colors—a style and color for everyone!

Crew members hold the mouth of the balloon open, while the pilot opens the blast valve of the gas burner. You will hear a load roaring noise, as the balloon inflates, the crew will turn the basket upright and you are ready to take off.

The wind pushes the balloon across the field and helps to lift it off the ground. You need the burning gas to heat the air in the balloon to make it rise off the ground. Other than the noise of the gas burning it is very peaceful and beautiful as you glide above the fields and treetops.

If you decide to take a balloon ride, you trust your life to the pilot. He has a compass and flight instruments on board the balloon. These help the pilot know the direction you are traveling and the altitude of the balloon.

As you are ready to land the pilot will use less gas so the air in the balloon will cool, letting you descend for a landing. Usually, the pilot will get permission from a farmer to use a field as a landing area.

When your flight is completed, you will help load the balloon into a cloth bag and place it all into a van or pickup for transport home.

Most people, having enjoyed the thrill of ballooning, would do it again. A ride in the sky is an outstanding experience.

While there have been many men working to break records in ballooning, many people enjoy ballooning just for fun. There are folks who are very enthusiastic members of the Balloon Federation of America. It started in 1961, and is considered a sport.

In my church there is a gentleman that owns his own balloon. At our picnic he offered balloon rides as part of the silent auction. People really bid quite high on this item.

If you and your audience need a break, play and sing the song "Around the World in 80 Days", or another appropriate song.

If you know a balloonist it would be interesting for the residents to have them visit your facility and talk about the balloon. If it is a nice day have the activity outside and let the balloonist bring his balloon for the residents to see.

The History of Ballooning

How did ballooning begin?

The Montgolfier brothers were the inventors of ballooning. They were French papermakers and experimented with a bag filled with heated air.

In 1783 the Montgolfiers drew a large crowd to see the first hot air balloon in flight in the village of Annonay, France. They named their balloon the aerostalic machine.

Two years later Jean Francois Pilahi de Rozier died when his hydrogen balloon caught fire. It was the world's first balloon tragedy.

Jacques Alexandre Charles, a French chemist, experimented with hydrogen filled balloons. He was actually able to take his balloon 9,000 feet up in the air. Others around the world began to work with balloons.

Jean Pierre Blanchard and Doctor John Jeffries crossed the English Channel with their hot air balloon. A man named Wise made a balloon with a rip panel. This section helped to release the air quickly when landing. He flew from St. Louis, Missouri, and flew for 809 miles.

During the Civil War, in 1861, hot air balloons were sent up to help gather information. Balloons were also used during World War I. They were attached to artillery trenches with heavy cables so soldiers could observe enemy troop positions.

The Montgolfier brothers were invited to show their machine to the King of France. Etienne Montgolfier made an oval-shaped balloon and called it the Revillion. Montgolfier decided to try out his balloon and took a duck, sheep, and rooster along as passengers. The Revellion II went down in the forest, the lid on the basket broke and the animals escaped in good condition. In fact, the sheep was found eating grass. A storm destroyed the Revillion.

The Montgolfier brothers wanted to send a human being up in their aerostat, so they built Revillion III. They coated the inside and outside with Alum (a metal), but the King forbid anyone to ride in the balloon unless it was tied down.

Finally, the King consented and on November 21, 1903, Pilatre de Rozier and Francois Laurent d' Arlandes made the first flight. They traveled over five miles and were 3,000 feet up in the air. They flew for 25 minutes and landed the basket with a thump.

In 1927 Captain Hawthorne C. Gray rose eight miles high in a balloon. Gray kept a log of his flight. Would you believe—he discovered at 31,000 feet the temperature was 32 degrees. Gray made his last entry at 44,000 feet. Later, he was found dead near Sparta, Tennessee. His diary and data are displayed at the Smithsonian Institute in Washington, D.C.

The Piccard brothers designed a huge balloon in 1931 and rose to over 51,000 feet. Albert W. Stevens and Orvel A. Anderson went up just before World War II. They departed from South Dakota and reached a height of 72,000 feet. They learned bacteria could be carried from earth for miles. The flies they brought along on an experiment died.

In 1950 monkeys and mice went on a flight 121,000 feet high. They returned to earth safely.

Each person that was trying to fly balloons tried to go higher. In 1957, Charles Moore, a meteorologist, went up to study weather. He took the first televised pictures during his ride.

In 1961 Victor Prather and Malcolm D. Ross went up over 113,000 feet. They landed in the Gulf of Mexico.

Nick Piantanida rose to 12,800 feet. He was killed on his second flight while attempting to break his first record.

In 1995, Steve Fossett went across the Pacific Ocean as the first balloonist to fly solo for 5,432 miles.

There are many balloon contests throughout the country. They began in 1906. Albuquerque, New Mexico, held the first Balloon Fiesta.

You may want to have some maps on hand to show the different locations where balloonists were experimenting with flight. Annonay, France; English Channel; Civil War locations; Sparta, Tennessee; South Dakota; Gulf of Mexico; Pacific Ocean; Albuquerque, New Mexico.

You might also pass around ballooning magazines so the residents can see the beautiful balloons. Here are two ballooning magazines:

Balloon Life, 2145 Dale Avenue, Sacramento, CA 95815.

Ballooning, P.O. Box 400, Indianola, IA 50125.

The National Association for ballooning is:

The Balloon Federation of America, P.O. Box 400, Indianola, IA 50125.

The National Balloon Museum is also in Indianola, IA.

Ballooning Terms

- *Pyrometer*—This instrument measures the temperature.
- *Variometer*—Measures the rate of the climb or descent.
- *Parachute Vent*—This small parachute plugs the hole to keep the hot air in the balloon until the time for descent.
- *Mouth*—A large opening at the bottom of the balloon's envelope.
- *Skirt*—The heat resistance fabric extension of the envelope that is designed to filter the heated air safely into the mouth of the hot air balloon.
- *Aeronaut*—The person who operates the hot air balloon.
- *Altimeter*—This instrument measures altitude.
- *Ballast*—The weight on the balloon to control altitude.
- *Gondola*—The basket the pilot and passengers ride in.
- *Maneuvering Vent*—A slot in the hot air balloon's envelope. The pilot pulls the cord to release air.
- *Envelope Nylon Bag*—Holds the gas in the balloon.
- *Appendix*—This is the tube at the bottom of the gas balloon. The appendix inflates the envelope.
- *Up Panel*—The part of the envelope that the pilot pulls open with a cord. This releases the air quickly for landing.

Hot Air Balloon Word Search

```
A P P E N D I X O P L M N T U V S T Y E M P T Y
S T U V W X Y M A N E U V E R I N G V E N T H T
T U S S C L O S E D H I T A E R O S T A T E I O
P A R A C H U T E V E N T A T T B A L L A S T C
B H I L B O T T O M D V A R I O M E T E R O P X
G N T R N B C D E O Y M S T F N I O K P Q A Y O
O B C S R S V O B R D O T P S B U E E X N L R E
N E X O M N K B O T O U I Y K Y X T N N S T O A
D R I F T I N G D M X T F D I W H V V A N I M E
O P T I F R E F I E E H A E R E B P E B S M E M
L E N V E L O P E A T P W M T L L C L O E E T P
A E R O N A U T I M E H O I E I L P O P X T E T
A L T I M E E E R S R O R P T O A P P F E E R Y
R A I N B O W B A L L O O N E P O R E B M R J E
V A R I O M M T E R I P P A N E L S T R S E K T
```

Hot Air Balloon Word Search:

Rainbow Balloon	Skirt	Envelope	Appendix
Empty	Altimeter	Pyrometer	Parachute Vent
Closed	Maneuvering Vent	Aeronaut	Ballast
Bottom	Rip Panel	Variometer	Gondola
Drifting	Mouth	Aerostate	

Hot Air Balloon Answer Key

```
A P P E N D I X O P L M N T U V S T Y E M P T Y
S T U V W X Y M A N E U V E R I N G V E N T H T
T U S S C L O S E D H I T A E R O S T A T E I O
P A R A C H U T E V E N T A T T B A L L A S T C
B H I L B O T T O M D V A R I O M E T E R O P X
G N T R N B C D E O Y M S T F N I O K P Q A Y O
O B C S R S V O B R D O T P S B U E E X N L R E
N E X O M N K B O T O U I Y K Y X T N N S T O A
D R I F T I N G D M X T F D I W H V A N I M E E
O P T I F R E F I E E H A E R E B P E B S M E M
L E N V E L O P E A T P W M T L L C L O E E T P
A E R O N A U T I M E H O I E I L P O P X T E T
A L T I M E E E R S R O R P T O A P F E E R R Y
R A I N B O W B A L L O O N E P O R E B M R J E
V A R I O M M T E R I P P A N E L S T R S E K T
```

Hot Air Balloon Word Search Key:

Rainbow Balloon	Skirt	Envelope	Appendix
Empty	Altimeter	Pyrometer	Parachute Vent
Closed	Maneuvering Vent	Aeronaut	Ballast
Bottom	Rip Panel	Variometer	Gondola
Drifting	Mouth	Aerostate	

June Activities

A Wedding Day Party

This activity will consume a whole half-day—either morning or afternoon. Plus the activity with the cake and decorating may take part of a prior day.

Items Needed:

Bridesmaid Dresses

Tuxedo

Wedding Dress with Train and Veil

Mother of the Bride Suits and Dresses

Fancy Hats

Old-Fashioned Hats (for the residents to wear)

Plastic Runner for the Fashion Show

Video of Wedding

Wedding Bells

Crepe Paper for Streamers

Wedding Cake and Top

Cake Knife and Server

White Tablecloth

Centerpiece for Buffet Table

Different Centerpieces for each Season

Residents' Wedding Pictures

Anniversary Pictures

Wooden Arch

Wedding Peace Plant

Bouquet of Flowers

Bottle of Champagne

In the morning before your fashion show, or in the days prior to the party, gather wedding pictures from the residents to use at the show. Sometimes someone has just celebrated a special anniversary, use that picture with their wedding picture—sort of a then and now.

Encourage the residents to show their wedding pictures and talk about their wedding day. One couple said they had eloped and, therefore, they didn't have any picture to show.

Show the wedding video and encourage the residents to comment on how it is different now from their wedding days.

Demonstrate how to set up a serving table with a cake. If you have a silver service use it on the table. Make it as real as possible, using napkins, nuts, mints, flowers, etc.

We made the wedding cake ourselves for the show. We started two days earlier and some of the residents, who could, helped with it. I gave a demonstration on how to frost and decorate a wedding cake. I also showed how to make frosting roses and leaves the day before the party. By working on something the days before the show everyone got involved in the planning and helping, making it more fun for all. If one of your residents did cake decorating when they were younger let them contribute some hints and unusual situations that happened to them.

Talk about other foods normally served at weddings, and find out what foods the residents had at their weddings. Was it good or a flop?

In years back, weddings were held at the home of the bride or at the church parsonage. Quiz the residents on this. Where was their wedding held? Why? Did they have a reception? Did they go on a honeymoon?

The Fashion Show

Select staff members or residents' family members to wear the dresses for the show. Some of them may like to wear their own dress. Ask some of the volunteers to wear tuxedos and play the part of the men in the wedding party, or find some men volunteers.

Have the staff and residents help decorate the room for the wedding with crepe paper streamers, bells, and the arch—don't forget the flowers! Use recorded music for the wedding march and all during the event.

When it comes to discussion of the Mother of the Bride dress, show several fancy dresses and ask the residents which one they would pick to wear if they were the Mother of the Bride, and why they would pick that one. They enjoy talking about clothes and fashion and seeing and feeling the fabrics.

Talk about the wedding preparation and the wedding cake. Find out what kind of cake the residents had at their wedding.

Have each resident select a hat to wear to the wedding, they enjoy dressing up!

Bring your camera and take pictures of the wedding party and the decorations.

One facility actually staged a Mock Wedding—minister and all. The residents got involved as part of the wedding party and had their pictures taken.

Reception

Now that the serving table is decorated, and the cake is finished it's time for the reception. Pop the cork on the champagne. Play romantic music and ask the residents to join in to sing. Maybe you'd like to take song requests for the sing-along.

If you have couples attending, find out how many years they've been married and honor them. For example: The ones married the longest, the ones married shortest, most recent anniversary, etc. Let them tell about their anniversary celebrations, or their honeymoons—that will be an interesting topic!

Now, you're ready to throw the bridal bouquet. Suggest that the residents who wish to, can sit in a circle (include wheelchair residents), put the bride in the middle. Have the groom cover the bride's eyes and when the music stops the bride should throw the bouquet.

Wedding Cake Recipe

Follow directions on a white cake mix for two 8-inch layers, and use three more cake mixes to make two 12-inch layers.

It takes $1^1/_2$ cake mixes to make a 12-inch layer, and 1 cake mix to make a 10-inch layer. Refer to my Picnics, Catering on the Move *cookbook, page 122 for a complete chart relating cake sizes to number of cake mixes.*

Let the residents mix the cake mix in a big bowl with a wooden spoon. It is very good exercise. Appoint one resident to break the eggs and add the oil and water. The residents can also grease and flour the baking pans (line the 12-inch pan bottom with wax paper, the cake will come out easier). Bake all cakes at 350 degrees.

For the 12-inch layers—let them bake for 50 minutes to one hour.

After the cakes are cooled slightly turn them out onto round cardboard to fit the size of each cake (don't forget to peel off the waxed paper from the 12-inch layer). You will need two 8-inch and two 12-inch cardboard rounds.

Refrigerate the cakes overnight.

Butter Cream Frosting

Yield: 5 pounds of frosting.

1	cup white margarine
$1^1/_2$	cups shortening
5	pounds powdered sugar
$^1/_2$	cup plus 2 tablespoons water
2	tablespoons almond flavoring
$^1/_2$	teaspoon salt

In a large quantity mixing bowl cream the shortening and margarine together. Add powdered sugar a little at a time alternately with the water and beat. Add the almond flavoring and salt and beat until smooth and creamy.

Starting with the 8-inch cakes:

To frost the cake, spread frosting over the bottom layer and smooth out with a spatula dipped in hot water. Place the second layer on top of the first layer and frost the sides and top. Smooth out again with hot-water spatula. Place the 8-inch cakes on a white 9-inch cake plate with four prongs on the bottom side. Pipe on a border with a number 28 tip. Repeat on the second layer.

12-inch cakes:

Place the 12-inch cake onto a 14-inch tray (don't forget to peel off the wax paper liner). Pipe on borders with the 28 tip. Place four clear cake risers one into each hole. Place these straight down into the cake, making sure they are centered. Place silk flowers in the middle of the cake. Place the 8-inch layers on top and place the cake topper on the top of the 8-inch layers and your cake is complete.

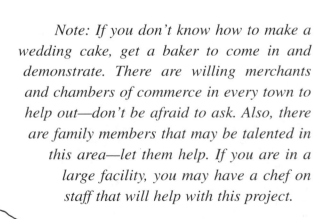

Note: If you don't know how to make a wedding cake, get a baker to come in and demonstrate. There are willing merchants and chambers of commerce in every town to help out—don't be afraid to ask. Also, there are family members that may be talented in this area—let them help. If you are in a large facility, you may have a chef on staff that will help with this project.

Flag Day Party

Flags are a good topic of conversation. Both men and women like to see flags and talk about the choices of design and colors. You can also sing patriotic songs and the national anthems of the various countries. Many of your residents have an ethnic background from a foreign country. It is interesting for them to see the flags of their ancestors' homeland.

I have an inflatable ball that has all the countries of the world printed on it like a globe. It is lightweight and easy to toss. It is good exercise for the residents. If you can find one, use it to toss to residents and have them find their homeland before they toss it on to the next person.

Alzheimer's patients will enjoy the colors of the flags and touching the fabric. Early stage Alzheimer's patients might know the shapes of the designs and be able to identify them for you.

For higher functioning residents display the national flags on a table. Hang up a colorful map displaying all the flags (these are like posters and should be available in your community).

Bake cupcakes and decorate them with a flag on a toothpick (available at party or paper stores). Pass the cakes around on a platter and have the residents identify the country the flag is from.

I encourage you to ask residents' families to help with the activities, or costs for supplies for the activities. Most families are happy to be involved with their loved one and will be eager to volunteer.

The men in your facility may be very knowledge about flag terminology. Use the trivia questions and word search exercises with this group. You can also use the flag exercise at the mens' luncheon.

You will be surprised how the residents get into this subject. Most folks don't really think much about flags. They see them wave and most do not recognize the majority of national flags. It is interesting to get a large globe or map of the world and identify the national flags of each continent. Flags are definitely a way of communication because as you study flags you will see that each one has symbols to express their history or feelings of the past. Flags also tell the story of war, promises of religions, political systems, and how states and countries came to be.

The American flag depicts freedom and liberty. Flags have been in existence for thousands of years. In the beginning, flags were only used by solders, priests, kings, and queens. But today, the poorest people have an attachment to their national flag and express this by flying their flag.

Many people refer to their flag as "the colours". It is a flag term and pertains to the colours of the flag.

Both flag colours and symbols have very deep meanings. There are common themes. Red frequently stands for revolution or courage of the heroes of liberation. Green is for hope, agriculture, the Islamic religion, and African heritage. Many countries use a plain background with a central design, and many also use horizontal or vertical strips. Stars are found on flags in every continent. Fierce animals and weapons suggest defense of the nation.

You can run off sheets of flags and discuss flag shapes and coats of arms with the residents. It depends on how much time and depth you want to go into with this activity. I found that residents were still discussing flags a week or two after we had the activity.

I usually serve dessert or treats at the end of an activity. It entices the residents' attendance! It is your choice.

Flag Word Search #1

```
C R O W N R D R E A D E T E D R H T I N W
A E W O R K R F A Z N T G W A T O Z X Y H
X D S L D F A G G C G C H Q E H R Q W Z E
C C R H G D G N L V H F H S A N S A R T A
R V T J I L O J E B R G M O D M E E X T T
O B H H H P N I J N T K A H R D M R T Y U
S J J N G U P K H M Y B E J G T A C V B N
S H C R E S C E N T M O O N B U N M E E T
C K B J T I E W M F L A M E O O T L D A D
E L V K H R W S T K A S T R I P E S I R T
R M N L G H E H O N X O V B D P U Q Z O R
T N K M F S V E R Y Z I C A S T L E A C N
Y G I K M D U J C Z R F R N U F E B I G Q
U F O E E S H N H E E V J I T J T K E E P
J U L F R Y D H D P W E A P O N S W Q A D
K T G T J O S B X O T S R S T A R S A S F
P A L M B R A N C H E S Y O U D A S D F M
```

Flag Word Search #1:

Stars	Lion	Weapons	Tree
Stripes	Sun	Crescent Moon	Horseman
Cross	Torch	Eagle	Crown
Anchor	Dragon	Wheat	Flame
Keys	Ship	Palm Branches	Castle

Flag Word Search #1 Answer Key

```
C R O W N R D R E A D E T E D R H T I N W
A E W O R K R F A Z N T G W A T O Z X Y H
X D S L D F A G C G C H Q E H R Q W Z E E
C C R H G D G N L V H F H S A N S A R T A
R V T J I L O J E B R G M O D M E E X T T
O B H H H P N I J N T K A H R D M R T Y U
S J J N G U P K H M Y B E J G T A C V B N
S H C R E S C E N T M O O N B U N M E E T
C K B J T I E W M F L A M E O O T L D A D
E L V K H R W S T K A S T R I P E S I R T
R M N L G H E H O N X O V B D P U Q Z O R
T N K M F S V E R Y Z I C A S T L E A C N
Y G I K M D U J C Z R F R N U F E B I G Q
U F O E E S H N H E E V J I T J T K E E P
J U L F R Y D H D P W E A P O N S W Q A D
K T G T J O S B X O T S R S T A R S A S F
P A L M B R A N C H E S Y O U D A S D F M
```

Flag Word Search #1 Answer Key:

Stars	Lion	Weapons	Tree
Stripes	Sun	Crescent Moon	Horseman
Cross	Torch	Eagle	Crown
Anchor	Dragon	Wheat	Flame
Keys	Ship	Palm Branches	Castle

Flag Word Search #2

```
W  S  C  R  J  F  U  I  S  J  M  F  B  A  S  E  H  U  F  S
A  D  O  V  C  H  L  J  K  T  N  N  G  V  Z  X  G  C  V  W
R  T  A  H  O  R  E  Y  C  V  A  Y  U  J  K  H  O  D  G  A
E  U  T  G  C  W  H  E  G  R  V  N  G  E  T  Y  N  F  G  L
N  B  O  B  K  S  R  O  T  Y  E  D  D  M  V  B  F  T  Y  L
S  A  F  N  A  C  T  H  I  H  X  S  J  B  S  E  L  H  A  O
I  N  A  M  D  W  F  A  B  S  C  T  T  L  A  R  O  A  S  W
G  N  R  J  E  T  V  T  F  Z  T  N  I  E  Z  T  N  L  D  T
N  E  M  U  Y  F  G  O  M  F  B  K  O  M  E  J  Q  F  F  A
Q  R  S  Y  C  O  L  O  U  R  S  L  J  Z  C  K  W  M  G  I
A  T  R  G  F  D  S  H  J  R  T  B  M  A  F  D  S  A  F  L
R  A  S  U  R  Q  U  A  R  T  E  R  P  J  C  L  Q  S  G  E
H  S  T  A  N  D  R  E  W  S  C  R  O  S  S  K  R  T  D  D
G  R  E  E  K  C  R  O  S  S  N  T  R  Y  D  Z  G  H  A  F
T  E  R  H  J  K  L  N  M  B  W  R  E  A  T  H  Y  A  S  L
Y  V  E  X  I  L  L  O  G  Y  E  O  R  H  A  C  P  T  D  A
N  H  J  K  M  E  R  C  H  A  N  T  F  L  A  G  O  S  B  G
K  F  I  E  L  D  E  R  C  A  N  T  O  N  V  B  N  M  T  Y
```

Flag Word Search #2:

Vexillogy	Field	Banner	Canton
Coat of Arms	Fly	Wreath	Emblem
War Ensign	Staff	Base	Crest
St. Andrew's Cross	Jack	Quarter	Colours
Half Mast	Stand	Gonflon	Greek Cross
Merchant Flag	Hoist	Cockade	Swallow-tailed Flag

Flag Word Search #2 Answer Key

```
W S C R J F U I S J M F B A S E H U F S
A D O V C H L J K T N N G V Z X G C V W
R T A H O R E Y C V A Y U J K H O D G A
E U T G C W H E G R V N G E T Y N F G L
N B O B K S R O T Y E D D M V B F T Y L
S A F N A C T H I H X S J B S E L H A O
I N A M D W F A B S C T T L A R O A S W
G N R J E T V T F Z T N I E Z T N L D T
N E M U Y F G O M F B K O M E J Q F F A
Q R S Y C O L O U R S L J Z C K W M G I
A T R G F D S H J R T B M A F D S A F L
R A S U R Q U A R T E R P J C L Q S G E
H S T A N D R E W S C R O S S K R T D D
G R E E K C R O S S N T R Y D Z G H A F
T E R H J K L N M B W R E A T H Y A S L
Y V E X I L L O G Y E O R H A C P T D A
N H J K M E R C H A N T F L A G O S B G
K F I E L D E R C A N T O N V B N M T Y
```

Flag Word Search #2 Answer Key:

Vexillogy	Field	Banner	Canton
Coat of Arms	Fly	Wreath	Emblem
War Ensign	Staff	Base	Crest
St. Andrew's Cross	Jack	Quarter	Colours
Half Mast	Stand	Gonflon	Greek Cross
Merchant Flag	Hoist	Cockade	Swallow-tailed Flag

Flag Terms:

Vexillogy—word for study of flags and their history. (Latin word is vexillum.)

Coat of Arms—figures forming the symbolic insignia of a nation, organization, family, or city.

   Elements of a coat of arms: crest, shield, wreath, helmet, supporters, compartment, and motto.

Ensign—a national flag displayed on a ship.

War Ensign—flag flown on a warship.

Civil Ensign—flag flown on a privately-owned vessel or cruise ship.

State Flag—flag flown on public buildings.

Civil Flag—is flown by private citizens on land.

State Ensign—flag flown on unarmed government vessels.

St. Andrew's Cross—is in the shape of an "x".

Greek Cross—has four equal arms.

Half-mast—flying the flag below the top of the flagstaff in sign of mourning.

Field—the background colour of a shield or flag.

Flag—a piece of cloth with different-sized shapes, colours, and symbols of a nation or city.

Fly—the outer edge of the flag.

Crest—the heraldic symbol above the wreath in a coat of arms.

Confalon—a swallow-tailed flag hanging from a horizontal bar attached to a staff.

Staff—the wood or metal mast that supports a flag.

Canton—a rectangular or square section of a flag or shield.

Compartment—the sustaining base for a shield.

Colours—a term used to denote a country's flag.

Jack—a flag flown at the bow of a ship that shows nationality.

Hoist—the measurement of the flag along the staff.

Quarter—divide the field of the flag or shield with horizontal and vertical lines placed in the center of both the length and width of the flag.

Base—lower portion of the shield in a coat of arms.

Charge—any figure, symbol, or emblem on the field of a flag or shield.

Cockage—a badge in the form of a ribbon rosette. This was a very popular political emblem in the nineteenth century.

Swallow Tail—used especially in the Scandinavian countries; it is the fly end of a flag, where a triangular portion has been cut out.

Scandinavian Cross—the vertical arms are closer to the staff of the flag.

Supporters—human or animal figures at the sides of a shield in a coat of arms.

Obverse—the more important side of a flag is the one visible when the flagstaff is to the left of the observer.

Motto—the saying on the bottom of the coat of arms.

Mantling—is the cloth which hung from the top of a knight's helmet.

Width—is the measurement of a flag made along the side of the staff.

Proportions—the width and length of a particular flag.

Flag and Geography Trivia
Circle the correct answer.

1. The oldest known flag was found at Khabis, Iran, and dates back to:
    a. 3000 B.C.   b. 1694   c. 1800

2. The only flag in the world that is not rectangular is the flag of:
    a. Nepal   b. Germany   c. United States

3. The St. Andrew's Cross is found on the:
    a. Spanish flag   b. Italian flag   c. United Kingdom of Great Britain and Northern Ireland flag

4. Two flags from Europe that are in a square shape are:
    a. France and Poland   b. Belgium and Switzerland   c. Greece and France

5. The following flag does not have a star:
    a. United States   b. Pakistan   c. India

6. The two countries that have "look-alike" flags are:
    a. United States and the United Kingdom   b. Cuba and Puerto Pico
    c. France and Belgium

7. Three countries found in Europe are:
    a. France, Belgium, and Poland   b. Iran, Egypt, and Japan
    c. Jamaica, Libya, and Sudan

8. Three countries found in Asia are:
    a. China, Japan, and Ethiopia   b. France, Italy, and Poland
    c. England, Russia, and China

9. The Chinese flag is:
    a. Purple with red stars b. Red with gold stars c. Red with five yellow stars

10. The following states are in South America:
    a. Brazil, Chile, and Peru   b. France, England, and Poland
    c. Iran, China, and Japan

11. The Virgin Islands are owned by:
    a. The United States   b. Spain   c. Great Britain

12. The flag of Liberia looks much like the:
    a. British flag   b. American flag   c. Polish flag

13. Some of the following countries are considered to be the Scandinavian countries:
    a. Norway, Finland, Sweden, and Scotland   b. Haiti, Jamaica, and Cuba
    c. Monaco, East Germany, and Austria

14. A country found in the Netherlands is:
    a. England   b. Holland   c. Asia

15. The name of the country that has a red maple leaf on its flag is:
    a. United States of America   b. South America   c. Canada

16. Canada is made up of the following:
    a. Provinces   b. Territories   c. Both of the above two answers
17. Some flags are designed in honor of:
    a. Presidents of countries   b. Queens of countries
    c. Both of the above two answers
18. The Polish flag has an eagle on its state arms dating back to:
    a. Thirteenth Century   b. Fifteenth Century   c. Nineteenth Century
19. Gibraltar is a peninsula on the southern coast of:
    a. France   b. Italy   c. Spain
20. Native Jamaicans are primarily:
    a. White   b. Black   c. None of the above
21. The flag of Switzerland bears a cross and is:
    a. Rectangular   b. Round   c. Square
22. The flag of Ireland is:
    a. Green, white, and orange   b. Red, green, and white
    c. Blue, green, and white
22. The following instrument has been adopted by the country of Ireland as an Irish symbol:
    a. Bagpipes   b. Harp   c. Flute
24. The country of Mautitus has a four-coloured flag of red, blue, yellow, and green and is found on which continent:
    a. Europe   b. Africa   c. Asia
25. The country of Egypt is found in:
    a. Asia   b. Europe   c. Africa
26. The following countries: Australia, Nauru, Kiribati, Guam, and New Zealand are considered the Oceania area and are located in the which of the following oceans:
    a. Atlantic   b. Pacific   c. None of the above
27. The total number of flags of the world is:
    a. 192   b. 193   c. 194

Answer Key:

1. a.	8. a.	15. c.	22. a.
2. a.	9. c.	16. c.	23. b.
3. c.	10. a.	17. c.	24. b.
4. b.	11. a.	18. a.	25. c.
5. c.	12. b.	19. c.	26. b.
6. b.	13. a.	20. b.	27. a.
7. a.	14. b.	21. c.	

Diagrams of Examples of Flag Layouts and Parts of Coat of Arms

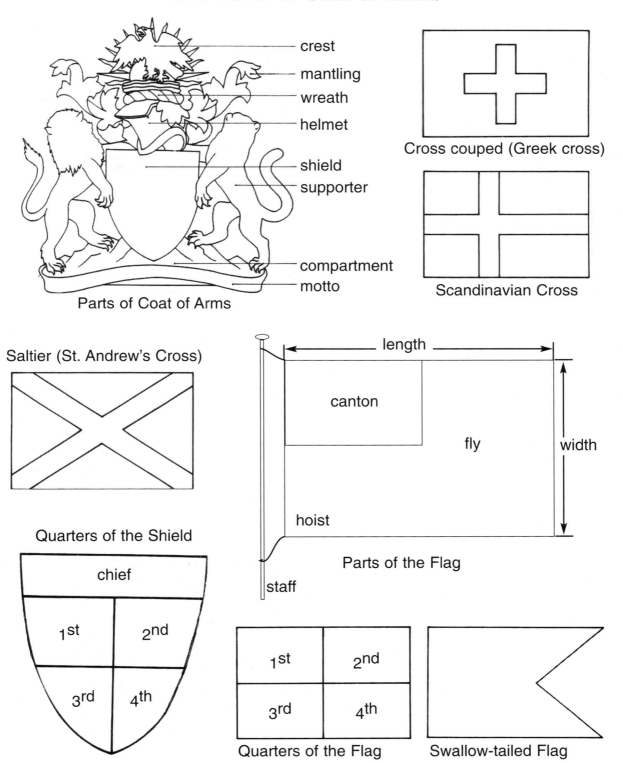

crest
mantling
wreath
helmet
shield
supporter
compartment
motto

Parts of Coat of Arms

Cross couped (Greek cross)

Scandinavian Cross

Saltier (St. Andrew's Cross)

Quarters of the Shield

chief

1st | 2nd

3rd | 4th

length

canton

fly

width

hoist

staff

Parts of the Flag

1st | 2nd

3rd | 4th

Quarters of the Flag

Swallow-tailed Flag

Selected Flags of the World

Please refer to the color section page 10-12 in the back of the book for flags.

United States of America:

The American flag has 50 white stars on the dark blue canton. The canton is a square section of the flag. There are 13 stripes to represent the 13 original states. Seven stripes are red and six are white. The first flag of the United States was made in 1776. The coat of arms dates to 1782. The American eagle holds an olive branch in one talon and 13 arrows in the other; these are symbols of peace and war.

France:

France uses three colours for its flag. They are vertical lines with blue on the left, white in the middle, and red on the right. These colours were used for the first time in 1794 during the French Revolution. White represents Joan of Arc, blue for Martin's cloak, and red for St. Denis and the imperial flag of Charlemagne.

Greece:

The Greek flag is made of a blue background canton with a white cross, and blue and white horizontal stripes. The blue and white colours were adopted during the Greek wars of independence and were confirmed in 1833. The blue and white were the colors of the Otto of Bavaria family. The cross shows the religious beliefs of Greece. The nine stripes is said to stand for the nine syllables in the translated Greek motto, "Liberty or Death".

Canada:

The flag of Canada has two vertical stripes of red on each side with a white vertical stripe in the middle. A red maple leaf is in the center of the white stripe. In the beginning Canada was made up of four provinces: Ontario, Quebec, Nova Scotia, and New Brunswick. This was considered the New Dominion in 1867. France owned Quebec in the early times, but it was taken by the British in 1763. Canada has 12 flags that denote the provinces and territories. Red and white were the heraldic colors of Canada. All the provinces and territories have arms and flags. They also have flags for their lieutenant governors. Canada did not have a distinctive national flag of its own until February of 1965. The modern coat of arms dates from 1921, and the motto is "From Sea to Sea".

West Germany:

West Germany's flag has three colours of horizontal stripes with the gold at the bottom, deep red in the middle, and black on the top. This flag was adopted in 1949. The colors were long associated with the pan-Germanic aspirations. They were used in the early nineteenth century in the uniforms of Baron Von Luitzow's famous Freikorps. Most of the countries on the Baltic coast have a swallow-tailed detail on their flags including Germany. Germany uses the black eagle for its state arms. The black is a symbol of authority from the Roman Empire.

Austria:

Austria's flag has two red horizontal stripes one at the top and the other at the bottom. The middle of the flag is white. The flag was adopted in 1945. The state arms has an eagle in the middle of the flag.

Poland:

Poland's flag has two horizontal stripes—half red and half white with the white on the top and the red on the bottom. The colours are also represented in the state arms. The eagle in the arms has been a Polish symbol since the thirteenth century and is white on a red shield.

Italy:

The Italian flag is a tri-colour of vertical stripes: green on the left, red on the right with white in the middle. Italy also has a state arms emblem and a war ensign. The Italian flag was designed by Napoleon during the Italian campaign of 1796. When the monarchy came to an end in 1946, the coat of arms was removed. The tri-colour replaced the older flag.

Denmark:

The Danish flag may be one of the oldest flags in the western world. It is said that Dannesbrog came from heaven to Vademar II during his campaign against the Estonians in 1219. The coat of arms dates back to the twelfth century. It is a red background with a white cross.

Ireland:

It was not until 1937 that Ireland was allowed to have its own president within the commonwealth. In 1949 Ireland became a republic. The Irish flag has three vertical stripes with the green on the left, white in the middle, and orange at the right. The flag was used as early as 1830 in honor of the French Revolution. The green symbolizes the Emerald Isle and its Catholic population. The orange symbolizes the Protestant religion, and comes from the colour of the House of Orange-Nassau. The white symbolizes the desire for peace between Catholics and Protestants. The harp has been an Irish symbol since the fifteenth century. No one really knows why the symbol was adopted.

Finland:

Finland became independent in 1917. The colours of the flag were adopted in 1918 and modified in 1978. The background is white with a blue cross. The white symbolizes snow and the blue is the sky. The coat of arms for Finland was granted in the sixteenth century when it became a grand duchy. The Aland Islands have their own flag with a blue background and yellow and red cross.

Sweden:

Sweden separated from Norway in 1905. In 1906 Sweden adopted their own flag. A similar flag was used by Gustav I in the sixteenth century. The background is blue with a gold cross. It is said that this was derived from the three gold crowns on a blue field, which made up Sweden's coat of arms in the fourteenth century. The swallowtail and the cross of the Swedish war flag depict the bonds that unite Sweden with other Scandinavian and Baltic countries.

Norway:

Norway's flag has a red background with a blue cross laying over the white Dannebrog cross. This flag is still used by independent Norway. Norway was under the control of Denmark from 1397 to 1814. The Norwegian lion was introduced into the flag when Norway was united with Sweden. The royal coat of arms has a golden lion surrounded by the collar of the Order of St. Olaf. The lion holds St. Olaf's battleaxe and has the crown. These two symbols were introduced in the thirteenth century.

United Kingdom of Great Britain and Northern Ireland:

This flag is red, white, and blue. The Union Jack consists of the superimposed crosses of St. George, St. Andrew, and St. Patrick. These saints are the patron saints of England, Scotland, and Ireland. St. George's cross is red on white. This was adopted by the English at the end of the thirteenth century. The symbol was carried during the wars against the Welsh and also during the Seventh Crusade. The white saltire on blue became the Scottish banner in the thirteenth century. The union of the kingdoms of Scotland and England was created in 1606 under James I. The St. Patrick's cross of red on a white field originated from the Fitzgerald family. Ireland was raised to the status of a kingdom in 1801 and the St. Patrick's cross was added to the flag. Notice the royal arms; the use of the three ensigns at sea—red, blue, and white—goes back to the time when the Royal Navy divided into three squadrons. Today, the red ensign is flown by merchant ships, the white ensign is reserved for the Royal Navy. The blue ensign is flown by some merchant ships commanded by reserve officers and unarmed government ships.

Switzerland:

The flag of Switzerland is the only square flag in the world. It is a contemporary chronicler that shows an urgent need to unite the Helvetic armies under one banner. This was accomplished in 1339 at the Battle of Laupen. The solders were marked with the Holy Cross, which was in white against the red shield. This flag was adopted officially in 1848. The civil ensign is flown on navigable rivers and lakes.

Nepal:

Nepal is the only nation in the world with a national flag that is not rectangular in shape. The sun and moon are symbols of hope, so the country may live as long as the two astral bodies. The entire flag is outlined with a blue strip. The background is red. The Nepalese landscape with the Himalayas in the background is the chief feature of the coat of arms. There is a white cow, a pheasant, and rhododendrons. There is an inscription on the bottom of the arms that, when translated, says: "The Fatherland is More Important Than the Kingdom of Heaven".

Cuba:

The flag of Cuba was adopted in 1902. It has a red triangle on the left side, with a white star. There are three horizontal blue stripes and two white stripes in between the blue stripes. The red triangle proclaims liberty, fraternity, equality, and the blood shed in the conquest and defense of freedom. The five-pointed star represents the country's independence. The blue and white stripes stand for purity of the revolution. General Narcisio Lopez tried to free the island from the Spanish colonial rule.

Puerto Pico:

The Puerto Rican flag has a blue triangle to the left with a five-pointed star. There are three red horizontal stripes and two white stripes in between the red stripes. The national flag was recognized in 1952. The United States and Puerto Rican flag are flown side-by-side. Puerto Rico was one of the first sites of Spanish settlement in the Western Hemisphere. Puerto Rico now has its own internal government.

Haiti:

Haiti is located in the western part of the island of Hispaniola. It became an independent republic in 1804. The first flag came from the heritage of France. But, in June of 1964, the flag took the vertical lines of black and red. In 1807 President Alexander Sabes Petion designed the coat of arms. The palm tree stands for liberty. The motto, *Unity Gives Strength*, is a reference of the spirit of cooperation between blacks and mulattoes in the struggle for independence.

Jamaica:

The Jamaican flag has a yellow St. Andrew's cross with two green triangles—one at the top and another at the bottom of the intersection of the cross. Spain owned Jamaica. Black stands for the past and the obstacles the country overcame, while the green stands for agriculture. Pineapples are found on Queen Elizabeth's personal flag for Jamaica.

Libya:

The flag of Libya is green. Originally the flag had stripes of gold and a coat of arms in the center. In 1977, the late President Anwar Sadat of Eqypt went to Israel to make plans for a peace treaty. But Qaddafi rejected the flag, so Libya used a plain green flag. The green is a symbol of the national religion, Islam. The color of the flag is also a symbol of the Green Revolution. The coat of arms of Libya shows the name of the country in Arabic script, and a hawk with the color of the country. The hawk is the totem of the Quarish tribe.

Sierra Leone:

The flag of Sierra Leone was accepted on April 27, 1961, when the country became independent. This flag has three horizontal stripes. Blue is at the bottom, green is at the top, and white is in the in the middle. The green stands for agriculture and the hilly countryside of Sierra Leone; white is for peace and justice; blue stands for the Atlantic Ocean, which washes the coast. The state arms has two lions with the saying, *Unity, Freedom, and Justice.* The arms is a definite reference to the name of the country and its past connection with Great Britain. The wavy blue lines and the three torches express the sea and freedom achieved through knowledge. The two palm trees refer to the importance of palm oil in the national economy.

Sudan:

Sudan is in the northeastern area of Africa. The Sudanese flag has three horizontal stripes. Black is at the bottom, white in the middle, and red at the top of the flag. A triangle of green is on the left side. While Sudan achieved independence in 1956, the official flag was not adopted until May 20, 1970. It was patterned after the flag of Egypt. Black stands for the name of the country (Sudan means black in Arabic). Green stands for prosperity (it is also a Islamic color). White stands for peace, and red denotes socialist revolution and patriot blood. The state arms is a secretary bird, which also appears on the presidential flag. There is an inscription on the state arms meaning *Victory is Ours.*

China:

The Chinese flag is red with one large star and four smaller stars around the large star. All the stars are yellow. The five-pointed star stands for communism. The number five also stands for wholeness and perfection in Chinese philosophy. The four smaller stars represent the four classes of workers: agriculture, industry, white collar, and management. The red also stands for the five colours of old Chinese flags: blue, white, black, and yellow are the other four colours.

Iraq:

The flag of Iraq has three green stars on a white horizontal stripe through the middle of the flag. The top stripe is red, and the bottom stripe is black.

Israel:

The flag of Israel is inspired by the talith, the Jewish prayer shawl. This flag was created by the Zionist movement. The flag has a white background with two medium blue stripes—one at the top and the other at the bottom. There is a six-pointed star of blue in the middle of the flag. The state arms has a seven-branched candelabra of the Temple of Jerusalem, there are also olive branches.

Japan:

The flag of Japan has an entire white background with a red disk. This symbol shows the rising sun of the land, it has been used for more than 1,000 years. The imperial arms consists of a stylized chrysanthemum with 16 petals.

Peru:

It is believed that General Jose de San Martin selected the colors for the flag of Peru. The General saw flamingos with white breasts and red wings in the air during the war against Spain in 1820, and he felt that those should be the colors of liberty. The flag has three vertical lines. The two outside stripes are red, with the middle stripe being white. The present flag was adopted in 1825. The state arms includes a cornucopia, llama, and cinchona tree.

Brazil:

Brazil's flag has a green background with a yellow diamond with a globe in the middle. The green and yellow were used in the first decades of the nineteenth century. The coat of arms was established in 1889. The stars in the arms stand for the 22 states and territories of Brazil. A star was added for every territory that became a state. The garland contains coffee and tobacco leaves.

Australia:

The first national flag of Australia was hoisted in 1901. It is almost identical to the one approved by Queen Elizabeth when she visited the country in 1954. The flag is British blue ensign with six white stars. The stars have seven points. Five of the stars represent the Southern Cross. The state arms is very elaborate with a kangaroo and emu (the national animals). The black swan represents Western Australia; the lion is for Tasmania; the Maltese Cross for Queensland; and the shrike for Southern Australia.

New Zealand:

The flag of New Zealand has a blue background with red and white cross. This cross is a variation of the British blue ensign. There are four stars representing the constellation of the Southern Cross. The stars are red with a white outline.

Western Daze Party

Meet with your facility administrator to get your Western Daze Party budget approval. If possible, allow funds to pay for entertainers such as a guitar player and singer, or a square dance caller. If approved, schedule the entertainers (find out if you need to pay part of their fee "up front"). *You will need 30-60 days advance planning.*

A month before the activity call a meeting with residents and the dietary department to select a western menu. Select items that your residents can help prepare—they will enjoy the preparation! Check with the nursing department on food limitations of some of the residents. Maybe special trays can be made up for those with limitations. Also, notify any volunteers that may be helping the residents of any food limitations. You don't want people to be upset, or not able to participate in this event.

Talk with regular volunteers and family members to have people available to grill hot dogs and to help the residents get to the picnic area.

Meet with your maintenance staff and schedule help to set up tables, chairs, and grills. If you need extra tables ask your volunteers to bring some, or set up rentals from a church, school, or rental center.

Publicize the party in the monthly activity calendar, the family newsletter, staff break room, posters, local newspaper, flyers around the facility, and bulletin boards. Be sure you get a count of people attending, maybe you need to send RSVP invitations to family members.

Suggested Entertainment:

A Petting Zoo. Is there one in your community that can bring some animals? Maybe a farmer? Contact your humane society, maybe their members can help with it.

Contact a guitar player and singer. Are there talented family members, or staff that would like to perform? Maybe a high school or middle school music group?

A square dance caller will definitely add excitement to your Western Daze activity. Inform your staff and volunteers they will need to help residents with the square dancing. This is something even the residents in wheelchairs can participate in.

Western Daze Party!!!

Day:

Date:

Time:

Where:

See ya' all there!

BE THERE FOR THE FUN

Penny Scramble,

Singing,

Storytelling,

Horseshoe,

Western Dancing,

Soft Drinks, Dessert,

and a Discussion on Decorating

for a Western Picnic.

Menu

Barbecued Pork Riblet Sandwiches

✫

Hot Dogs and Buns

✫

Potato Salad

✫

Potato Chips

✫

Calico Baked Beans

✫

Deviled Eggs

✫

Watermelon

✫

Pickle Relish, Ketchup, Mustard, Chopped Onions,
Pickles, and Olives

✫

Buffalo Chip Cookies

✫

Drinks

Recipes:

Barbecued Pork Riblet Sandwiches

Place 4-ounce riblets on a large cookie sheet. Baste with commercial, bottled barbecue sauce. Cover with foil and bake at 350 degrees for 45 to 60 minutes.

Watch the ribs carefully so they don't dry out, or burn. Your dietary department can take charge of this duty.

Your dietary department can also order individual size packages of potato chips for your picnic. They usually come 60 packages to a case.

Potato Salad

Yield: 40 servings or 12$\frac{1}{2}$ pounds.

10	pounds potatoes, cooked, peeled, diced
7	hard-cooked eggs (reserve 2 eggs for garnish)
2	cups diced celery
$\frac{1}{3}$	cup diced onion

Dressing:

6	cups mayonnaise
$\frac{1}{4}$	cup distilled vinegar
3	tablespoons yellow mustard
2	tablespoons plus 2 teaspoons sugar
$\frac{3}{4}$	teaspoon salt
$\frac{3}{4}$	teaspoon pepper

Garnish:

2	hard-cooked eggs, peeled and sliced
	paprika
	dehydrated parsley

Cook the potatoes in their jackets until tender. Pierce with a fork to check for doneness. When cool, peel and cut the potatoes. Dice 5 hard-cooked eggs. Reserve 2 eggs for garnish. Dice the celery and onion. Mix all ingredients.

In a large bowl mix all dressing ingredients until smooth and creamy. Add the dressing mixture to the potato mixture. When thoroughly mixed place in two serving bowls. Place one peeled, sliced, hard-cooked egg on top of each salad. Sprinkle with paprika and parsley.

You may substitute low-fat mayonnaise if you wish.

Resident Involvement:

Residents can help with peeling the potatoes and eggs. Maybe some can even help with dicing the celery and onion. A couple of residents can measure and mix the dressing. Of course, you need to plan for volunteers or staff members to supervise each one or two residents.

Calico Beans

Yield: 45-50 servings.

2	cans each (15.8-ounces each) great northern beans, lima beans, pinto beans
1	can (3 pounds 5 ounces) baked beans
2	pounds ground beef
1	pound bacon
$3/4$	cup diced onion
$1/2$	cup brown sugar
1	cup ketchup
2	tablespoons vinegar
2	tablespoons yellow mustard

Drain and rinse all the beans and combine in a full-size steam pan.

Brown ground beef and drain. Fry the bacon until crisp and drain and crumble. Fry onions in the bacon drippings and drain. Add the beef, bacon, onion, brown sugar, ketchup, vinegar, and yellow mustard to the beans. Cover with foil and bake at 350 degrees for 30 to 35 minutes.

Resident Involvement:

Maybe some of your residents can open and rinse the beans, place them in the baking pan, and mix them when all ingredients are together.

Deviled Eggs

Yield: 50 deviled eggs.

25	hard-cooked eggs
$1^1/4$	cups salad dressing
1	tablespoon lemon juice
$1/2$	teaspoon salt
$1/2$	teaspoon pepper
2	teaspoons sugar
1	tablespoon yellow mustard
$1/2$	teaspoon Worcestershire sauce

Hard-cook the eggs. When cool, peel eggs and cut in half, lengthwise. Scoop out the yolks. Beat the yolks in a 5-quart mixer until they are fine particles. Add salad dressing and beat until smooth. Add the seasonings and mix again until smooth.

Insert cake tube number 1E into a 12-inch pastry bag. Fill the bag $^3/_4$ full with the egg mixture. Fill each egg half. Garnish with paprika and parsley.

The cake tube will give the deviled egg a professional touch.

Buffalo Chip Cookies
Yield: $2^1/_2$ dozen cookies.

1	cup butter softened
1	cup shortening
4	eggs
1	pound brown sugar
2	cups granulated sugar
1	teaspoon vanilla
1	teaspoon almond flavoring
4	cups flour
2	teaspoons baking powder
2	teaspoons baking soda
2	cups quick oatmeal
2	cups rice krispies
1	cup chopped almonds, walnuts, or pecans
1	package (6 ounces) white chocolate chips
1	cup coconut

Preheat the oven to 350 degrees.

Combine the butter and shortening until creamy. Add the sugars and flavorings and mix until creamy and smooth. Blend in the flour, baking powder, and baking soda; then blend in the cereals, nuts, chips, and coconut.

Using a $^1/_4$ cup ice cream scoop, scoop out cookies and place 6 per ungreased cookie sheet (12 if you have a commercial baking sheet). They will spread. Bake for 15 minutes. Let the cookies cool on the pan for five minutes before removing.

Work with your dietary department to get the cookies baked during one of their down times. If they have a commercial oven, maybe they can bake them all at one time.

Miscellaneous Picnic Menu Items

Purchase a number 10 can of dill pickle spears and 4 (16-ounces each) cans of large, black olives. A number 10 can of pickles should contain about 75 pieces.

Purchase a large watermelon. Wash and cool. Cut into wedges and place on a tray the day of the party. A 23-pound watermelon will yield 128 3 x 4-inch slices; 50 pieces 8 inches long should fit on a 16-inch tray. If you are good with the knife, you may want to slice the watermelon in front of the residents. They will enjoy watching!

You may want to purchase picnic paper or plastic plates, cups, and plastic silverware for your picnic. Or see if you can use the dishes and silverware from your dining room.

Don't forget the coffeepot and something for a cold drink. Your dietary department can help with these items, also.

Coffee Chart

Regular Strength Coffee:

Water in cups:	20	30	40	50	60	70	80	90	100
Coffee in cups:	$1^1/_4$	$1^1/_2$	2	$2^1/_2$	3	$3^1/_2$	4	$4^1/_2$	5

Time to cook coffee in a 100-cup coffeemaker:

Cups:	20	30	40	50	60	70	80	90	100
Minutes:	20	25	30	35	40	45	50	55	60

Check the coffee before you leave to set up the picnic area to make sure it is perking properly. If you plan to plug it in at the picnic locate an extension cord and electrical outlet. If there is no electricity available at the picnic site you will need to transfer the coffee into insulated carriers with a spigot. These will not keep the coffee as hot as a coffeepot.

Tip: Clean out the bottom of the coffeepot, especially the hole where the stem fits. Otherwise, the coffee does not perk properly. Use cream of tartar with water and perk to clean the coffeepot. There are coffeepot cleaners on the market, but they are expensive. Use the long thin brush that comes with the pot to clean the tube.

Decorations

The day of the picnic decorate the buffet table with a red checked tablecloth. (You will need two 8-foot tables for your picnic. We had so much food at our picnic that we needed *three* tables!) Use a horse and cowboy hat for table decorations. You can place the individual potato chip bags around the hat brim.

Other decorations you may want to use include: covered wagon, cowboy, cowboy boots. If you don't have them yourself, ask your volunteers to help with finding these things.

A day or two before your picnic, check again with your entertainers to remind them to come and what time you need them. It would be nice if you would also include them in the picnic. Plan to have the musical entertainment immediately after lunch when everyone is gathered together and they don't need to gather again. The petting zoo and square dance can follow the music.

You might also plan a watermelon seed-spitting contest. It can be pretend if you are concerned about the residents swallowing the seeds.

Father's Day Luncheon

In most care facilities, the women outnumber the men. I've tried to have activities that will reach out to the men, as well as the women.

We had a Father's Day Luncheon especially for the men. I contacted the dietary department and arranged for the mens' luncheon to be delivered at noon to the classroom. I covered the tables with tablecloths and centerpieces. We had sent special invitations to all the men residents to come to the classroom for their lunchtime. I supplied non-alcoholic beer and wine to celebrate the occasion.

My neighbor was a deacon in our church. He came and had lunch with the men and gave a little talk on what it means to be a Father, since he had six children he had some experience! He was very good with the residents. He got them talking and reminiscing about happenings in their own families with children and grandchildren.

I'm sure you know someone in your community, or a resident's family member, who could supply an interesting and interactive program for your men residents.

Paul Bunyan Breakfast for Men

Menu

Lumber Camp Sunrise Orange Juice

Lumberjack Pancakes with Forest Maple Syrup

Sawmill Choice Eggs

Timberline Jack's Potatoes

Buck's Bacon and Sausage

Hungry John's Sugar Donuts

He-man Toast and Wild Berry Jelly

Mountain Grown Coffee, Tea, and Ice Water

There were only 15 men in the facility where I worked. The majority of men did attend this activity. We did a breakfast once a month. Since we were a fairly small group we met in a small kitchen area. You probably have a small area in your facility you could use for your mens' group. We always supplied a daily newspaper so the men could keep up with current events and sports scores. (This is a good conversation starter.) The men liked the idea that they could choose what they wanted to eat at our breakfasts, and also they could have their eggs the way they liked them best.

We advertised the event each month. If you need to know what quantities to prepare for your mens' breakfast, you may take their menu requests a day or two before the event. However, we found sometimes they changed their mind after they got to breakfast. Just have a little extra prepared, and it won't be a big deal if someone wants pancakes instead of eggs, or both.

We always set up the tables family style and let the men help themselves. But we waited until they arrived to do the eggs and toast to order—just like downtown! It took three of us to prepare and serve our mens' breakfast.

We worked with the CNAs to make sure the men were up and dressed, so they could attend this activity. For the most part they were great at getting the men ready and to the breakfast.

This is a great event for the men.

Make sure the men can feed themselves, or try to find volunteers to help those who can't. Also, check their diets to make sure the food is within any special dietary needs.

A Father's Day Fishing Trip with Grandchildren

We contacted residents' families to see if they could locate and bring fishing poles for their fathers and grandfathers. One of our volunteers even brought her children along to help. The people enjoyed the children. Of course, invite the residents' grandchildren!

We hired a bus to transport the residents. We were close to a river so it wasn't a long ride.

We packed sandwiches, fruit, cookies, and drinks for each resident. Someone brought a small tent for shade in case anyone got too much sun. (Check to see if the residents may have a sun hat they can bring with them.) We also brought chairs for the ones who weren't in wheelchairs. We had purchased bait and the children helped the residents bait their hooks and threw out the lines, they also took the fish off the hook for the lucky ones who caught something.

Be sure you don't do this activity on an overly hot day, you don't want anyone to get sick from too much heat or sun. The people relaxed and enjoyed the day. When we returned to the facility those who had stayed home were eager to hear about the fishing expedition.

Don't forget to take pictures!

Petting Zoo

We were able to contact a gentleman that has a petting zoo at his ranch. He came with donkeys, horses, and goats and set up a petting zoo on our terrace. (See page 13 in the color section.)

In the beginning, only a few residents came to see the animals. However, the buzz got around and many came later with several family members or friends.

There are always residents who say they can't come to an activity because they don't feel good today, or are too busy, or just don't feel like it. This day was different! Those people were wheeling themselves in to see the animals. They all petted the goats and fussed over the animals.

The administrator came up to me and said, "What are you going to do next? I can't believe how the residents are so excited about the animals."

I took a lot of pictures and the entire facility enjoyed the day. The workers and family members came with the residents, too. Just *dare to be different* to get your residents involved. You will be successful. Continue to keep in mind you need to play to the interests of every resident to reach a high degree of success in your activity program.

Square Dance Party

See page 13 in the color section for a Square Dancing Party photo!

If you don't know anyone who calls square dancing, ask around at your facility and community and check the Yellow Pages® in the telephone directory. Square dancing is quite popular in my area.

Assemble your residents in a large area (maybe move the tables and chairs back in the dining room). Enlist the help of staff and family members to push the wheelchairs around. Some residents just enjoyed watching—but some wanted to get in there and dance. Our caller and his wife showed the residents the steps.

We had an hour of great music and fun. Some of our residents recalled square dancing in their younger days. Get them talking among themselves and sharing good memories.

After the dance we served punch.

This was an easy event to organize and was enjoyed by all.

Pasta Art Project

The purpose of this project is to learn the names of the various pastas on the market and also to taste one kind of pasta of their choice. The Alzheimer's residents enjoyed the spaghetti.

I got the cardboard and wallpaper at no cost. I asked my local home decorating store to save old wallpaper books. I used cottage cheese and non-dairy whipped topping containers for the various kinds of pasta.

Supplies needed:
Cardboard.
An oval-shaped pattern.
Wallpaper.
Glue Stick.
Multi-purpose Glue.
Scissors.
Variety of ribbons.

Variety of pastas such as: sea shells (large and small) rigatoni, pasta bows, spaghetti, mostaccioli, elbow macaroni, wagon wheels, whole-wheat noodles. A variety of shapes makes interesting designs for the projects.

Place pastas in a variety of containers within arm's reach of the residents seated around the table. Place scissors, glue, and wallpaper books on each table. Gather the residents around the table.

Run off extra patterns so each resident can have one. Cut out the pattern and place it on the cardboard, trace around the pattern and cut out the cardboard following the oval pattern. Choose 2 pieces of wallpaper and trace the pattern on them. Cut out the wallpaper. Using a glue stick, glue the wallpaper on each side of the cardboard backing. Select the desired shapes of pasta, arrange on the oval picture, and glue in place.

You can hang the decoration up by putting a hole through the picture and using yarn for a hanger, or you can buy a frame to fit the picture and frame it.

The day before the party we spent time discussing the various kinds of pasta, and I made a large poster board with the samples glued on so they learned all the different types. I also boiled some wheat noodles, added butter, pasta seasoning, garlic, and onion. They enjoyed the good smells, and eating the pasta, of course!

Measurements for Projects Pictured in Color Section:
Square = $4^1/_2$ x $4^1/_2$ inches with fish and sea shell shapes.
Oblong = 7 x 11 inches, farm picture is a piece of wallpaper.
Chicken scene = 4 x 7 inches, with top corners cut diagonally.
Pasta spaghetti picture = $5^1/_2$ x 11 inches.

Pattern for the Pasta Art Project

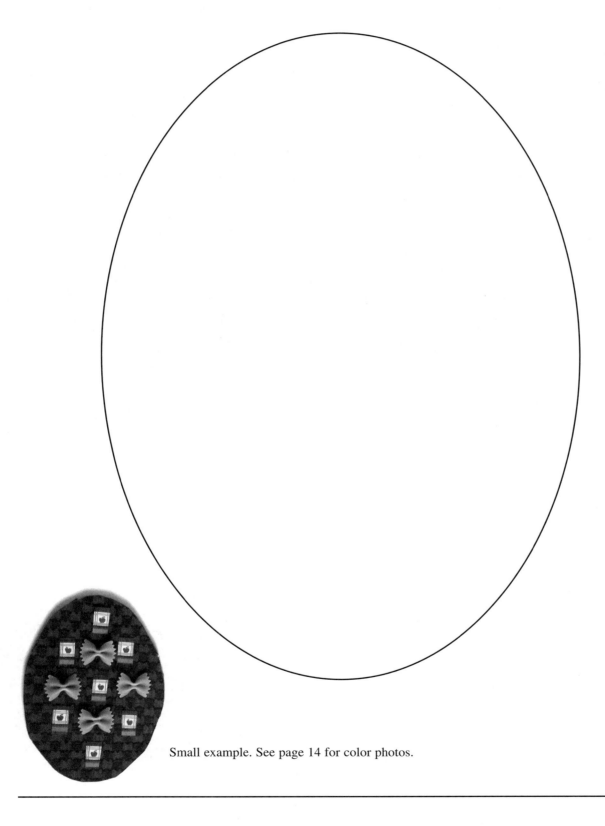

Small example. See page 14 for color photos.

Residents' Special Days

Sometimes your residents will have "special days", such as a 90th birthday, a 60th wedding anniversary, etc. It's nice if, on times like this, you can take them and their friends at the facility out to a restaurant for lunch or coffee. Of course, their family would also like to attend this special occasion. Our residents were allowed to order from the menu (this is special in itself!). We always sang "Happy Birthday" or whatever fit the occasion, congratulated them, and took pictures. The residents are able to socialize in a different environment and this was always a joyful success.

A Shopping Field Trip and Sandwich Lunch

Contact one of your local discount stores and make arrangements to bring your residents for a shopping trip. Most of the larger stores will have staff members to help your residents with their shopping and even push their wheelchairs. If your store doesn't have such folks, contact your regular volunteers or family members and see if they are available to help. You will also need nursing assistants to help with bathroom duty.

We took the residents' sandwich orders when we first arrived at the store and got the order started with the lunch counter so it would be ready when we were ready to eat. After eating we helped the residents checkout their purchases. Everyone had a great time—being able to go out and shop.

I was amazed at how little the residents bought for themselves. They bought little gifts for their grandchildren. One lady had been given money and she was able to purchase new slacks and a blouse. This was a big deal to her and made her day!

This event was a blessing for me. Now you know how little it takes to make the elderly happy. Yes, it is a big deal to please them and serve them with love!

Time is My Friend
by Pat Nekola

Make the most of time each day.
For as long as you live,
When asked about time you can say
Time is my invisible friend, come what may.

For one more birthday
The song remains the same,
With another year unfolding,
I have another year's memories to gain.

Cherish the seven days a week.
Relish the seasons, and garden's bounty—
Full of pretty flowers and crisp vegetables,
Always beautiful—never dowdy.

Greet the days and months passing by,
Full of life and cheer.
All the happy memories
You'll always hold dear.

Watch the birds,
Feed the fish,
Pet the dog,
And fill the cat's dish.

Hug your family,
Read a favorite poem,
Seek comfort from a homily,
Be happy with life, whatever will come.

Time tells the past and present,
What the future holds unknown to us.
Be hopeful that the time left on Earth
Will be full of surprises—so never fuss.

As long as there is time,
Hold that invisible friend in your heart.
With the guidance of our Lord,
Each day is a gift until we depart!

Time for a Friend

by Sue Schmitzer

Day by day by day,
Time moves us gently along.
As we grow older,
Some of us will thoughtfully say:

Time is our every loyal friend,
Always constant, always measured.
The calendar bookmarks the days and unfolds the months,
Stacking them up behind us marking yet another year's end.

Relish the seasons and the bounties they provide,
From flower-filled gardens to vegetable harvests;
From colorful carpets of leaves underfoot,
To the sparkle reflected off a snowy hillside.

Pet the dog; run your fingers through his thick fur.
Watch the birds; feed the fish; hear the frog croak.
Follow the butterfly fluttering from flower to flower.
Bend down to the cat and serenely absorb his soft gentle purr.

Treasure your loved ones with hugs to your family,
Read that novel you put away on the bookshelf,
Lean back in your chair and listen to the music you enjoy.
Seek the comfort, when needed, from a familiar homily.

Enjoy the months, one-by-one, as they pass quickly by.
Each week is an original, each day is unique.
There will be sad times—there will be bad times,
But it is the happy times that carry us, and on which we rely.

Time can explain the Past and define the Present.
But the future, looming ahead, is unknown to most.
Proceed optimistically knowing that the time left on earth
Will be unpredictably filled with surprises ever so pleasant.

Time is immortal, always a friend close to our heart.
It surrounds and engulfs us like the water in the womb,
Buoyed by guidance from our Lord and Master above.
Best of all, time creates the gift of memories, to be cherished after we part.

It's All About Time Party

(See colored photos of clocks in the colored section pages 5 and 6.)

People through all the ages were aware of time. They used the stars, moon, and sun to help tell time. Time has always been a precious commodity to mankind.

Remember: "A Stitch in Time Saves Nine".

People have always watched the moon change from full, to half, to crescent, and even oval. The moon and sun helped primitive man tell time.

It was the Greeks and Romans that gave us the name "calendar". Other cultures used various methods to calculate time.

Julius Caesar worked at making a calendar that would be the same each year. He forged ahead some others on this project, but never got it completed.

Time dates back to the Romans. They invented a calendar in 753. It is believed that the legendary King Romulus was responsible for the calendar.

The Aztec calendar had 18 months with 20 days per month and an additional 5 days to make up the year. Within the 365-day calendar they had 260 days for the religious calendar. This calendar was used for a 52-year cycle.

The Babylonians divided their year into 7-day weeks. They worshiped when there was sun and moon. Their lunar calendar was 354 days. There were 12 alternating months of 29 and 30 days.

The Chinese are considered the oldest continuous civilization in the world. China uses the Gregorian calendar today. There is still the ancient, traditional lunar-solar calendar. This determines the Chinese New Year and special Chinese events.

Egyptian Calendar

The Egyptians had a 360-day solar calendar. There were 12 months to the year and 30 days to each month. They added 5 days to the last month of the year to make it come out. Their high priest would not allow the people to correct the calendar with a leap year, as a result the calendar was not in line with the seasonal flooding.

During the French Revolution religious holidays and Sundays were taken away from the calendar. This calendar had 12 months. Five extra days were added to make up 365 days. Napoleon Bonaparte got rid of this type of calendar in 1806 and went back to the Gregorian calendar.

Gregorian Calendar

In the sixteenth century it was very obvious the Julian calendar was a problem for the Catholic Church. Easter was to be celebrated the day the sun crosses the equator and should be celebrated in the spring. It was Pope Gregory XIII who ordered the calendar to be changed to correct the mistakes. He kept New Year's on January 1, but he did not want to observe leap year every four years.

Two hundred years went by before England and Germany would accept the Gregorian calendar. Russia did not accept this calendar until 1918. Almost the entire world accepts the Gregorian calendar today.

Hebrew Calendar

For many years the Hebrew calendar was based on the lunar month. When they were captured by the Babylonians in 586 B.C. they did adopt a lunar-solar calendar like their captors. For the Hebrew (Shabbat) or (day of rest) and the Babylonians came to a calendar of a 7-day week and 24-hour days.

Islamic Calendar

The Islam religion is very strong with about 500 million believers. There was a prophet called Mohammed (570-632) that taught there was only one God, Allah. The Islamic year had 354 days and 12 months. They also had 7-day weeks. The Moslems ended their day at sundown, just like the Jews. The Moslem world uses the Islamic calendar.

Julian Calendar

Julius Caesar ruled in 49 B.C. He had trouble getting March to fall in springtime. The farmers disregarded his calendar because of the planting season, Caesar asked a Greek astronomer to put together a new calendar using a 365-day solar year. Every fourth year there would be a leap year in February, the other three years would have 365 days. Over a 300-year period the calendar developed an error because they didn't observe the leap years.

Mayan Calendar

The Mayan people had symbols called hieroglyphs to show an idea. They did not have a written language. They used a solar calendar—actually they had two calendars. One was called the xiuhmolphilli and the other was the haab. This calendar was 365 days long with 18 months of 20 days each. Five extra days were added to make up the 19th month.

Roman Calendar

Romulus invented a calendar of 305 days. His calendar was only 10 months long. Then Numa Pompilius (the second king of Rome) decided to add two more months to the calendar (Januarius and Februarius, or as we know them—January and February.) While Numa ruled his calendar became unreliable. He had labeled his calendar with the Roman numerals I to XII.

World Calendar

The Gregorian calendar was considered fairly accurate. In 1930 a world calendar was designed to be exact for each year. Every year started on a Sunday. Each quarter contained 3 months. One of the problems with this calendar was, there were religious groups that used the lunar calendar. They were very strict about observing their holy days.

The world calendar of 1930 went from January through December. The weekdays were Sunday through Saturday. Originally there were 30 days in February and the leap year day every fourth year was in June.

Time Trivia

- Name the pope that instructed the Catholic Church to use the leap year cycle in 1582. (Pope Gregory XIII)
- What day in February was George Washington really born? (February 11, 1731)
- What day do Americans celebrate George Washington's birthday? (February 22)
- What were the names of George Washington's parents? (Augustine and Mary)
- Which Roman ruler marked much of the calendar by month's names? (Julius Caesar)
- Which pope in the 1500s was responsible for the Gregorian calendar? (Pope Gregory XIII)
- Which religion persisted in using the moon instead of the sun for telling time? (Islamic)
- A 12-month cycle with 28 to 31 days per month is called a? (Calendar)
- Before a 7-day week was established there were 8 days used by what group? (Romans)
- The calendar used today in most western countries including the USA. (Gregorian)
- In B.C. times people used what resources to tell time? (Moon and Sun)
- Not only did the Roman Julius Caesar make the calendar in 45 BC, but also a Greek-Egyptian designed a calendar. What was his name? (Sorsigeners)
- The monks also worked on calendars. Where did they live? (Monastaries)
- Which holiday in the spring did the scholars in early times have the most trouble placing in the calendar? (Easter)
- In order to make the cycle of days balance out, it was decided that February needed an extra day. This came every four years and was named: (Leap Year)
- Establish that leap year comes every 4 years and then figure out the answer to this—If you were born in 1920 on leap year—How old are you? Take today's leap year date and subtract it from 1920—then divide it by 4 to get your answer.
- While working on your calendar what mountain grown hot beverage could you drink. It is served with cream and sugar or a sweetener. (Coffee)
- What was the *Poor Richard's Almanac* comprised of? (Sayings and Proverbs—Rising and Setting Times for the Moon—Weather Reports)
- Who was the author of the *Poor Richard's Almanac*? (Benjamin Franklin)
- Who was the person responsible for suggesting we call daylight savings time by that name? He also invented bi-focals. (Benjamin Franklin)
- Who was really responsible for inventing daylight savings time? (William Willett in 1907) *He was a British construction manager and wrote a pamphlet called* The Waste of Time. *He wanted to get as much work done as possible in the daylight.*
- In 1675 the Royal Greenwich Observatory (RGO) was founded regarding time. What group of people was this directed at? (Navigators and Sea Captains)
- Which famous captain in 1772, sailed and used the Royal Greenwich Observatory method? (Captain Cook)
- Describe the method. (If the captain timed the eclipses of Jupiter's four large satellites or measured the separation of the moon and bright stars it gave the captain the time.)
- What type of device was used to tell time by the hour using sand in a glass? (Hour Glass)
- Which president in the Depression valued time? (F. D. Roosevelt)

Time Questions:

- Each birthday you are: (one year older)
- 12 months equals: (one year)
- 24 hours equals: (one day)
- 7 days equals: (one week)
- 60 seconds equals: (one minute)
- 15 minutes equals: (1/4 hour)
- 30 minutes equals: (1/2 hour)
- 45 minutes equals: (3/4 hour)
- 60 minutes equals: (1 hour)
- 1 year equals: (365 days)
- Leap year is in which month? (February)
- Leap year occurs every: (4 years)
- February has how many days in a leap year? (29)
- Leap year has how many days? (366)
- Name the months that have 30 days: (April, June, September, November)
- Name the months that have 31 days: (January, March, May, July, August, October, December)
- Name the month that generally has 28 days: (February)
- Name the days of the week: (Sunday, Monday, Tuesday, Wednesday, Thursday, Friday, Saturday)
- Name the first day of the week: (Sunday)
- Name the day usually reserved for washing clothes: (Monday)
- Name the day usually reserved for ironing clothes: (Tuesday)
- Name the days that are considered the weekend: (Saturday, Sunday)
- Which date starts the new year? (January 1st)
- Which date ends the year? (December 31st)
- When the hands on the clock move they make a (circle) around the clock face to display the time.
- The secondhand circles the face every: (minute)
- What kind of clock or watch does not have hands? (digital)
- What do the digital clocks or watches show? (numerals of time)
- On a digital clock or watch the first number tells you the: (hour) and ends in two (zeros).
- What instrument did the people use to tell time before clocks or watches? (hour glass)
- A (sundial) was used to tell time, but did not work at night or on cloudy days.
- When the sun moves across the sky, the shadow on the face of the sundial moves and the (shadow) marks the (time).
- A (stopwatch) is used for measuring a race.
- A stopwatch is started when the race begins. Once the winner crosses the finish (line) the (watch) is (stopped).
- When a person travels by airplane and crosses over the time lines they may get (jet lag).
- How long does it take to bake an 8-inch cake? (30 minutes)

- How long does it take to bake a loaf of banana nut bread? (55-60 minutes)
- How many minutes does the nightly news usually run? (30 minutes)
- How many minutes does it take to move the minute hand to the next number on the clock? (5)
- How many minutes does it take for the minute hand to go all the way around the clock? (60)
- The time between midnight and noon is called: (a.m.)
- The time between noon and midnight is called: (p.m.)
- When the minute hand is halfway around the clock face and it points to the number 6 it is said to be: (half past)
- The imaginary line where the water or land meets the sky is called: (horizon)
- A (stop watch) is a special watch that measures short periods of time in seconds for a (race).
- A (horologuim) is a combination water and sundial clock.
- (Marharran) pertains to the Islamic calendar meaning 30 days.
- How many hours are there between noon and midnight? (12)
- Mid-day is also called: (noon)
- How many seasons are there in the year? (4)

Calendar Art Project
(See my calendar example in the colored section page 16.)

Each resident can fill in the day numbers and month name and then show their scheduled activities for the month.

Supplies needed:
Paper.
Pen.
Ruler.
Colored Pencils.

Examples to fill in:
Visitors, friends, and family.
Birthdays of family and friends.
Appointments for hair, doctor.
Social activities: cards, music, sports, coffee, lunch, club meetings.
Time to get up and go to bed.
Mealtime.

Pattern on next page to copy and fill out per month.

	BIRTHDAYS THIS MONTH:

SUNDAY	MONDAY	TUESDAY	WEDNESDAY	THURSDAY	FRIDAY	SATURDAY

THIS MONTH'S UPCOMING EVENTS:

It's About Time Music Bingo

B	I	N	G	O
Anniversary Waltz	Star Spangled Banner	Shall We Dance	Camptown Races	Goodnight Irene
Sunrise, Sunset	Shine on Harvest Moon	Lazy River	Sugartime	Fly Me to the Moon
Summertime	Red Sails in the Sunset	**FREE**	My Old Kentucky Home	The Things We Did Last Summer
Now is the Hour	Grandfather's Clock	Get Me to the Church On Time	On the Sunny Side of the Street	Try to Remember
Blue Skys	Winter Wonderland	It's a Most Unusual Day	Oh What a Beautiful Morning	Sunrise, Sunset

I played my accordion at a facility each week for three years. There was one gentleman that wouldn't participate—the staff and I had tried many different approaches.

I always made a special effort to find him and greet him and personally invite him to our music program. We would say, "I'll only come if you promise to play 'Good Night, Irene' for me." I said, "Certainly." Each week he came and each week I played 'his song'. One time my curiosity got the best of me and I asked him why he liked that song so much. He said he fell in love with a beautiful lady, named Irene, in his younger days. "Did you marry her?" I asked. "No, I let her get away," he replied. "I shouldn't have let her get away from me, either!" I continued talking with him each time I came, and finally we got him involved in cooking activities and playing cards.

Music Appreciation Group

Select several songs about time from the following list. Play the tunes on the piano or accordion and let the residents "Name That Tune". You can give them hints with the following words written on papers for each of them—or write them on a bulletin board or chalkboard.

Sun	Moon	Day	July	Sunshine
Morning	Night	Monday	Sunday	Time
Supper	Moonlight	May	Years	April
Evening	Light	Noon	September	Season
Autumn	Lights	Nights	Nine	January
February	June	Summer	Mornin'	Month

List of Songs:

"Anniversary Waltz" (years)

"East of the Sun" (sun, moon)

"It's a Most Unusual Day" (day)

"I'm a Yankee Doodle Dandy" (July) (summer) (season)

"My Melancholy Baby" (sunshine)

"Pennies from Heaven" (sunshine)

"Get Me to the Church on Time" (time) (morning)

"Wouldn't It Be Lovely" (night)

"I Could Have Danced All Night" (night)

"I Have Dreamed—from The King and I" (evening)

"Shall We Dance—from the King and I" (night)

"You Are My Sunshine" (sunshine)

"On a Clear Day" (day)

"We Kiss in a Shadow—from the King and I" (moon)

"Whispering Hope" (sunshine)

"Blue Skies" (sun)

"Oh! What a Beautiful Morning—from Oklahoma" (morning)

"Fiddler on the Roof" (noon, night, day, time)

"Grandfather's Clock" (time, hours, tick-tock, day, morn, ninety years)

"Sunrise, Sunset—from Fiddler on the Roof" (sunrise, sunset, days, years, season, night)

This song is excellent because it reflects on the time that has passed. The words are: "Is this the little girl I carried? Is this the little boy at play? I don't remember growing older, when did they?"

"To Life—from Fiddler on the Roof" (Monday, Sunday)

"Sugartime" (time, morning, evening, supper)

"California Here I Come" (sun)

"Moonlight Bay" (moonlight)

"Wait 'Til The Sun Shines Nellie" (sunshine)

"Star Spangled Banner" (night) *the line says, "our flag was still there".*

"Dixie" (frosty morning) *line says, "I was born one frosty morning.*

"Battle Hymn of the Republic" (evening dews and damps)

"America the Beautiful" (years)

"Nine Hundred Miles" (Saturday, night)

"I've Been Working on the Railroad" (day, time)

"Down in the Valley" (sunshine)

"In The Good Old Summertime" (summertime)

"Silver Threads Among the Gold" (May)

"On a Sunday Afternoon" (Sunday, afternoon, June, month, Monday)

"Alley Cat Song" (night)

"The Sheik of Araby" (night)

"Autumn Leaves" (autumn)

"Till We Meet Again" (night)

"It's Only a Paper Moon" (moon)

"April in Paris" (April)

"Blue Hawaii" (moon)

"Blue Orchids" (light, night)

"My Romance" (moon, month, May)

"Lucky Day" (day)

"By the Light of the Silvery Moon" (moon)

"Ida, Sweet as Apple Cider" (moonlight)

"Shine on Harvest Moon" (moon, January, February, June, July)

"Summertime" (summertime, mornin')

"Camptown Races" (night)

"Help Me Make It Through the Night" (night)

"Edelweiss—from the Sound of Music" (snow)

"Goodnight, Irene" (night)

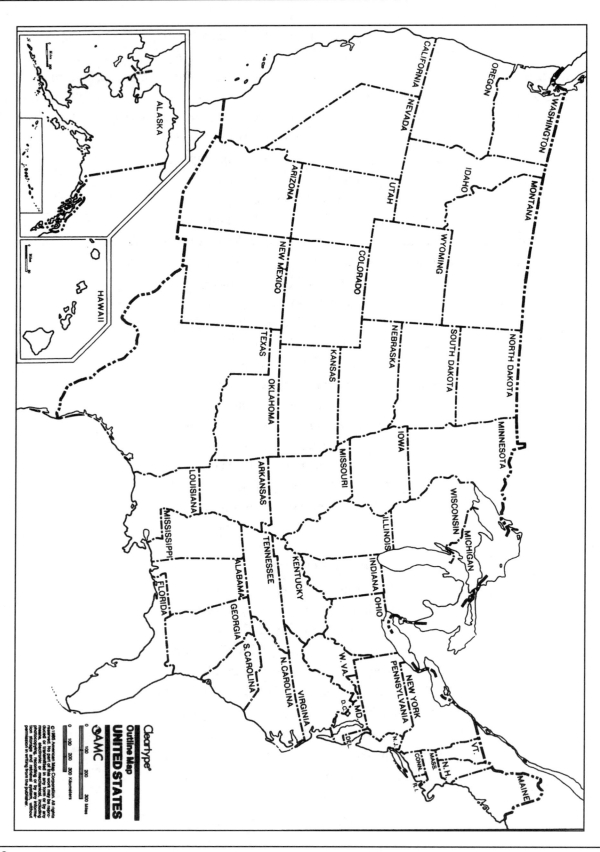

Time in the U.S.

Time Spelling Bee

Easy:

dawn	tick-tock	time	morning	shade	year	noon	second
week	sun	moon	month	minute	season	zone	evening
hour	night	cycle	Roman	Greek	clock	shade	midnight
measure	quarter	winter	summer	spring	fall	watch	digital
weekend							

Brain Teasers:

imaginary line	calculate	calendar	measurement	hourglass
longtime	hemisphere	Gregorian	astronomers	deliberation
sundial	hibernation	afternoon	shadows	birthday
sunshine	nocturnal	migrate	equinoxes	midday
sunlit	daylight	computus	horologium	

Time in the U.S.

Give each resident participant a map of the Unites States. Discuss with them that there are four time zones. (Eastern, Western, Mountain, Central)

Since I live in Wisconsin I will use this state as an example. We have the slogan, "Fall back and spring ahead". We change time twice a year (daylight savings time).

Indiana's time varies throughout the state. Southern Indiana is one hour ahead of Wisconsin. Cities in Northern Indiana, near Chicago, are on Wisconsin and Chicago time. South Bend, and Mishawaka, Indiana, are one hour ahead of Wisconsin. Fortunately, the entire state of Wisconsin is on the same time. Michigan and Ohio are one hour ahead of Wisconsin. Illinois, Iowa, Minnesota, and Missouri are on the same time as Wisconsin, or Central Time.

California, Oregon, and the state of Washington are two hours behind Wisconsin. When it is 8:00 a.m. in Wisconsin it is only 6:00 a.m. in the West. These states are on Western Time.

Colorado is on Mountain Time. Wisconsin is one hour ahead of Colorado. When it is 6:00 p.m. in Wisconsin it is 5:00 p.m. in Colorado.

The Southeastern states and Eastern states are on Eastern Time. For example: when it is 7:00 p.m. in New York it is 6:00 p.m. in Wisconsin.

Did you know there are 24 different time zones in the world? Why? The 24 time zones represent one for each hour of the clock. Think of the following places: New York, London, Moscow, and Tokyo as time lines. When it is 7:00 a.m. in New York, it is 3:00 p.m. in Moscow. When it is 12:00 p.m. (midnight) in London, it is noon in Chicago. When it is 9:00 p.m. in Tokyo, it is 12:00 p.m. (midnight) in London.

Did you ever think about the fact that there are 24 hours in a day, but a clock only has 12 hour numbers on it?

Exercises:

1. Call out a state name and ask what time it is in that state now. Using four colored pencils, mark the four time zones on the map.
2. Pass out paper and pencils. For each exercise the person with the most answers will get a prize.
3. Using a stopwatch, ask the residents to write down as many of their favorite foods as they can in 2 minutes.
4. Ask the men to write down various sports in 3 minutes.
5. Ask the ladies to write down the names of their children, grandchildren, and great grandchildren in 4 minutes.
6. Ask the group to write down all the holidays in a year in 4 minutes.
7. Ask them to write down all of their favorite movies in 5 minutes.
    I'm sure you can think of other categories. I use quarters for prizes. They are very popular.

Time to Exercise

Line up two rows of people in wheelchairs (6 in a row) facing each other. Use a big soft volleyball. Set the stopwatch to 5 minutes. Encourage them to pass the ball back and forth without dropping it on the floor. I found they enjoyed this outside on warmer days. The sun is good for them, as long as they are not out very long.

Serve juice at the end of the exercise.

References:

Mapping Time, The Calendar and Its History (427 pages) by E.G. Richards.
This book goes into detailed explanation of calendars. It is very interesting. However, if a person is not interested in this history you may lose them. But maybe you have someone that who *really* interested—get the book from the library for them!

Marking Time by Duncan Steel.
Calendar, Humanity's Epic Struggle to Determine a True and Accurate Year by David Ewing Duncan.

Index

Addresses, Telephone Numbers, Email and Website Addresses

Applewood Ink
Division of Catering by Design
P.O. Box 181
Waukesha, WI 53187
Pat Nekola's story: www.bookzone.com

Balloon Federation of America
P.O. Box 400
Indianola, IA 50125

Folk Music from Norway: info@arcmusic.co.uk
Arc Music
P.O. Box 2453
Clearwater, FL 33757-2453

Genealogical Center and Naeseth Library (608) 255-2224
415 W. Main
Madison, WI 53714

Kentucky Derby: info@derbymuseum.org.

Native Ground Music: www.nativeground.com
1-800-752-2656
109 Gell Road
Ashville, NC 28805

Nordic Fest: www.nordicfest.com 1-800-382-3378
Decorah, IA 52101

"Norway" Video from Lonely Planet Publications
1-800-275-8555
150 Linden Street
Oakland, CA 94607

Other Scandinavian Travelogues:
Travel the World by Rick Steves
Questar, Inc.
P.O. Box 11345
Chicago, IL 60611
and
Traveloguer Collection
3301 W. Hampden Avenue, Ste. N.
Englewood, CO 80110

Penzey's Spices 1-800-741-7787

Vesterheim Norwegian-American Museum
www.vesterheim.org (563) 382-9681
Decorah, IA 52101

Other Helpful Resources

Alzheimer's Association: www.alz.org/
(312) 335-8700 or 1-800-272-3900

Alzheimer's Disease Information Center:
http://webmd.lyco.som

Alzheimer's Disease Education and Referral Center
(ADEAR): 1-800-438-4380

American Association of Retired Persons (AARP):
(202) 434-2277 or 1-800-424-3410

Area Agency on Aging (AAA): (202) 296-8130

Assisted Living Federation of America: (email)
lc@alfa.org (website) www.careguide.net (703) 691-8100

Children of Aging Parents: (215) 945-6900

Elder Abuse Hotline (national number) and Eldercare
Locator: 1-800-677-1116

Insurance Consumer Helpline: 1-800-942-4242

Medicare: www.medicare.gov

Medicare Wisconsin: 1-800-362-3002 (hard of hearing)
1-877-486-2048

National Association for Continence: 1-800-252-3337

National Certification Council of Activity Professionals:
www.nccap.org (757) 552-0653

National Council on the Aging Inc.: (202) 479-1200

National Hospice Organization: (703) 243-5900 or
1-800-658-8898

National Institute on Aging: (301) 496-1752

National Kidney Foundation: www.kidney.org
1-800-622-9010

Railroad Retirement Board: 1-800-808-0772

Social Security Administration (SSA): www.ssa.gov
1-800-772-1213 (hard of hearing) 1-800-325-0778

Veteran's Administration: 1-800-827-1000

Wisconsin Geriatric Education Center: (414) 288-3712

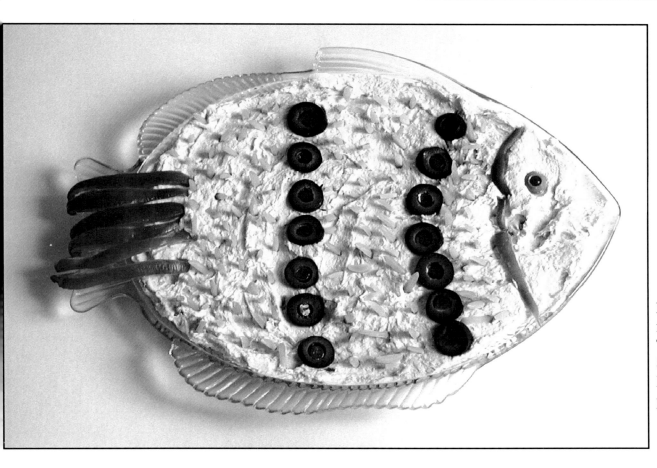

Recipe
for St.
Thomas
Seafood
Dip on
page 10.

Directions on how to make a
shell pin on page 20.

Directions on how to make a
Caribbean Hat Band for Straw
Hat for Party Leaders on page 21.

The Sunny Caribbean Saying Sheet on page 19.

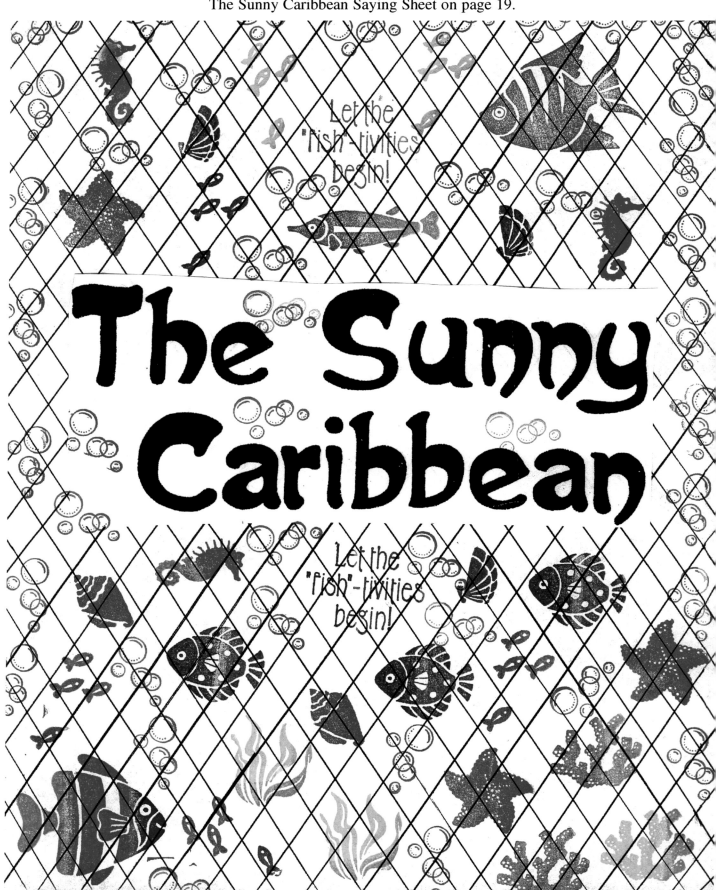

Decorations for a Caribbean Party
Directions for the Following;
1. Hat on page 21.
2. Starfish on page 22.
3. Flag on page 23.
4. Napkins on page 23.

Wishing Well Activity from page 45.

Zucchini
Bread recipe
on page 52.

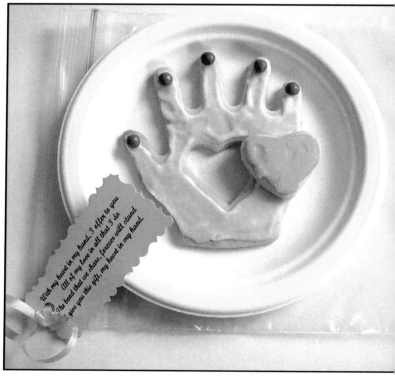

Hand and Heart Cookie recipe on page 55.

Easter Bunny Cake from page 93.

Hour Glass for It's All About Time Party on 243.

Bird Clock from Clock Party on page 141.

Different Clocks from
Clock Party on page 141
or It's All About Time Party on 243.

Windsock
Art Project
from
page 65-66.

Mexican Maracas Art Project from page 157.

Pose and a
Rose from
page 171.

Tulip Flowerpot Centerpiece Art Project from page 187.

Animals from Norway from page 195.

Polar bear

Reindeer

Baby
seal

Fjord horses

Selected Flags of the World from page 222.

Barbados

American Virgin Islands

St. Maarten

Grenada

Antigua & Barbuda

Saba

St. Eustatius

St. Kitts & Nevis

Monserrat

Anguilla

British Virgin Islands

Dominica

St. Lucia

Trinidad & Tobago

Guadeloupe, Martinique

St. Vincent & the Grenadin

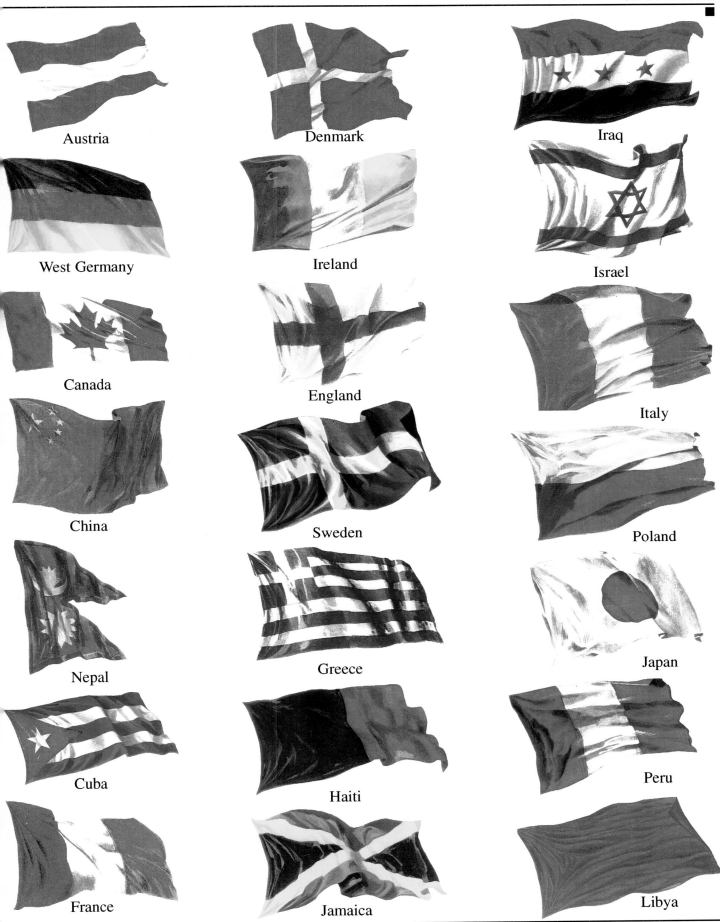

Austria

Denmark

Iraq

West Germany

Ireland

Israel

Canada

England

Italy

China

Sweden

Poland

Nepal

Greece

Japan

Cuba

Haiti

Peru

France

Jamaica

Libya

New Zealand

Switzerland

Sudan

Brazil

Puerto Rico

United Kingdom

Australia

Sierra Leone

United States

Norway

Petting Zoo from page 236.

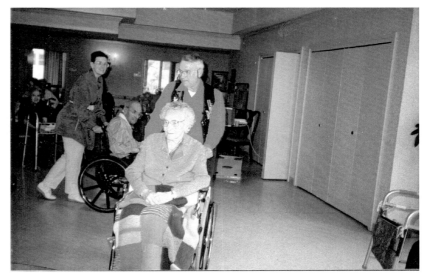

Square Dancing from page 237.

Pasta Art Project from page 239.

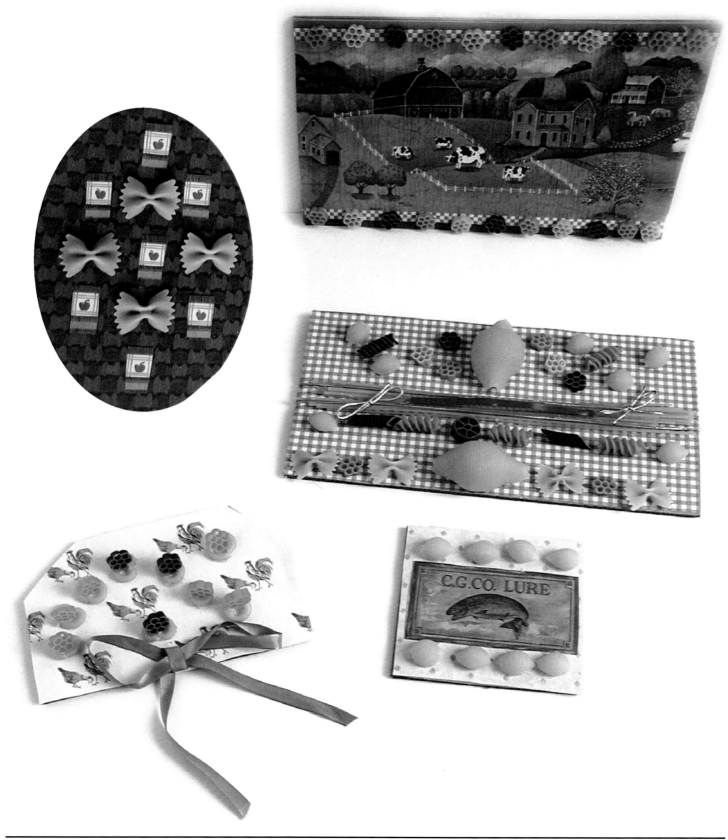

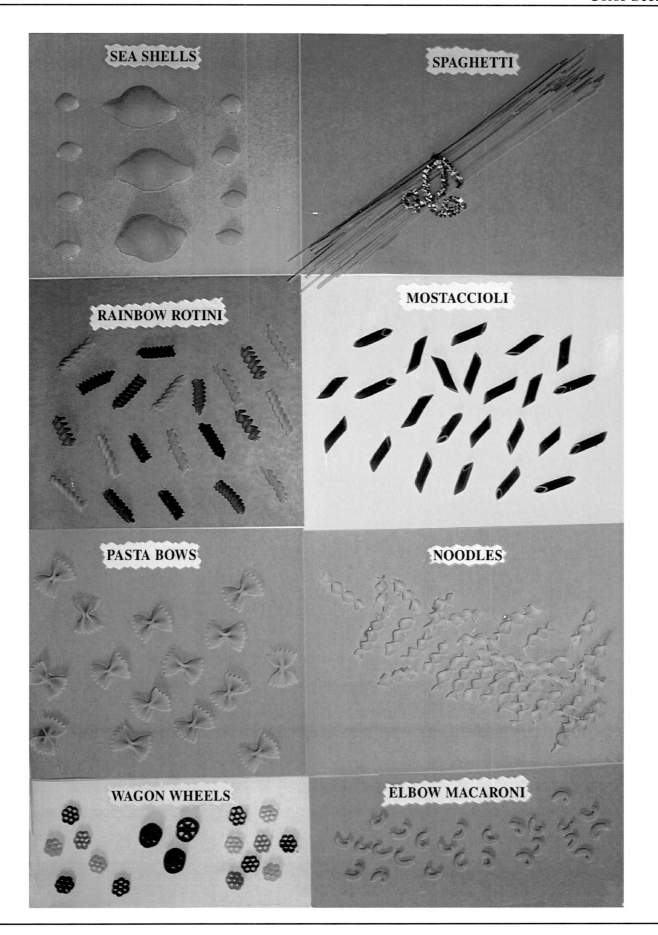

SEA SHELLS

SPAGHETTI

RAINBOW ROTINI

MOSTACCIOLI

PASTA BOWS

NOODLES

WAGON WHEELS

ELBOW MACARONI

Calendar Project

Each person can make a calendar month of their schedule. Let the residents choose their favorite month. Show and tell about everyone's calendar. What are some dates in your calendar month that you would like share with the group?

Supplies Needed:
Paper.
Pen.
Ruler.
Colored pencils.

Examples:
1. When to start and end a day.
2. Meal time.
3. Visitors, friends, and family.
4. Birthdays of family and friends.
5. Season of the year.
6. Play bridge or other card games.
7. Take a nap.
8. Watch a favorite show on TV.
9. Feed the Fish or other pets.
10. Watch or feed the birds.
11. Go shopping with the resident.
12. Go to lunch.
13. Dinner with family or friends.
14. Go fishing.

SUNDAY	MONDAY	TUESDAY	WEDNESDAY	THURSDAY	FRIDAY	SATURDAY
		1 Day Out!	2	3	4 Concert	5
6	7 Doctor	8	9 Coffee with Joe	10	11	12
13	14	15 Pizza Party	16	17 Pie Social	18	19
20	21 Bake Bread	22	23	24	25	26 Ball Game
27	Haircut 28	29	30 My B-day	31		

This calendar was created with the template on page 7 by copying part of it.